GOVERNORS STATE UNIVERSITY LIBRARY

3 1611 00154 1090

W9-AFU-456

LANDMARK
J·U·S·T·I·C·E

UNIVERSITY LIBRARY
GOVERNORS STATE UNIVERSITY
UNIVERSITY PARK, IL. 60466

LANDMARK
J·U·S·T·I·C·E

The Influence of
William J. Brennan
on America's Communities

Charles M. Haar
and
Jerold S. Kayden

Published in cooperation
with the
Lincoln Institute of Land Policy

THE PRESERVATION PRESS
National Trust for Historic Preservation

UNIVERSITY LIBRARY
GOVERNORS STATE UNIVERSITY
UNIVERSITY PARK, IL. 60466

KF 5697 .A52 B74 1989

Brennan, William J. 1906-

Landmark justice

242659

The Preservation Press
National Trust for Historic Preservation
1785 Massachusetts Avenue, N.W.
Washington, D.C. 20036

The National Trust for Historic Preservation is the only private, nonprofit organization chartered by Congress to encourage public participation in the preservation of sites, buildings and objects significant in American history and culture. Support is provided by membership dues, endowment funds, contributions and grants from federal agencies, including the U.S. Department of the Interior, under provisions of the National Historic Preservation Act of 1966. The opinions expressed in this publication do not necessarily reflect the views or policies of the Interior Department. For information about membership in the National Trust, write to the above address.

Library of Congress Cataloging in Publication Data
Brennan, William J. (William Joseph), 1906–
       Landmark justice : the influence of William J. Brennan on
America's communities / Charles M. Haar and Jerold S. Kayden.
       p.   cm.
    Includes index.
    ISBN 0-89133-132-8 : $34.95
    1. Land use—Law and legislation—United States—Cases.
    2. Historic sites—Law and legislation—United States—Cases.
    3. Judicial opinions—United States. I. Haar, Charles Monroe,
    1920– . II. Kayden, Jerold Seth, 1953– . III. Title
    KF5697.A52B74   1989
    346.7304'5—dc19
    [347.30645]   87-35986

Copyright © Charles M. Haar and Jerold S. Kayden. All rights reserved.
No part of this book may be reproduced in any manner without written permission from the publisher, except for brief quotations used in reviews.

Printed in the United States of America
98 97 96 95 94 93 92 91 90 89 5 4 3 2 1

Edited by Diane Maddex, director, and Janet Walker, managing editor, The Preservation Press, with assistance from Janet Mullaney.

Designed by DRPollard & Associates, Washington, D.C.
Line illustrations prepared by Carolynn Leaman.
Composed in Trump Mediaeval by BG Composition, Baltimore, Md.
Printed by McNaughton & Gunn, Saline, Mich.

∞   The paper used in this publication is Glatfelter Offset and meets the minimum requirements of the American National Standard for Permanence of Paper for Printed Library Materials Z39.48-1984.

Jacket: Grand Central Terminal, New York City. (William D. Middleton from *Grand Central: The World's Greatest Railway Terminal*) Justice William J. Brennan, Jr. (Supreme Court Historical Society)

CONTENTS

PREFACE

This book is for people interested in the future of our cities and suburbs, how we live in them and what kinds of communities will emerge from the battles between contending forces. By what rules are we to arrive at decisions about how metropolitan land resources are to be allocated? How dramatically can society's demand for fashioning the physical environment reshape the entrepreneur's role in land development? Can city governments require private owners to maintain vacant land as open space for the benefit of the public? Should city governments have the authority to dictate who may live together in a residence? Must suburban towns allow for the construction of low-income housing for poor families? Can society compel owners of historic buildings to preserve them? Do communities have the power to ban billboards? Does the public have a right to walk along ocean beaches, even if they are privately owned? Can municipal officials choose who will be allowed to open a store within their town and who will be denied that right? Should government pay damages to private owners when its regulations cut too deeply into their economic expectations? Indeed, where should the line be drawn between private property and the social welfare?

Landmark Justice explores these and other difficult questions through the eyes of a justice of the Supreme Court of the United States, one who has written most extensively and influentially about the use of land. During his 40 years of state and federal court service, Justice Brennan has written 21 opinions—13 majorities, two concurrences and six dissents—that collectively describe the major land use disputes of our day. The book's first three chapters present an analysis of the approaches he has taken toward resolution of conflicts over the uses of land. Commentaries on Justice Brennan's state cases and excerpts from his state opinions constitute chapters 4, 5 and 6, while chapters 7 through 9 treat in like fashion his U.S. Supreme Court opinions. Finally, a brief conclusion measures his land use contribution against the backdrop of his larger role in American law and life. Extended notes following the chapters are designed for the legally inclined reader.

Some general comments are in order. For purposes of this book, we reviewed all of Justice Brennan's state and federal court opinions and selected those that, in our view, most directly touch on land use issues. Of course, his influence on America's communities extends well beyond this single area, important as it may be. His decisions involving freedom of the press, voting rights and sex discrimination, for example, also define the nature of our communities. We have chosen to concentrate on the singular role land use plays in establishing what may be called the territorial foundation of citizenship.

One purpose of scholarship is to broaden attitudes and perspectives. It is our conviction that, by focusing on one judge, one area, and one cumulative contribution, a powerful message is conveyed. Taken individually, a land use judicial decision is a world unto itself, written in response to conflicts posed at a particular time, decided in the midst of a full docket that includes contract, criminal, tort, corporation and constitutional law cases. Taken together, Justice Brennan's 21 opinions make visible surprisingly unified approaches to land use controversies not readily apparent from the consideration of one or two cases. It is our sense, too, that Justice Brennan's land use jurisprudence deserves to be added to the list of legal contributions normally associated with him.

Judicial opinions, all too often buried in chronologically arranged dusty volumes, accessible only at specialized libraries and serving as primary source material for lawyers, can be eye-opening reading material to all interested in the stuff of democracy in action. Embodying snapshots of society at any given moment, they reveal and pronounce upon the major conflicts between individual and community. Judicial opinions—our neglected national essays—reflect the moral values and norms of our evolving society in their narration of the democratic give and take. Written more than 30 years ago, Justice Brennan's New Jersey opinions, for instance, paint a fascinating portrait of small towns confronting explosive post–World War II population growth. The story, of efforts to control the social, economic and physical environment in the face of change and of Justice Brennan's weighing of competing public and private rights, provides as much a sense of the time as any history book, topical novel or newspaper article. His more recent United States Supreme Court opinions encapsulate equally well the drama of the current era, a time of technological, environmental and social complexity demanding sophisticated awareness of land use as an ingredient of human existence.

But let Justice Brennan speak for himself. Our commentaries aim at placing his cases in the general context of planning theory and law. The extended excerpts from his opinions are stripped of legal citations, procedural discussions and other technical barriers to the general reader, for that is the intended audience. Rather than paraphrasing, we hope thereby to capture the flavor of a judge at work, struggling with the tough decisions that bear so heavily on how we as individuals live in our communities. In his careful balancing of interests, thoroughly explained and justified for all to see, a hallmark of a civilized democracy is magnified.

ACKNOWLEDGMENTS

Justice William J. Brennan, Jr., is unequaled for the many legal opinions he has written having profound implications for land use in the United States. This is why, in 1986, he was an obvious choice for an award presented periodically by the Lincoln Institute of Land Policy to individuals making distinguished contributions to the development of land policies in the public interest. He joined an eminent group—whose members include Lewis Mumford, Sir Desmond Heap and Sir Frank Layfield—notable for its impact on the use of land as a vital social, economic and natural resource. Justice Brennan received this honor in person at a small ceremony in Cambridge, Mass. On that occasion, the idea for a book, which would collect and evaluate his judicial opinions relating to the use of land, was conceived.

We are grateful to the Lincoln Institute of Land Policy for its support. We especially thank past and present directors: Arlo Woolery, who helped initiate this work, and Ron Smith, who has encouraged its completion. Katie Lincoln presided at a small symposium discussing some of our early conclusions. The National Endowment for the Arts has provided assistance for some of the photographs in the book.

We also would like to thank Diane Maddex, director of the Preservation Press, and Janet Walker, managing editor, for their thoughtful editing. Michelle LaLumia, Elizabeth Merritt, Tracey Black and Joyce Miller contributed needed technical assistance. Margaret Byrne Heimbold, vice president and publisher of the National Trust for Historic Preservation, and Ian Spatz, of the Trust's legal department, also were helpful in their suggestions.

Above all, this book is a salute to Justice Brennan, a wise and generous human being.

Charles M. Haar and Jerold S. Kayden

PART I

STRIKING THE ELUSIVE BALANCE BETWEEN PRIVATE AND PUBLIC RIGHTS

Proposed nuclear power plant site, which San Diego wanted to maintain as open space. From San Diego Gas & Electric Co. v. City of San Diego.
(Jerold S. Kayden)

1 DEFINING A LAND USE JURISPRUDENCE

Grand Central Terminal, the Beaux Arts masterpiece designed a landmark by New York City in 1967. From Penn Central Transportation Co. v. New York City.
(Jerold S. Kayden)

Distilled to its essence, a land use case presents a clash between private and public rights. Property owners assert that the government has impermissibly interfered with that bundle of rights called private property.[1] Governments respond that they are properly exercising their authority in order to advance the public welfare.[2] Under our constitutional system, the judicial branch is left to referee this contest and draw the line demarcating private and public domains. In so doing, judges must consult broad constitutional and statutory clauses providing only the vaguest guidelines for assessing the propriety of the contested government action.[3]

Judges must decide whether the government's purpose is legitimate and whether the means chosen to achieve it are reasonable.[4] They must ascertain whether the asserted purpose is the real one or whether it is being used as a mask for illegitimate motivations.[5] They must assess whether the property owner's refrain of economic catastrophe is the proverbial boy crying wolf or whether an excessive deprivation of value has occurred.[6] They must determine when government power, exercised to enforce the will of the majority, nevertheless must bend to higher principles and when the interests of minorities—even highlighted as the interest of one—must take precedence over the interests of the many.[7] Judges must, in the final analysis, answer the most slippery of all land use questions (slippery because its answer depends on defining the relationship between the individual and the community): what is private property?[8]

During his eight years (1949 to 1956) as a state court judge in New Jersey and his 32 years (1956 to the present) on the Supreme Court of the United States, Justice William J. Brennan, Jr., has faced virtually all of the thorny questions that manifest themselves in land use cases.[9] Over this 40-year span he has written 21 land use opinions: 13 majorities, two concurrences and six dissents. His state court years include 12 majorities and one dissent. In contrast, his federal output includes only one majority, albeit in his most famous land use opinion, upholding the preservation of Grand Central Terminal in New York City.[10] The bulk of his federal opinions shows him concurring twice or dissenting five times.

Doubtless, Justice Brennan's long tenure as a judge has itself provided him an unusual opportunity to write many land use opinions. But far more than length of service explains the quantity and quality of his contribution. His Supreme Court decisions in particular indicate a keen interest in land use matters, because, unlike the assigned authorship of majorities, the writing of concurring and dissenting opinions is largely at the discretion of the individual justice.[11] He has expressed his views in a surprisingly large share, over one-third, of the relatively few land use cases making their way onto the Supreme Court's oral argument docket.[12] Moreover, by virtue of their persuasive reasoning and thoughtful presentation, these opinions—although not binding precedent in all but one case—have strongly influenced the development of federal and state land use law.[13] Justice Brennan, more than any of his federal and state colleagues on the bench, justifiably can be called a "Landmark Justice."

Theme, Propositions and Temperament

Justice Brennan's land use opinions[14] reveal one central theme: an attempt, over time, to discover, elaborate and strike an appropriate balance between competing private and public rights.[15] In land use cases, private rights encompass all that is implied by the freedom to enjoy property, for example, to develop land for a profit, to exclude others from one's property, to choose one's housemates, to alter or demolish existing buildings, to live anywhere in a city or suburb, to post signs and erect billboards, to show adult movies commercially. Public rights gain content from notions of a collective good, and their enjoyment is shared by groups of individuals. In land use cases, public rights may suggest the preservation of historically valuable buildings, the protection of environmentally sensitive lands, the promotion of certain moral values, the maintenance of small-town character. Frequently, they are described as part of a community's efforts to ensure its social, economic and physical well-being.[16]

The tension between spheres of public and private rights arises because expansion of one usually results in contraction of another. By employing a balancing test, Justice Brennan necessarily suggests that neither right shall automatically assume precedence over the other. For him, then, assignment of the proper weight to these competing interests presents the major intellectual challenge. He relies on two fundamental sources to illuminate and assess the importance of interests. First, he examines the language, prior judicial interpretation and, especially, the purpose of relevant constitutional and statutory provisions, while at the same time staying attuned to their pragmatic meaning and application to human beings in modern-day life.[17] Intolerant of legal positivism,[18] he prefers an eyes-open inclusionary approach that systematically gives each of these factors its due consideration. For example, Justice Brennan reads the broad purposes set forth in state zoning legislation to support an accommodating, rather than restrictive, judicial attitude toward community exercises of the zoning power.[19] And, understanding the complex reality of today's regulated land market, Justice Brennan interprets the word "taking" in the just compensation clause[20] neither so broadly as to prohibit any government diminution of private property value nor so restrictively as to cover only traditional eminent domain condemnation of land for a public use.[21]

Justice Brennan's second font for assigning weight is intriguing: he looks to the parties themselves—local governments and private property owners—for evidence of the importance they invest in their interests. Self-serving articulations of importance, particularly made in the courtroom and unaccompanied by historical proof of seriousness, are less likely to swing the balance. Conversely, the maxim that actions speak louder than words finds a sympathetic ear in Justice Brennan. Attempting to understand the true motivations of actors and to ferret out unsubstantiated claims, he pays an unusual degree of attention to the facts in the record, a recognition that land use cases present unusually fact-dependent tableaux.

Governments and landowners, faced with daily decision making, are less interested in the conceptual underpinnings of a balancing test. They share an understandable desire to know the rules of the game and a healthy distaste for the wild card of uncertainty. They want to determine where the courts stand on the major issues of the day. Justice Brennan does not give them all they want. He refuses to oversimplify the complicated, recognizing that clarity for clarity's sake alone is a false compass. In areas where clear-cut answers are elusive, he candidly acknowledges ambiguity.[22]

Nevertheless, a review of Justice Brennan's opinions reveals four recurring land use propositions.

1.   Although commonly accepted land use regulatory techniques such as zoning can improve the social, economic and physical well-being of a community, their legitimacy hinges on the support of sound planning and a comprehensive approach in order to mitigate the threat of arbitrary and discriminatory government action against the individual.[23]

2.   Although judicial deference to land use regulations is normally due, regulations affecting fundamental personal rights cloaked as private property rights (such as regulations banning billboards and adult movie theaters or defining who can live together in a house) demand greater judicial scrutiny and place a higher burden of justification on government.[24]

3.   Although the need to be flexible and to tailor regulations to individual fact patterns is legitimate, discretionary government procedures are inherently capable of being arbitrary, discriminatory and noncomprehensive and must be more carefully reviewed by the courts.[25]

4.   Although the individual's right to develop and use private property may be severely limited by rights of the community, the individual in all events is entitled to an expectation of reasonable economic use and must receive compensation for loss of value if a regulation goes too far.[26]

A reading of Justice Brennan's land use opinions also allows the observer to draw several conclusions about his judicial temperament.

1.   Justice Brennan is an innovative problem solver, willing to suggest new approaches to old puzzles.[27]

2.   Justice Brennan is a logical writer, presenting arguments in a step-by-step organized structure.[28]

3.   Justice Brennan is an effective advocate, highlighting the weaknesses of opposing arguments and using the well-chosen dramatic line to bolster his point.[29]

4.   Justice Brennan is a careful craftsman, paying particular attention to the facts that illuminate land use cases in particular.[30]

5.   Justice Brennan is a humane jurist, frequently imbuing the U.S. Constitution's vision for a just and free society in ideas and language transcending technical legal prose.[31]

State Versus
Federal Court Judging

In his eight years as a New Jersey judge, Justice Brennan wrote 13 land use opinions, almost twice as many as the eight written during his federal years.[32] Since most land use contests raise state, rather than federal, law questions, the disparity is hardly surprising. Even when land use cases contain a federal constitutional component, the issues presented are mostly run-of-the-mill challenges to the application of a bylaw to a particular parcel of land, not the cutting-edge constitutional questions normally considered by the U.S. Supreme Court.[33]

Still, the role of a state appellate judge interpreting state and local land use laws does not differ altogether from that of a U.S. Supreme Court justice engaged in heady constitutional inquiry. State judges have been forced to give content to legislative language initially no more yielding of substantive meaning than federal constitutional provisions. If the due process, equal protection and just compensation clauses are the guiding lights of federal constitutional land use jurisprudence,[34] then the state statutory requirements of uniform treatment and comprehensiveness and the prohibitions against arbitrary and capricious action rise to the level of a *de facto* constitution.[35] Furthermore, although Congress maintains published records of legislative history, most state legislatures document their proceedings leading to statutory enactments poorly, if at all. Thus, even as state judges pay lip service to supposed legislative intent, state judges themselves must frequently intuit the legislature's motivation. By giving content to abstractions, state judges become the real enumerators of the law.[36]

That said, significant differences do exist between state supreme court and U.S. Supreme Court judges.[37] Unlike their federal counterparts, state supreme court judges do not face pressure to serve as national unifiers of the law.[38] A state high court opinion, no matter how well reasoned and persuasive, is binding only in the state in which it is delivered. U.S. Supreme Court opinions are literally the law of the land and, consequently, preclude the possibility of other approaches. This fact can be at once liberating and limiting for state judges. The comparative lack of national importance may empower them to take more risks, to be more innovative and not to worry about divergence from the national culture. On a more prosaic level, their decisions are not subject to the same level of academic and media scrutiny accorded U.S. Supreme Court pronouncements.[39] The importance of state autonomy under our federalist system of government[40] and the Brandeisian concept of state laboratories[41] reinforce the notion of experimentation at the state level. Of course, the same federalist system that accords states their substantial governing role serves as the ultimate check on local innovation, for the U.S. Constitution itself, as interpreted by the Supreme Court, remains the supreme law of the land. State courts run the risk of reversal by the U.S. Supreme Court whenever they innovate in interpretations of the U.S. Constitution. That Sword of Damocles hangs ever more precariously the more a state court, forever bound by the principle of *stare decisis*,[42] diverges from accepted constitutional doctrine. The penalty of reversal is not, however, the world's worst fate for a state high court judge bent on experimentation.

Perhaps Justice Brennan's initial freedom as a state judge helped forge his willingness to find innovative solutions to problems. His careful craftsmanship surely received early honing in the detailed exposition of factual records so characteristic of his state court opinions. But in his eight U.S. Supreme Court opinions, one especially sees the logical writer, effective advocate and humane jurist. Justice Brennan, of course, had almost two decades of additional judicial experience under his belt before writing his first Supreme Court land use opinion. Another explanation for these evident judicial qualities lies in the nature of his opinions. All but one of his New Jersey decisions were majorities, with few written dissents to defend against. All but one of his Supreme Court decisions were dissents or concurring opinions, in which exposing the illogic of the majority, characterizing and limiting its meaning and reach, laying the groundwork for future opinions and persuading public followers of the Supreme Court were the major objectives. Not surprisingly, his only New Jersey dissent (also his last state land use opinion) came closest to auguring the judicial style and temperament illustrated by his later Supreme Court opinions.

2 EARLY EXPLORATIONS IN NEW JERSEY

*Area in light industrial zoning district, New Providence,
N.J., where a developer sought to build a shopping
center against the wishes of town planners. From
Katobimar Realty Co. v. Webster.*
(Jerold S. Kayden)

A s a judge in the trial and appellate divisions of the New Jersey Superior Court, and as a member of the New Jersey Supreme Court, Justice Brennan decided questions pitting landowner against community. Framed in the technical language of the land use field, the cases involved zoning amendments and variances, special permits and nonconforming uses, public use doctrines and billboard regulation. His opinions, although written early in his judicial career, provide inklings of approaches that emerge fully in his major constitutional efforts written years later as a member of the U.S. Supreme Court. As such, the state opinions are a rich ground for the legal anthropologist in search of roots, themes, explanations and insights about the growth of a major jurist.

When Justice Brennan served in New Jersey, small communities in the state were first sensing post–World War II rumblings of the explosive growth that ultimately would produce the sprawling megalopolis extending from Boston to Washington, D.C.[1] New federally financed highways and federally insured Federal Housing Administration and Veterans Administration mortgage loans made the suburb an increasingly attractive and affordable place to live.[2] Zoning ordinances adopted in the 1930s and 1940s, when economic depression, world war and real estate quiescence ruled the day, had never been put to the test as mechanisms to guide and control substantial growth.[3] Nervous at the prospect that runaway development in the early 1950s would forever change town character and wreak havoc with the provision of municipal services, communities turned with new enthusiasm to their zoning ordinances for protection previously afforded by moribund land markets. Faced with applications from developers for multifamily housing, commercial buildings and industrial plants, towns retooled their bylaws to deal with the new reality.[4]

As zoning changed from lamb to lion, lawsuits brought by property owners, couched in terms of unfairness to the individual or general irrationality, importuned the New Jersey courts to exercise a searching review of local ordinances.[5] Such requests did not always fall on deaf ears. A majority of New Jersey Supreme Court judges sometimes exercised heightened scrutiny of land use regulations to overturn local decisions.[6] For Justice Brennan, however, New Jersey's state zoning statute, enacted by its legislature, was designed to give local communities broad powers to ensure a balanced and well-ordered environment.[7] Its purposes of promoting health, safety, morals and the general welfare were to be liberally construed to allow municipalities to confront anticipated growth. The terse utterances of state law were amplified fully by Justice Brennan's interpretation.

Coupling Sound Planning with Zoning

The principal land use proposition to emerge from an examination of Justice Brennan's New Jersey opinions is his view that, properly supported by sound planning, zoning is a positive instrument for the social, economic and physical well-being of communities. His attitude was upbeat about the potential of zoning to ensure a quality environment, and he viewed cautiously judicial restrictions on its use. Where New Jersey judges sometimes exercised a "Lochnerian" review over zoning,[8] willing to substitute their substantive views for those of elected legislators, Justice Brennan believed that courts were not meant—statutorily, constitutionally or institutionally—to be "super-legislatures." Local innovation was not to be stifled by a judge's view of the "right" way to zone. Community responses to community problems were to receive due deference, as the state legislature intended.

At the same time, however, Justice Brennan was unprepared to abandon judicial review of zoning altogether: the court's role should be limited, but only as long as there was evidence that zoning was the product and reflection of sound planning. Justice Brennan's coupling of zoning with sound planning—planning as both necessary and sufficient for regulatory action—became crucial to his presumption in favor of local action. If the courts were to defer to localities, and uphold their restrictions on exercise of private property rights, then the prerequisite to such deference was assurance that regulations were neither arbitrary nor unfair. By showing that local action was predicated on sound planning—objective, carefully thought out, comprehensive—communities were able to provide that assurance.

At its best, sound community planning involves several critical steps. Data about existing land uses, population, housing, jobs, topography and other characteristics are carefully collected. Present and expected trends of growth and decline are extrapolated from the collected data. Competing visions of what the community might be like are assembled from its citizens, planners and designers, politicians and business leaders. The data, trends and visions are compared and integrated to assemble a geographically specific plan. The final product, most frequently expressed through text and maps, enjoys a variety of labels, including comprehensive plan, master plan, general plan, community plan and city plan. The zoning ordinance itself is usually a reflection of the plan, and its trio of use (residential, commercial), shape (height, setback) and bulk (four units to the acre) regulations implement the plan.

Ever the realist, Justice Brennan did not demand that communities demonstrate textbook perfect planning and zoning decisions. However, he required more than a community's conclusory assertion, without proof, that it conducted planning. His travail included the parsing of testimony, planning reports, traffic surveys, demographic statistics, land appraisals, economic trends and any other evidence presented in the trial court. Once satisfied that sound planning occurred, he declined to second-guess the substance of the local regulatory decision.

Critics who scoff at Justice Brennan's reliance on planning label this reasoning simplistic. They know planning's methodological weaknesses and can cite chapter and verse documenting its failures. The bulldozing of livable neighborhoods for massive urban renewal projects and highways[9] and the building of inhumane public housing highrises[10] are but a few of the most notorious planning failures. But this view misses the point. Justice Brennan did not focus on evidence of planning because of its substantive success. His reliance instead derived from the procedural and institutional protections it guaranteed to the exercise of private rights,[11] as well as its insights into the community's commitment to public rights. Planning involves some degree of community participation, and the importance of private rights may be articulated and considered. Planning takes time and money and shows that decisions are not taken in a totally arbitrary way. Planning leaves tracks, and permissible and impermissible motivations may be more easily detected. In short, with the protections afforded by an overall planning effort, Justice Brennan was more confident about the seriousness and nonarbitrariness of local zoning.

Interestingly, Justice Brennan's most famous state land use opinion articulating his basic philosophy is his only state land use dissent. In *Katobimar Realty Co. v. Webster*,[12] the borough of New Providence, seeking to enhance its economic base by creating exclusive areas for industrial parks (at the time a revolutionary real estate concept), amended its zoning ordinance to prohibit residential and retail uses within light industrial zoning districts.[13] A developer, seeking to build a shopping center in such a light industrial district, attacked the amendment as "unreasonable, arbitrary and capricious" and a deprivation of his property "without due process of law,"[14] and brought suit to compel New Providence to issue a building permit.

Siding with the developer, the majority overturned the amendment, finding that there was no "rational distinction referable to the fulfillment of the statutory zoning considerations, all or any of them, between the contemplated shopping center and the uses permissible in the limited industrial district."[15] The majority reasoned that the developer's "projected business center and light industrial uses are not incompatible in nature; they are generally, so far as zoning policy goes, wholly congruous uses, and if in special circumstances a distinction may reasonably be made to serve an overriding public interest, such showing is not made here."[16] Thus, concluded the majority, "[t]here is no reasonable basis for the classification."[17] In effect, the majority substituted its own judgment—that retail commercial uses would not conflict with industrial uses—for that of the local community. The majority also enshrined the rationale and practice of "cumulative" or "pyramidal" zoning—where districts permitting more intense uses (industrial) automatically permit less intense uses (commercial)[18]—as statutory law. Attuned to the time-honored, albeit voluntarily adopted, cumulative format of most local zoning, the judges were bewildered by the new attitude of New Providence's planners.

Rejecting such judicial law making, Justice Brennan welcomed the innovation.[19] In stark contrast to the majority's crabbed view of the zoning power, he accepted the unprecedented:

New Jersey has witnessed a marked and salutary change in the judicial attitude toward municipal zoning over the past decade. Long overdue recognition of the legitimate aspirations of the community to further its proper social, economic and political progress, and of the propriety of requiring individual landowners to defer to the greater public good, have replaced the narrow concepts held by former courts. . . . Present-day decisions rightly give maximum play to the philosophy underlying our constitutional and statutory zoning provisions that localities may decide for themselves what zoning best serves and furthers the local public welfare, subject only to the rule of reason forbidding arbitrary and capricious action.[20]

Having announced his general principle, he went on to attach his safeguard condition that zoning be supported by sound planning. To guarantee that the community had met this condition, Justice Brennan delved into the record. He cited statistics showing that New Providence's population virtually doubled in five years, from 3,500 persons in 1950 to 6,000 in 1955.[21] Tax revenues from the community's modest residential properties would be unable, standing alone, to support mounting costs of schooling and municipal services.[22] Thus, his dissent recounted, the community decided to attract non-nuisance industries to bolster its property tax base.[23] It chose as its strategy the creation of limited industrial zones prohibiting residential and commercial uses. According to expert opinion and evidence in the record, Justice Brennan noted, residential and commercial uses incompatible with light industrial uses would hinder the ability of New Providence to attract non-nuisance industry, thereby thwarting its plan.[24] In short, he warned,

> If well-conceived and carefully thought out zoning plans such as this, so obviously and peculiarly appropriate to further the well-being of the community of New Providence, are to be struck down in this fashion, a grievous blow will be dealt the forward progress of zoning as an instrument for the enhancement of the overall social and economic welfare of our municipalities.[25]

Again, in one of his earliest opinions as an appellate judge, the role of planning played an important part in Justice Brennan's approval of a rezoning. In *Birkfield Realty Co. v. Board of Commissioners*,[26] a landowner in the city of Orange, sought permission to build garden apartments in an area zoned for single-family homes.[27] The owner claimed that changes in the land uses surrounding his parcel had made the comprehensive plan on which the zoning was based obsolete.[28] In rejecting this argument, Justice Brennan emphasized the community's efforts to address growth and change through its master planning process and zoning ordinance.[29] Showing keen appreciation for the difficulties facing planners, he noted that "attainment of planning objectives cannot be achieved overnight, particularly in a long-settled community like Orange, founded in 1664, where the immediate effort must be in large part a struggle to preserve 'such beneficial features as may have survived the period of spontaneous and uncontrolled growth' of the city."[30]

Justice Brennan contrasted two areas in Orange, one a "striking example of the baneful consequences of planless growth and haphazard development,"[31] the other salvageable through planning and wise residential zoning. A planning board study had concluded that, " 'in a city such as Orange, where there exists little vacant land, where the population growth has remained on the decline, it is most important to protect those areas and investments that are good, while encouraging new constructions in those areas in need of rejuvenation.' "[32] After carefully studying the neighborhood surrounding the landowner's parcel, the planning board decided that it needed protection as a single-family district " 'based upon the character of fine homes still standing in this area.' "[33] Because the community produced evidence that its decision was a reflection of sound planning, Justice Brennan deferred to the views of the planners and local officials.

Protection of Comprehensiveness

For Justice Brennan, one of the most significant indicators of sound planning is comprehensiveness. Comprehensiveness has both spatial and temporal dimensions: spatial in the sense of large geographic areas, temporal in the sense of application over a substantial period of time. Comprehensive planning commonly describes a process in which the locality studies and plans for the long-term interests of major sections of the community.[34] Under most state zoning enabling acts, including New Jersey's, zoning ordinances and amendments must be enacted in accordance with a comprehensive plan.[35] Thus, in reviewing challenges to local zoning actions, judges must determine whether the zoning follows or reflects a comprehensive plan.[36]

The potential protections afforded by such a requirement are manifold. By definition, comprehensive planning is contrary to piecemeal planning, where the singling out of individuals may be, or may appear to be, unfair and arbitrary. The comprehensive planning process encourages all voices in a community to be heard, thereby democratizing planning through citizen participation. Where the push and pull of a specific controversy can ignite passions overriding long-range thinking, comprehensive planning elevates the discussion to a higher and detached plane. The expenditure of energy and funds in a comprehensive effort can help assure the reviewing court that the community itself values its stated goals.

In his first land use opinion as an appellate judge, Justice Brennan cited comprehensiveness as one reason for upholding the zoning decision of a small community grappling with new growth patterns. In *Guaclides v. Borough of Englewood Cliffs*,[37] a property owner agreed to sell 13 acres of land in Englewood Cliffs to a developer for a proposed garden apartment project.[38] In response to objections from residents, the town rezoned most of its jurisdiction, including the 13 acres, to single-family use and limited multifamily dwellings to one area.[39] Writing for the court, Justice Brennan first recited boilerplate language familiar to the land use lawyer: a presumption of validity attaches to local legislative action, the burden is on the challenger to establish that the legislative action is illegal and if the validity of the action is fairly debatable, then the legislative judgment prevails.[40] He emphasized that no violation of the state enabling legislation had occurred, as the zoning amendment was "clearly comprehensive," embracing much of the land in the borough and not just the parcel of the landowner.[41] Thus, as well, the amendment did not constitute spot zoning aimed only at the landowner's property.[42] And because neighboring land was either undeveloped or occupied by single-family housing, a prohibition on multifamily housing in the general vicinity was hardly unreasonable.[43] Justice Brennan also observed that, unlike other communities in New Jersey, Englewood Cliffs had experienced neither a large increase in its population nor the building of many new homes.[44] Its 1932 population of 900 had remained constant, and until the year before the lawsuit, when five new houses were built, not more than one or two houses had been constructed annually since 1932.[45] Indeed, no multi-family housing existed in the community, he added, and whatever demand existed could be accommodated in the area zoned for it.[46] Thus, the community's purpose of preserving small-town character did not interfere with a surging demand for residences.

The comprehensiveness requirement could also cut the other way. In *Conlon v. Board of Public Works*,[47] the city of Paterson changed the zoning use restriction on a single lot from residential to business to permit the construction of a bank.[48] However, the definition of the business zone included not only the bank use, but also many other business uses admittedly not desired by the locality.[49] Justice Brennan commented that the zoning change was "not made with the purpose or effect of establishing or furthering a comprehensive zoning scheme calculated to achieve the statutory objectives."[50] Instead, he pointedly observed, it was designed merely to help the landowner avoid alleged "particular harshness" caused by the original residential restriction.[51] For this purpose, the correct avenue available to the landowner was an application for a variance from the existing zoning,[52] not a change in the underlying zoning and planning. To accomplish a delicate and specific task (helping one landowner), the municipality had used too blunt an instrument, Justice Brennan maintained, one that impermissibly ignored the comprehensive plan.

In *Casper v. City of Long Branch*,[53] the town's apparent comprehensive plan again played an important role for Justice Brennan. There, the city refused to grant a permit for the use of a structure as a boarding house.[54] In upholding the town's decision to stop further encroachments on its plan, he approvingly cited evidence of the city's attempt to "maintain the integrity of the zoning scheme" by prosecuting a number of zoning violators.[55]

Plans, Variances and Nonconforming Uses

Since its early days, zoning has been attacked by persons straining to release its "Euclidean" grip. Named after the famous 1926 case *Village of Euclid v. Ambler Realty Co.*,[56] in which the U.S. Supreme Court first upheld the constitutionality of zoning, Euclidean zoning refers to the traditional ordinance in which municipalities divide their land into districts defined by use, shape and bulk classifications. One way to avoid uniform, inflexible and static prohibitions is through discretionary exceptions, and the history of zoning is nothing if not a history of variances and special permits.[57] More than anything else, the variance escape valve has been used—and misused—to avoid the requirements of the local plan. Most variance provisions, including those found in New Jersey's zoning enabling act, allow the grant of a variance only when it is "without substantial detriment to the public good and will not substantially impair the intent and purpose of the zone plan and zoning ordinance" and when the applicant can demonstrate both that exceptional physical property conditions exist and that strict application of the ordinance would cause undue hardship unique to his or her land.[58] The board of appeals, a town's variance-granting body, operates independently from a town's planning board or zoning commission.

Because of his ever-present emphasis on sound planning and comprehensiveness, and his related wariness of discretionary governmental action, Justice Brennan cast a watchful—some may say antagonistic—eye on devices designed to temper zoning's inherent rigidity. Indeed, his opinion in *Leimann v. Board of Adjustment*[59] overturned the issuance of a variance that had "the effect not simply of substantially impairing the intent and purpose of the Cranford zoning ordinance: the grant for so large an area as 9.5 acres [for construction of a garden apartment complex of eight buildings with 140 units] in a district where single-family dwellings are built usually on moderate sized lots virtually shatters, if indeed it does not wholly nullify, the general scheme of the zone."[60] In *Rexon v. Board of Adjustment*,[61] Justice Brennan approved the denial of a variance for a machine shop use in a residential area.[62] As with *Leimann*, however, he emphasized that care should be taken that the granting of a variance, by frustrating the general scheme, should not end up usurping the planning and zoning power embodied in the original ordinance.[63] And in *Cobble Close Farm v. Board of Adjustment*,[64] Justice Brennan again displayed a chariness about variances, especially where the property owner, with eyes open, buys into a situation requiring one.[65] There, the "controversy grows out of plaintiff's desire to convert the manure barn into a one-family dwelling and the group of buildings around the cobbled court into eight one-family residences,"[66] even though the owner knew in advance that the zoning would not permit such a development. Justice Brennan tolerated no exception to the zoning unless the owner had clean hands and reasonable expectations for the desired use,[67] and the integrity of the plan was maintained.

When zoning ordinances are initially adopted or subsequently amended, existing land uses previously allowed may be prohibited by the new zoning. These existing uses are classified as "nonconforming" and are usually permitted to continue for a reasonable period of time. *Struyk v. Samuel Braen's Sons*[68] involved an attempt by an owner to expand the operations of its quarry, itself already a nonconforming use, to a newly acquired neighboring property.[69] Justice Brennan stated the familiar rule that "[t]he policy of the law is to restrict rather than to increase non-conforming uses," under the theory that the current zoning plan should be followed as much as possible.[70] He thus approved the denial of the expanded quarry operation. Furthermore, as in *Cobble Close Farm*, he noted that the landowner purchased the property "with full knowledge of the restrictions imposed thereunder" and the effort to extend the nonconforming use was "in effect an attempt to circumvent the prohibition of which [the landowner] was fully aware."[71] Since no legitimate private property expectations were shattered, government permission for the expanded quarry was not required.[72]

Through the lenses of today's glasses, Justice Brennan's reliance on zoning coupled with planning may seem not only naive but conservative. Skepticism about the ability of planners to predict the future or create superior environments clouds the willingness to rely on planning-supported zoning.[73] Perhaps more significant, it is now evident that the ramification of zoning retoolings by many New Jersey communities—and other towns across the country—was the exclusion of low-income and minority families from suburban areas. But if the 1960s and 1970s were the decades of exclusionary zoning litigation, the 1950s witnessed only the commencement of the exodus to suburbia. No one at that time was making claims that suburbia should affirmatively zone for the development of their fair share of low- and moderate-income families.[74] Had such claims been in the zeitgeist, it is interesting to speculate what Justice Brennan's response would have been. One suspects that he would have lent a sympathetic ear and fashioned responsive legal remedies.[75]

Dangers of
Standardless Discretion

In one of his last state land use opinions, Justice Brennan articulated concerns about standardless municipal discretion that would echo in his later U.S. Supreme Court opinion *Metromedia, Inc. v. City of San Diego*.[76] In *Weiner v. Borough of Stratford*,[77] a local ordinance provided that no person could engage in any business within the community unless he or she obtained a license from the borough clerk and paid a fee.[78] Under a discretionary scheme established by the law, the application for a license went to the planning board, which forwarded findings and recommendations to the borough council, which in turn granted or denied the license.[79] An individual sought a license to open an auction store at a location permitted by the applicable zoning, but the borough council rejected the application.[80]

In his majority opinion, Justice Brennan overturned the entire licensing provision. He wrote that "unless the provisions . . . vesting discretion in licensing officials to grant or deny a license provide adequate standards to govern the deliberations of the officials having the discretionary power," the ordinance was fatally flawed.[81] Without explicit directions in the law, the administering body could arbitrarily and capriciously grant or deny the license. Indeed, the specific facts of this case demonstrated the problem, for the council apparently denied the license to the new store for an impermissible reason: it wanted to protect the business interests of existing auction establishments.[82] This was a " 'subversion of competition . . . not in the public interest,' " scolded Justice Brennan.[83]

Billboards
and the Crystal Ball

One New Jersey opinion by Justice Brennan directly presaged a later federal opinion. In *United Advertising Corp. v. Borough of Raritan*,[84] the issue involved government regulation of billboards, just as it later would in *Metromedia, Inc. v. City of San Diego*.[85] Interestingly, his treatment in one does not predict his treatment in the other. In *United Advertising*, the borough of Raritan adopted a local zoning provision banning the traditional free-standing billboard.[86] Many communities nominally justified billboard regulations on grounds of traffic safety: after all, if billboards did their job, then drivers were distracted from the task of driving. Of course, the real reason for the ban was that billboards were perceived as aesthetically unattractive. In the *United Advertising* case, the billboard company complained that the ban illegally discriminated against billboards while ignoring other unattractive urban uses.[87] Why should the company's signs be banned in business and industrial zones where manufacturing plants, junk yards, and coal and coke yards were allowed?[88] That very argument was made some 30 years later by none other than Justice Brennan in his *Metromedia* opinion.[89] Here, however, he rejected it with an uncharacteristically terse conclusory statement: "It is enough that outdoor advertising has characteristic features which have long been deemed sufficient to sustain regulations or prohibitions peculiarly applicable to it."[90]

The contradiction between *United Advertising* and *Metromedia* is understandable only against the backdrop of developments in first amendment law. *United Advertising* was decided before the U.S. Supreme Court concluded that commercial speech, including advertisements on billboards, was entitled to some degree of protection under the freedom of speech clause of the first amendment.[91] Without free speech protection, however, the billboard owner was like any other property owner subject to traditional classifications under zoning. If an ordinance could ban business uses in residential districts, then surely it could also prohibit billboards from certain districts. Applying the "minimum scrutiny" test appropriate for review of socioeconomic legislation under the equal protection clause,[92] Justice Brennan necessarily concluded that the billboard ordinance was constitutional.

Public Use Doctrine

Just as private property owners are not free to do whatever they like with their property, government faces limitations on use of government-acquired property. The rules applicable to public property differ, however, from those affecting private property. They are traceable to limitations governing an ancient and honorable privilege enjoyed by the sovereign since the time of the Magna Carta: the power to take private property *for public use* on payment of just compensation, known as the power of eminent domain.[93] Codified in the just compensation clause of the U.S. Constitution's fifth amendment,[94] and in state constitutions as well, traditional public uses justifying the exercise of eminent domain include highways,[95] public buildings,[96] urban renewal,[97] schools,[98] parks[99] and housing.[100]

In recent years, courts have chipped away at the fringes of the public use limitation, rarely disqualifying a taking of land on the basis that it is not for a public use. The surprising notion that government may take land from one private owner to give to another private owner is now a judicial commonplace. Indeed, courts have approved takings that destroyed an entire residential neighborhood to accommodate a new General Motors automobile manufacturing plant in Detroit[101] and that broke up large Hawaiian estates for redistribution to smaller private owners.[102] Each of these takings had an underlying public purpose—jobs in Detroit, oligopoly bashing in Hawaii—that satisfied the public use requirement.

Although a liberal interpretation of the public use doctrine is now standard, the early 1950s presented a more conservative judicial hue. Some judges rigidly distinguished between public and private and struck down government actions involving private sector participation. Justice Brennan was not among such formalists. Just as U.S. Supreme Court Justice William O. Douglas in 1954 pronounced the magisterial extent of public purpose justifying government authority in *Berman v. Parker*,[103] a well-known urban renewal case from the District of Columbia, so, too, did Justice Brennan that same year in a New Jersey Supreme Court case. The question in *Camden Plaza Parking, Inc. v. City of Camden*[104] involved the propriety of leasing public land to private parties who would then construct and operate a parking garage.[105] Justice Brennan made short shrift of a cramped reading of the public use limitation on government exercises of power: "Action by a municipality to relieve traffic congestion through the establishment of off-street public parking facilities is the exercise of a public and essential governmental function, and publicly-owned lands used for such purposes are devoted to a public use."[106]

On the additional issue that the facility was to be operated by a private party, Justice Brennan concluded that this was not a violation of the public use requirement, noting "the land and facility do not cease to be used for a public purpose when leased to private operators for operation as a public parking facility."[107] There would be no exaltation of form over substance here.

Run-of-the-Mill Jurisprudence

A state judge is frequently faced not with substantial land use legal questions, but with mundane ones making up the less significant part of that area of law. Some of Justice Brennan's opinions, although deeply affecting the parties, are, frankly, uninteresting from a legal point of view. Still, initial indications of the careful craftsman, concerned with untangling and deciphering the facts, emerge from these simple cases. In *Tice v. Borough of Woodcliff Lake*,[108] the question of the moment was the definition of an "amusement park" as that term was used in the zoning ordinance.[109] Justice Brennan concluded that the proposed project—a swimming pool with bath houses and a refreshment stand —did not fall within the terms of the definition and thus was not prohibited by the zoning ordinance.[110]

If Justice Brennan's 13 New Jersey land use opinions are neither individually nor cumulatively earthshaking, they are thoroughly representative of land use issues faced by state court judges across the country. Perhaps therein lies their ultimate significance for the professional and personal development of Justice Brennan's sensibilities. The prosaic conflict of *Tice* no less than the growth-preservation controversies of *Birkfield* and *Guaclides* provided opportunities to hear genuine aspirations of private property owners and local communities. Forced to learn the intricate details of one state's land use regulatory system, Justice Brennan would be better able years later to gauge the majestic but indeterminate phrases of the Constitution against the realities of local government practice. Not surprisingly, his eight Supreme Court opinions are animated by the intuition of a seasoned, confident practitioner entering a world made familiar by past experience. In retrospect, his New Jersey days constituted the proving ground from which a major land use jurist would emerge.

3 LATER VIEWS FROM WASHINGTON

Ventura County, Calif., beachfront property, along which the state attempted to require a public right of access. From Nollan v. California Coastal Commission.
(Jerold S. Kayden)

Following his appointment in 1956 to the U.S. Supreme Court, Justice Brennan did not write another land use opinion for 19 years. This fact reflects not change in interest on his part, but scarcity of land use cases accepted for full consideration by the Supreme Court. After a flurry of four zoning opinions announced in the late 1920s,[1] the Court did not issue another substantial land use regulatory opinion until the early 1960s.[2] And even that case was a restatement of prevailing principles first articulated around the turn of the century.[3] The evolution of land use law was left to the states.

Like a judicial version of Rip Van Winkle, however, the Supreme Court in the mid-1970s reawakened from its land use slumber with a vengeance. Over the past 14 years, the Court has heard 23 land use cases,[4] and Justice Brennan has written substantial opinions in eight of them. Given the opportunity, Justice Brennan shows vigorous interest in the field, recognizing how land use restrictions directly affect the quality of community and private life.

In the zeal of discovery, the legal anthropologist may succumb to the serious temptation of constructing *post hoc* a latticework of legal thinking, magically linking together four decades of opinions into seamless themes and approaches. Mindful of that danger, one may, nonetheless, detect in Justice Brennan's eight Supreme Court opinions clear reverberations from his state court days. In particular, the importance he attached to comprehensiveness resurfaced over 20 years later in two different areas: land use regulations affecting first amendment free speech rights and land use regulations challenged as takings. In the first amendment cases, the existence of a comprehensive effort to meet aesthetic concerns provided Justice Brennan with a measure of assurance that the community was serious about its goal (actions speak louder than words). In the takings area, the comprehensive approach helped secure the guarantee against arbitrary and discriminatory actions affecting individual property owners.

Comprehensiveness Revisited: Land Use, the First Amendment and Billboards

In his concurring opinion in *Metromedia, Inc. v. City of San Diego*,[5] Justice Brennan first introduced the idea of a comprehensiveness test in first amendment land use cases, a concept that received further elaboration in two subsequent Brennan first amendment land use opinions about restrictions on posting signs and on adult theaters.[6] Six justices (joining Justice Byron R. White's plurality opinion or Justice Brennan's concurring opinion) chose to strike down San Diego's citywide ban on the traditional free-standing billboard in *Metromedia*.[7] In its result, the case is another in a line of decisions applying first amendment protections to commercial speech.[8]

Because the first amendment expressly protects speech, government actions that directly or indirectly impinge on that right must be carefully reviewed. The critical clash in *Metromedia* was between the billboard owner's claim for free speech, exercised through the private property right of erecting a billboard, and the community's right to a safe and attractive physical environment. Lurking in the wings was everyone's right to communicate and receive messages through the medium of billboards. Justice Brennan's balancing test allowed a total ban on commercial speech billboards if a city "can show that a sufficiently substantial governmental interest is directly furthered by the total ban, and that any more narrowly drawn restriction, i.e., anything less than a total ban, would promote less well the achievement of that goal."[9]

Applying that test to San Diego, Justice Brennan, joined by Justice Harry A. Blackmun, found that the city had failed.[10] San Diego asserted two government interests supporting its billboard ban: traffic safety and aesthetics.[11] Justice Brennan acknowledged that, in the abstract, these government interests were sufficiently substantial.[12] It is because he found no evidence in the record showing that San Diego itself held these interests to be sufficiently substantial that he overturned the law.[13]

After a brief discussion about the failure of evidence on traffic safety,[14] Justice Brennan turned to the knotty question of aesthetics. After all, he implicitly wondered, how does a city prove that it has a substantial interest in aesthetics? His answer was reminiscent of his New Jersey thinking: "[B]efore deferring to a city's judgment, a court must be convinced that the city is seriously and comprehensively addressing aesthetic concerns with respect to its environment. Here, San Diego has failed to demonstrate a comprehensive coordinated effort. . . ."[15] Simply mouthing the word "aesthetics," so easy to do when courts today routinely accept aesthetics as a legitimate justification for government regulation,[16] is not enough for Justice Brennan where the heightened interests of the first amendment are involved.

As in his New Jersey days, he looked to the parties themselves to see what weight they placed on their interests. What effort, other than the billboard ban, had San Diego made to deal with its aesthetic concern? Justice Brennan made clear that he was not demanding a massive city program: "Of course, this is not to say that the city must address all aesthetic problems at the same time, or none at all. Indeed, from a planning point of view, attacking the problem incrementally and sequentially may represent the most sensible solution."[17] He added, "On the other hand, if billboards alone are banned and no further steps are contemplated or likely, the commitment of the city to improving its physical environment is placed in doubt."[18]

To the argument that it is inherently obvious that billboards are eyesores, Justice Brennan declined to take judicial notice of this fact and responded, "It is no doubt true that the appearance of certain areas of the city would be enhanced by the elimination of billboards, but 'it is not immediately apparent as a matter of experience' that their elimination in all other areas as well would have more than a negligible impact on aesthetics."[19] For example, he noted, a "billboard is not necessarily inconsistent with oil storage tanks, blighted areas, or strip development," areas that admittedly existed in San Diego.[20] Lest he be accused of substituting his views for that of the legislature, he subsequently remarked, "Of course, it is not for a court to impose its own notion of beauty on San Diego."[21]

Inevitably, those unpersuaded of the utility of Justice Brennan's standard will deem the preceding qualification conclusory and self-serving. And, indeed, there remains something unsatisfactory about a quest for objectivity in the inherently subjective world of aesthetics. The quandary for judges, and especially sequestered and secluded appellate ones, involves an uncertain navigation between the Scylla of perfunctory rubber stamp review and the Charybdis of visceral decision making. In a sense, what Justice Brennan proposed is a middle ground: reliance on the existence of an articulated plan of action that judges can measure for signs of public commitment and integrity. Some irreducible amount of subjective judicial second-guessing of legislative choices is the price he appears willing to pay to guarantee meaningful review of first amendment restrictions. Reminding the reader that this is a case where important first amendment private rights are at stake, he recapitulated his test:

> By showing a comprehensive commitment to making its physical environment in commercial and industrial areas more attractive, and by allowing only narrowly tailored exceptions, if any, San Diego could demonstrate that its interest in creating an aesthetically pleasing environment is genuine and substantial. This is a requirement, where, as here, there is an infringement of important constitutional consequence.[22]

Justice Brennan's view that a "billboard is not *necessarily* inconsistent with oil storage tanks, blighted areas, or strip development" recalled the apparently contrary statement from his New Jersey *United Advertising* opinion some 30 years earlier that "there also exists no invidious discrimination in the provisions of the ordinance barring plaintiff's signs in the business and industrial zones while allowing therein manufacturing plants, junk yards, coal and coke yards and other uses suggested by plaintiff as also having undesirable attributes."[23] This apparent inconsistency is not a real one and instead reflects the Court's conclusions, adopted years after the *United Advertising* case, that commercial speech is entitled to protection under the first amendment and thus to heightened scrutiny.[24]

A secondary issue in *Metromedia* involved the exercise of municipal discretion, something Justice Brennan addressed once before in his New Jersey *Weiner* opinion.[25] There, he struck down a local regulation giving standardless discretion to the city government to grant or deny a business license to an auction house.[26] In *Metromedia*, the issue arose from dictum in Justice White's plurality opinion about the contours of a constitutionally acceptable billboard ban. The first amendment extends its maximum protection to political and ideological speech, while according commercial speech, such as advertising, less protection. For Justice White, the San Diego ordinance effectively inverted this constitutional hierarchy by, for example, allowing businesses to erect identifying signs on their premises while banning all political or ideological billboard messages.[27] His opinion suggested approval for a city ordinance that totally banned commercial speech billboards but allowed noncommercial speech billboards.[28]

Justice Brennan was troubled by this distinction, because "it gives city officials the right—before approving a billboard—to determine whether the proposed message is 'commercial' or 'noncommercial.'"[29] He observed, "Because making such determinations would entail a substantial exercise of discretion by a city's official, it presents a real danger of curtailing noncommercial speech in the guise of regulating commercial speech."[30] To demonstrate just how difficult it is for courts, let alone city officials, to distinguish between commercial and noncommercial messages, Justice Brennan offered an instructive string of increasingly noncommercial billboard messages involving an imaginary Joe's Ice Cream Shoppe: "Visit Joe's Ice Cream Shoppe," "Joe's Ice Cream Shoppe uses only the highest quality dairy products," "Because Joe thinks that dairy products are good for you, please shop at Joe's Shoppe," and "Joe says to support dairy price supports: they mean lower prices for you at his Shoppe."[31] Which is commercial and which is noncommercial, he implicitly asked?

Comprehensiveness, Poster Bans and Erogenous Zoning

The comprehensiveness seed, planted in New Jersey and blooming in *Metromedia*, fully blossomed in two subsequent dissenting opinions by Justice Brennan.[32] In *Members of City Council v. Taxpayers for Vincent*,[33] the Court upheld against first amendment challenge a citywide ban on the posting of signs on public property.[34] In that case, a political committee supporting Roland Vincent's candidacy for election to the Los Angeles City Council hired a company to post signs on utility poles throughout the city.[35] Relying on Justice Brennan's *Metromedia* reasoning, the U.S. Court of Appeals for the Ninth Circuit concluded that Los Angeles's interest in aesthetics was not sufficiently substantial to outweigh the constitutional interest in free expression.[36] The court of appeals observed that the city failed to prove that it had undertaken a comprehensive and coordinated effort to remove other elements of visual clutter within its boundaries.[37]

Although a majority of justices overruled the court of appeals and upheld the poster ban, Justice Brennan, dissenting, won a third adherent, Justice Thurgood Marshall, for his *Metromedia* test. This time around, he elaborated more fully on his views. His reasoning in the *Metromedia* case, he observed, was "premised largely on my concern that aesthetic interests are easy for a city to assert and difficult for a court to evaluate."[38] He acknowledged that "'beauty is in the eye of the beholder'" and that "[a]s a consequence of this subjectivity, laws defended on aesthetic grounds raise problems for judicial review that are not presented by laws defended on more objective grounds. . . ."[39] But this just made the job of review that much more central and thus strengthened his resolve: "In short, we must avoid unquestioned acceptance of the City's bare declaration of an aesthetic objective lest we fail in our duty to prevent unlawful trespasses upon First Amendment protections."[40]

Justice Brennan criticized the majority for deferring to the city's assertion of interest, a deference suitable for land use regulations having no first amendment impacts but inappropriate for a poster ban.[41] Instead, he employed his *Metromedia* test, noting that a comprehensive and coordinated effort addressing community aesthetics provided the reviewing court with a reliable indication of the government's own assessment of substantiality.[42] Only when the government itself demonstrates seriousness can a court be reasonably assured that there is no underlying discrimination against the content of the banned messages.[43] And, after all, the *Vincent* case was the ideal vehicle in which to raise that specter, as the banned posters urged the election of candidate Vincent to the same city council that, sometime in the past, had enacted the poster ban.

In *City of Renton v. Playtime Theatres, Inc.*,[44] the Court upheld a local ordinance prohibiting adult motion picture theaters from locating within 1,000 feet of residential zones, single- or multifamily dwellings, churches or parks, or within one mile of any school.[45] In dissent, Justice Brennan once again applied his *Metromedia* test, this time stating that Renton, Wash., must demonstrate that it was seriously and comprehensively addressing secondary land use effects, such as impacts on neighborhoods, associated with adult movie theaters.[46] Otherwise, no reviewing court would be sure that no impermissible motivations relating to the content of speech were behind enactment of the regulation.[47] Since, among other failings, Renton had made no studies demonstrating such secondary effects, Justice Brennan would have struck down the law.[48]

Comprehensiveness, Takings and Historic Preservation

The most famous legal showdown involving the historic preservation movement had its high noon at the Supreme Court in 1978. In the landmark case on landmarks, *Penn Central Transportation Co. v. New York City*,[49] Justice Brennan delivered one of his most influential opinions (his only Supreme Court land use majority), which saved New York City's Beaux Arts masterpiece, Grand Central Terminal (1913, Reed and Stem; Warren and Wetmore), and, more broadly, upheld the constitutionality of historic preservation laws across the country. His majority was noteworthy as well for its detailed recapitulation of almost a century of Supreme Court takings jurisprudence and for its contribution of several innovative legal theories.

The city of New York enacted a landmarks preservation law through which it attempted to preserve historic landmarks and districts.[50] Landmarks were defined as buildings 30 years old or older, with special character or special historical or aesthetic interest, while historic districts were singled out as areas containing landmarks and representing styles of architecture typical of the city's history.[51] More than 400 landmarks and 31 districts had been designated by the New York landmarks commission.[52] Once designated, a property's exterior appearance could not be modified by its owner without the commission's approval.[53]

The Penn Central Transportation Company owned Grand Central Terminal, which in 1967 was designated a landmark by the commission.[54] The company wanted to build an office skyscraper over the terminal, but two of its proposals were rejected by the commission as harmful to the landmark qualities of the terminal building.[55] Penn Central claimed a taking of its property without just compensation, a violation of the fifth and fourteenth amendments of the U.S. Constitution.[56] Because New York's landmarks law, although different in detail, mirrored the basic structure of local landmark legislation across the country, an adverse ruling on its constitutionality would severely undermine the national effort to save architecturally and historically significant places.

With refreshing candor, Justice Brennan acknowledged how the Court "has been unable to develop any 'set formula' for determining when 'justice and fairness' require that economic injuries caused by public action be compensated by the government, rather than remain disproportionately concentrated on a few persons."[57] Nevertheless, Justice Brennan adumbrated two key concerns that should guide the Court in its "essentially *ad hoc*, factual inquiries".[58] the "character of the governmental action" and the "economic impact of the regulation on the claimant and, particularly, the extent to which the regulation has interfered with distinct investment-backed expectations."[59]

In applying the character criteria, Justice Brennan was impressed by the comprehensiveness of the government action in this case.[60] He observed that, "[i]n contrast to discriminatory zoning, which is the antithesis of land-use control as part of some comprehensive plan, the New York City law embodies a comprehensive plan to preserve structures of historic or aesthetic interest wherever they might be found in the city . . . ."[61] He cited the number of landmarks (400) and historic districts (31) designated under the plan.[62] Comprehensiveness here served an additional purpose beyond establishing the seriousness of the government's interest. In the takings context, comprehensiveness helped ensure that individuals were not singled out, that government was not "forcing some people alone to bear public burdens which, in all fairness and justice, should be borne by the public as a whole."[63]

The scope of comprehensiveness was at the heart of the dispute between Justice Brennan's majority and Justice William H. Rehnquist's dissent.[64] Although obviously burdened more heavily than nonlandmark property owners, Justice Brennan observed, the landmark owner derives some benefit from the comprehensiveness of the restrictions on other landmarks throughout the city.[65] If the Constitution does not guarantee exact equality, it still sets a baseline best expressed by Justice Oliver Wendell Holmes's 67-year-old concept of an "average reciprocity of advantage."[66] As long as enough persons are similarly restricted, then everyone has received some benefit, even if some are burdened more substantially than others. Although Justice Rehnquist agreed that comprehensiveness is important, he disagreed about its applicability to New York's landmarks program. In an undocumented but telling calculation, Justice Rehnquist noted that New York imposed landmark designations on "less than one one-tenth of one percent of the buildings in New York City for the general benefit of all its people."[67] That can hardly be called comprehensive, he argued.

The second inquiry—economic impact—always creates the most confusion because no court has a simple answer about how much is too much.[68] The extremes are known: owners are not constitutionally entitled to the highest and best or most profitable use of their land[69] but are entitled to an economically viable use.[70] Following Justice Holmes's 1922 *Pennsylvania Coal Co. v. Mahon* opinion,[71] courts traditionally assess the "diminution of value" to the property caused by the regulation to determine whether a taking has occurred.[72] If the property value drops sufficiently, then courts will find a taking. However, they rarely do.

Justice Brennan introduced a novel element to the economic inquiry in the *Penn Central* case by requiring consideration of "the extent to which the regulation has interfered with distinct investment-backed expectations."[73] Believing that the regulatory impact on landowner expectations is more relevant than the impact on absolute property values,[74] he shifted the central point of view from property to property owner. To take expectations out of the realm of the ethereal, they must be "distinct" and "investment-backed." Under Justice Brennan's formulation, a property severely devalued in its regulated state theoretically may still not support a takings claim if the landowner cannot demonstrate legitimate investment-backed expectations for a higher use. Such a scenario may arise, for example, when an individual purchases property whose economic viability is contingent upon the government's willingness to amend applicable zoning.[75] Since the individual's investment decision is based on the mere hope of favorable public action, the individual's takings complaint may be discounted when expectations do not transform into reality.[76] After all, the just compensation clause does not guarantee profits, only the possibility of profits. This retooling of the economic impact inquiry—giving it a modern-day financial gloss—dovetails with one of the most commonly used real estate financial analysis measures: the return on equity invested.[77] Only recently have courts begun to explore the true significance of this shift in focus.[78] Because the Penn Central Transportation Company (in what may, with the wisdom of hindsight, be dubbed a strategic error) expressly admitted that it earned a reasonable return on its investment in the terminal building,[79] impacts on its distinct investment-backed expectations by definition could not rise to the level of a taking.

The highlighting of expectations in *Penn Central* as a central determinant of private property rights resonates fully with Justice Brennan's path-breaking definition of so-called new property rights under the due process clause. The new property refers primarily to statutory entitlements created by government such as welfare benefits or a public job.[80] Because individuals reasonably develop expectations about the existence and continuation of such entitlements, Justice Brennan has argued, entitlements assume some of the attributes associated with traditional private property. And the mere fact that new property rights may be characterized as creatures of government beneficence is not dispositive, for government and the society it represents have made them part of the social contract binding together the citizenry. Thus, the Constitution requires that government may not deprive persons of these rights without "due process of law," usually a hearing, statement of reasons or other procedural device.[81]

Justice Brennan first announced this functional view of property in his 1970 *Goldberg v. Kelly* decision, where he wrote that "[m]uch of the existing wealth in this country takes the form of rights that do not fall within traditional common-law concepts of property," and that "[i]t may be realistic today to regard welfare entitlements as more like 'property' than a 'gratuity.' "[82] Where subsequent Supreme Court cases limited new property rights to instances where legislatures have expressly defined rights as such,[83] Justice Brennan rejected this overtly positivist view (that the state may deprive individuals of rights merely because laws do not expressly define them as property) and instead adhered to his pragmatic expectations-based divining rod. For example, in a case involving the firing of a policeman, he commented that "before a state law is definitively construed as not securing a 'property' interest, the relevant inquiry is whether it was objectively reasonable for the employee to believe he could rely on continued employment."[84] After all, he noted, " '[i]t is a purpose of the ancient institution of property to protect those claims upon which people rely in their daily lives, reliance that must not be arbitrarily undermined.' "[85]

In another practical slant to property rights, Justice Brennan directed the Court's economic inquiry in *Penn Central* to the regulation's impact on the "parcel as a whole."[86] Penn Central argued that the landmarks law rendered the air space above the terminal completely valueless and thus took that discrete part of the company's property.[87] Even if that assertion is true,[88] suggested Justice Brennan, the regulation had not necessarily effected a taking. As long as the landowner is able to make reasonable use of the entire property—and Penn Central admitted that it could—then that was enough. The wisdom of the "parcel as a whole" rule is readily observed. Zoning laws frequently prohibit development of parts of a parcel, for example, to guarantee sufficient front, side and rear yard setbacks from the street and sidewalk. Owners would be able to challenge these and other requirements as takings without the "parcel as a whole" qualification.

Justice Brennan also cast a favorable eye at what was then a relatively new and innovative land use technique, transfer of development rights (TDR), which held promise for preservation of historic properties, agricultural land and open space. Traditionally, land and the air above it had been viewed as unseverable for purposes of ownership. A transfer of development rights program severs ownership by allowing owners to sell (transfer) unused development rights to other owners. The selling owner's property is then restricted by the amount of development rights sold, while the buying owner can use the additional development rights on a different property to construct buildings larger than otherwise permitted by applicable zoning rules. Recognizing that its restrictions imposed costs on landmark owners, and that sale of unused development rights could help compensate them, New York City permitted transfers to nearby properties.[89] Indeed, Penn Central owned eight properties to which it could transfer some of the air rights above Grand Central Terminal.[90] Willing as always to let local governments innovate for the social, economic and physical well-being of the community, Justice Brennan embraced the transfer option and counted it as a mitigating factor in evaluating the economic impact of the landmark designation.[91] Even as Justice Rehnquist argued that the landmark regulation effected a taking, he agreed with Justice Brennan that the transfer of development rights provision might be valuable.[92] However, he would have sent the case back to the lower courts to determine whether a transfer would constitute just compensation to Penn Central.[93] In late 1986, much to the unhappiness of New York officials, the unused Grand Central Terminal air rights finally came home to roost: First Boston Corporation proposed to use at least 800,000 of the 1.9 million square feet of unused rights and transfer them to a Madison Avenue lot several blocks away from the terminal for a 74-story office tower, more than twice as large as would otherwise be permitted under the zoning.[94]

Putting to one side the legal innovations of the *Penn Central* decision, its practical effect was to validate, indeed to encourage, the proliferation of landmarks laws across the country.[95] Justice Brennan can take significant credit for enhancing what planners and citizens today take for granted as an essential aspect of communities: their history.

Takings and Just Compensation: A Novel Constitutional Rule

San Diego Gas & Electric Co. v. City of San Diego[96] is a case that demonstrates the crucial role of dissents in the Supreme Court's history.[97] Here, Justice Brennan squarely faced a question answered only indirectly by earlier Court decisions: can a land use regulation such as zoning effect a taking within the meaning of the just compensation clause, and, if so, must just compensation be paid? This controversy, at the heart of decades of disputes between local governments and landowners, was especially exacerbated by Justice Holmes's mercurial phrase in his 1922 *Pennsylvania Coal* opinion: "[I]f regulation goes too far it will be recognized as a taking."[98]

In the *San Diego Gas & Electric Co.* case, the five-member majority failed to reach this burning question because it found technical jurisdictional barriers in the way.[99] In his dissent, Justice Brennan and three other justices addressed the merits, found that a regulation can effect a taking and proposed a new just compensation remedy.[100] What gave Justice Brennan's dissent added force was a brief concurring opinion by Justice Rehnquist.[101] While joining the majority, Justice Rehnquist also wrote separately to say that, had he reached the merits, he "would have little difficulty in agreeing with much of what is said in the dissenting opinion of Justice Brennan."[102] Some vote counters interpreted Justice Rehnquist's opinion as a *de facto* fifth vote for the Brennan view.[103] Thus, the dissent has been widely followed by an impressive number of lower federal and state courts persuaded by its reasoning and by the possibility that it represents the views of a majority of the Supreme Court.[104]

The facts of the case are simple enough. In 1966 the San Diego Gas & Electric Company assembled a 412-acre parcel of land north of San Diego near the coast as a possible site for a nuclear power plant.[105] At the time of purchase, 116 acres were zoned industrial, with much of the balance zoned agricultural.[106] In 1967 the city of San Diego adopted a general plan designating most of the company's site industrial.[107] Six years later, in 1973, San Diego took three actions that together formed the predicate for subsequent litigation. First, the city downzoned some of the parcel from industrial to agricultural use.[108] Second, San Diego adopted a new open space plan designating 233 acres of the company's land for open space use and recommending that the city acquire the parcel for parkland.[109] Third, the city prepared to issue bonds that would finance the purchase of the property, although the bond issue never took place.[110]

Alleging a regulatory taking and seeking $6 million in damages, the company sued the city.[111] A California trial court held that the city's actions effected a taking of a portion of the company's land and, following a jury trial on the compensation question, awarded more than $3 million plus interest and other fees to the electric company.[112] The California Court of Appeal affirmed, but the California Supreme Court transferred the case back to the appellate court for reconsideration in light of a new California Supreme Court decision holding that property owners may seek only invalidation of, not compensation for, an unconstitutional land use regulation.[113] The appellate court subsequently reversed the trial court's judgment of a taking, the California Supreme Court denied further review, and the U.S. Supreme Court noted probable jurisdiction.[114] Writing for the majority, Justice Harry A. Blackmun held that the decision of the California Court of Appeal was not final, thus depriving the U.S. Supreme Court of jurisdiction to review the case.[115]

Justice Brennan found a final judgment and therefore reached the merits.[116] He first posed a threshold question that neither the parties to the litigation nor virtually any of the numerous amicus briefs[117] had addressed: "whether a government entity's exercise of its regulatory police power can ever effect a 'taking' within the meaning of the Just Compensation Clause."[118] The importance of this question can be quickly appreciated, for if a regulation can never effect a taking, then a regulation can never trigger operation of the just compensation clause. Whatever else a landowner may claim, he or she may not demand just compensation within the meaning of that constitutional clause.[119]

The theory that a regulation can never effect a taking was hardly chimerical: it had received judicial validation not only in California, but also in New York.[120] Indeed, the state court opinion in the *Penn Central* case, from which the railroad appealed to the U.S. Supreme Court, was partially based on just such a theory.[121] These courts, and supporting commentators, did not argue that land use regulations were always constitutional, only that they never effected takings.[122] They contended instead that overbearing regulations violated the due process clauses of the fifth and fourteenth amendments, violations for which, unlike the just compensation clause, the U.S. Constitution failed to specify an explicit compensatory remedy. Justice Brennan directly rejected this conclusion. He cited U.S. Supreme Court precedents (including his own *Penn Central* decision) where the Court explicitly inquired whether the challenged regulation effected a taking under the fifth amendment's just compensation clause.[123] Why, Justice Brennan queried, would the Court analyze these regulations as potential takings of private property were an affirmative answer foreclosed? For those commending a metaphorical reading of Justice Holmes's "if regulation goes too far it will be recognized as a taking" aphorism, Justice Brennan remained unpersuaded.

Furthermore, he argued, there is an essential similarity between regulatory and other takings: "Police power regulations such as zoning ordinances and other land-use restrictions can destroy the use and enjoyment of property in order to promote the public good just as effectively as formal condemnation or physical invasion of property."[124] In the traditional taking, the government exercises its power of eminent domain for a public use, condemns the property, takes physical possession and legal title, pays compensation and builds its highway, civic center, public housing or other facility. If a regulation totally prevents an owner from using property for any economic purpose, however, it is of little solace that the owner retains formal title. The fact that the government may not intend to take property when it regulates— as distinct from government intentions in formal condemnation proceedings—was of no constitutional moment for Justice Brennan.[125] Stripping away empty formalisms,[126] he implicitly disputed what is sometimes called the two-track theory, whereby police and eminent domain powers follow separate tracks that, by definition, never intersect.[127] Instead, he introduced the pragmatic notion of a "de facto exercise of the power of eminent domain," sensibly suggesting that an overzealous exercise of the police power may concurrently be an exercise of the eminent domain power.[128]

With this predicate in place, Justice Brennan turned to the second issue: whether just compensation must be paid when a regulation effects a taking. Before San Diego Gas & Electric Co., the only assured remedy for the property owner under Supreme Court precedent was invalidation of an unconstitutional regulation. Put another way, the landowner was not constitutionally entitled to receive money damages for the harmful impact of the regulation.

Landowners customarily argued that a judicial finding of taking automatically required an award of just compensation, measured by the full fair market value of the taken property.[129] Municipalities countered that, even upon a judicial determination of a taking, invalidation, not damages, was the proper remedy.[130] As frequently happens in constitutional litigation, both sides relied on policy considerations to buttress their positions. Owners noted that mere invalidation provided no real incentive for government bodies to eschew overreaching regulations. Indeed, Justice Brennan's dissent quoted the unfortunate exhortation of a California city attorney speaking at a National Institute of Municipal Law Officers conference: "If all else fails, merely amend the regulation and start over again."[131] If anything, urged owners, a monetary remedy would encourage cities to provide a proper margin of safety in their regulatory activities.

Municipalities responded that the threat of damages would chill innovative land use planning, that planners would no longer take the risks essential to good planning. Where the past penalty was the nonfinancial remedy of invalidation, a financial penalty would shift the economic loss caused by an unconstitutional regulation from landowner to government regulator, and the public ante would be undesirably raised. Furthermore, argued municipal officials, a monetary remedy would wreak havoc with budgetary planning by imposing huge and unanticipated liabilities.

Accepting neither the property owner position of permanent fee simple transfer and fair market value compensation nor the government position of invalidation, Justice Brennan offered a different constitutional interpretation: "[O]nce a court establishes that there was a regulatory 'taking,' the Constitution demands that the government entity pay just compensation for the period commencing on the date the regulation first effected the 'taking,' and ending on the date the government entity chooses to rescind or otherwise amend the regulation."[132] For him, the fact that a regulatory taking is temporary and reversible made untenable the landowner position that the government entity must pay full fair market value for the taken property and become a fee simple owner.[133] By the same token, however, this temporary and reversible quality made it no less a taking for its duration,[134] and the express words of the just compensation clause required an award of just compensation when a taking had occurred.[135] And the fundamental purpose of the clause—to redistribute to the public costs improperly borne by the individual—was served through compensation.[136] Thus, compensation for the period of taking[137] was required by the language, past judicial interpretation and underlying purpose of the just compensation clause. Justice Brennan wisely neither spelled out a detailed procedure for landowners to follow in seeking compensation, leaving to a later day and concrete conflict the further elaboration of this rule,[138] nor did he specify what methodology is appropriate to calculate the temporary just compensation payment.[139] Finally, it should be noted, he did not decide whether or not San Diego's regulatory actions in this case effected a taking: he simply made clear that, when facts justify a conclusion of regulatory taking, compensation must be awarded.[140]

The *San Diego Gas & Electric Co.* dissent dramatically increased the cacophony of debate on this most fundamental of land use questions. Some observers were perplexed at his position, even as they were familiar with and might applaud his opinions ensuring individuals the right to sue government for constitutional violations relating to life, liberty and other express constitutionally specified rights,[141] if not private property. Others found it difficult to reconcile the dissent with his opinion upholding government land use regulation in *Penn Central*, even as that case dealt with the definition of a regulatory taking, not the delineation of the remedy for a regulatory taking.[142] Simplistically, some liberals had trouble understanding why he (and Justice Marshall) would side with property owners.[143] But just as environmentalists could worry about the chilling of wetland and open space regulations, low-income housing advocates could celebrate the chilling of exclusionary zoning masked as environmental controls. Liberal and conservative political labels, so easy to attach, frequently obscure rather than reveal true meaning. As Justice Brennan rhetorically asked in one of his most pungent—and quoted—lines, "After all, if a policeman must know the Constitution, then why not a planner?"[144] The bottom line for him is, and always has been, the absolute necessity of meaningful remedies, for without them, the Constitution's guarantees are merely precatory.[145] In the case of the just compensation clause, the remedy happens to be explicit.

Many state and federal circuit courts followed Justice Brennan's dissent as a veiled majority or as a persuasive approach to the issue.[146] Land-owners stopped urging courts to award full fair market value and instead asked for temporary damages. Cities continued to push for invalidation rather than compensatory relief. After two subsequent failures to reach the compensation question[147]—attempts that set the land use lawyer bar buzzing over a seeming inability, or unwillingness, to face the music[148]—the Supreme Court adopted Justice Brennan's *San Diego Gas & Electric Co.* dissent lock, stock and barrel[149] in 1987 in *First English Evangelical Lutheran Church v. County of Los Angeles.*[150] What Justice John Paul Stevens called a "novel" constitutional theory[151] had now become official constitutional law.

Takings and Beach Access: A Classic Debate

Public access to the waterfront, and especially to ocean beaches, is a major issue in many states. Private owners of beachfront property want to exclude the public, while state and local governments usually support efforts to open the shoreline. Although *Nollan v. California Coastal Commission*[152] factu-ally concerned this debate, its legal significance for all land use regulations is potentially far more profound. Justice Antonin Scalia for the majority and Justice Brennan in dissent squared off in an argument about the proper stan-dard of review to be applied by courts in evaluating government regulation of private property. Justice Scalia's approach was substantially less deferential to government than Justice Brennan's and thus more likely to invalidate reg-ulatory efforts. Some 33 years after his New Jersey *Katobimar* dissent, Justice Brennan found himself once again attacking a majority for overturning a gov-ernment land use restriction designed to promote the public good.

The Nollans had a property interest in a small beachfront lot on the California coast with a 504-square-foot bungalow.[153] They wanted to replace the bungalow with a larger, 1,674-square-foot, three-bedroom house and attached two-car garage.[154] Under California law, they were required to apply to the California Coastal Commission, a state land use regulatory authority, for a permit.[155] Indeed, all development along the coast required a permit from the commission.[156] The Nollans applied for and were given a permit, but subject to the condition that they grant the public an easement to walk up and down the beach in front of their proposed house.[157] This would allow individuals to pass along the coast between two public beaches, one-quarter mile to the north and one-third mile to the south of the Nollan property.[158]

In the five-to-four decision written by Justice Scalia, the Court struck down the easement condition as a taking of private property under the just compensation clause.[159] The Court noted preliminarily that the commission could not have required the Nollans to provide the public easement on their existing bungalow property, because that would be a " 'permanent physical occupation,' " the most extreme violation of settled takings law.[160] Thus, the "question becomes whether requiring [the easement] to be conveyed as a condition of issuing a land use permit for the new house alters the outcome."[161] The Court held that the condition imposed was unconstitutional because it failed to substantially advance legitimate state interests:[162] the commission's asserted public interest of preserving visual access to the beach was in no way furthered by the north-to-south access requirement.[163]

The majority assumed, without deciding, the legitimacy of the commission's asserted purposes of "protecting the public's ability to see the beach, assisting the public in overcoming the 'psychological barrier' to using the beach created by a developed shorefront, and preventing congestion on the public beaches."[164] Given these purposes, the Court reasoned, the commission "unquestionably would be able to deny the Nollans their permit outright if their new house (alone, or by reason of the cumulative impact produced in conjunction with other construction) would substantially impede these purposes, unless the denial would interfere so drastically with the Nollans' use of their property as to constitute a taking."[165] Thus, concluded Justice Scalia, permit conditions serving the same legitimate public purposes as those met by forbidding construction of the new house altogether would likewise be constitutional.[166] Among acceptable conditions enumerated by the Court that would protect the public's ability to see the beach, notwithstanding construction of the new house, were height and width limitations, a fence ban and, most intrusively, a "viewing spot" literally on the Nollan property for passersby.[167]

The problem for the majority was the lack of connection between the asserted commission goals and the actual condition. Justice Scalia wrote, "It is quite impossible to understand how a requirement that people already on the public beaches be able to walk across the Nollans' property reduces any obstacles to viewing the beach created by the new house."[168] He added, "It is also impossible to understand how it lowers any 'psychological barrier' to using the public beaches, or how it helps to remedy any additional congestion on them caused by construction of the Nollans' new house."[169] In short, he concluded, "unless the permit condition serves the same governmental purpose as the development ban, the building restriction is not a valid regulation of land use but 'an out-and-out plan of extortion.' "[170]

The majority imposed a surprisingly taut requirement of connection between means and ends. After all, the commission's concerns about psychological barriers and additional congestion (if not visual access) were arguably addressed by the easement condition. What Justice Scalia did, quite openly, was to increase the amount of scrutiny to be accorded land use restrictions. He wrote that abridgment of private property rights must be justified as a " '*substantial* advanc[ing]' of a legitimate State interest,"[171] a formulation destined to appear in countless plaintiff briefs challenging even the sort of run-of-the-mill local land use regulations Justice Brennan reviewed as a state court judge. Virtually no land use scholar or lawyer has thought that the word "substantial," used by Justice George Sutherland in *Village of Euclid v. Ambler Realty Co.* (the 1926 Supreme Court case upholding the constitutionality of traditional zoning),[172] actually stood for a higher standard of review than that implied by the words "reasonable," "conceivable" and "rational," adjectives used loosely and interchangeably by courts to describe the necessary nexus between means and ends. But Justice Scalia, in a bombshell footnote, announced that "substantial" meant more than "reasonable," and that past judicial indications to the contrary were wrong.[173] Thus, one may argue that land use regulations are no longer clothed with a comforting (to the government) presumption of validity.

In his dissent, 50 percent longer than the Court majority, Justice Brennan employed a classic style of argumentation: attack the basic assumptions of your opponents; then show how, even under their own assumptions, they are wrong. For Justice Brennan, the majority adopted an improperly heightened "standard of precision" for government land use regulation instead of the correct test of whether the government could rationally have decided that the regulation might achieve its objective.[174] Fighting footnote with footnote (his own footnote 1 versus Justice Scalia's footnote 3), he cited past opinions and observed that, while the Court's "phraseology may differ slightly from case to case . . . these minor differences cannot, however, obscure the fact that the inquiry in each case is the same."[175] Under the "correct" test, Justice Brennan concluded, the easement condition was clearly constitutional.[176] This debate is broadly reminiscent of the New Jersey *Kato-bimar* case, where, it may be recalled, Justice Brennan criticized the majority for substituting its ideas of proper zoning for the new ideas of the locality.[177] Here, he observed in a similar vein, the majority's "narrow conception of rationality . . . has long since been discredited as a judicial arrogation of legislative authority,"[178] and its stringent test "could hamper innovative efforts to preserve an increasingly fragile national resource."[179]

Even applying the majority's test, Justice Brennan continued, the easement condition was legitimate.[180] He implied that the majority had set up a straw person through its near-exclusive focus on the view blockage justification,[181] as the commission had also justified its action more generally on the basis of burdens resulting from "an increase in private use of the shorefront."[182] And, indeed, courts can virtually predetermine the outcome of cases by selecting those parts of the record supporting their position, while ignoring those that do not. Here, Justice Scalia will never be accused of a comprehensive exploration of the commission's position. Ever the careful craftsman, Justice Brennan systematically reviewed the record prepared by the commission, a record outlining in detail concerns with encroaching private development.[183]

In attempting to blunt every argument of an opponent, adversaries are sometimes unwisely drawn into debate about how many angels can dance on the head of a pin. Thus, Justice Brennan's attempt to show that the visual access burden itself was mitigated by the easement condition is less convincing. He asserted that view blockage caused by "a phalanx of imposing permanent residences, including the [Nollans'] new home," would be offset if people from the road and public beaches to the north and south could see people walking up and down the coastline.[184] This reasoning fails to blunt Justice Scalia's principal contention that the problem with new houses along the coast is that they prevent people on the road from seeing the beach at all, let alone from seeing people walking along it by virtue of the public easement.[185]

A portion of Justice Brennan's opinion incorporated his *Penn Central* takings analysis, inquiring about the character of the government action and its economic impact on the Nollans.[186] His argument here is also only partially convincing. Referring to the width of the proposed public pathway and its topographic relationship to the Nollan house, he described the physical intrusion authorized by the easement as "minimal."[187] But determination of a taking does not depend on the size of the physical invasion. Indeed, a 1982 Supreme Court decision held that a television cable less than one-half inch thick and 30 feet long and running 18 inches above a building rooftop effected a taking.[188] And everyone agrees that the right to exclude others from one's property is among the most fundamental strands of the bundle of rights.[189]

As for economic impact, Justice Brennan highlighted the failure of evidence showing any diminution of value.[190] Furthermore, the distinct investment-backed expectations of the Nollans have not been diminished, he asserted, because they never should have expected to exclude the public from their land.[191] Forty-three permits for new developments near the Nollan property had previously included public easement conditions, and the Nollans and prior users of their property never objected to past public access.[192] Furthermore, because Justice Brennan read the state constitution and statutes as preventing beachfront owners from excluding the public, coastline private property rights simply did not include the right to exclude.[193] Indeed, in an interesting reversal-of-expectations analysis, Justice Brennan argued that public expectations, not private ones, were being upset.[194] He suggested that private landowners were the "interlopers" on the coastline, and that the "public's expectation of access considerably antedates any private development on the coast."[195] "It is therefore," he concluded, "private landowners who threaten the disruption of settled public expectations."[196]

Reliance on state law alone for discerning expectations of owners is at once interesting and troublesome. Justice Brennan premised this reliance on a simple proposition: "It is axiomatic, of course, that state law is the source for those strands that constitute a property owner's bundle of property rights."[197] This axiom goes too far, however, because it implies that government may adopt laws abolishing private property altogether. The U.S. Constitution itself protects "private property" from being "taken for public use" without "just compensation."[198] If government may, by legislative enactment, define the words "private property" into oblivion, then the just compensation clause itself becomes precatory. In addition, there is no small irony—and inconsistency—in Justice Brennan's willingness to rely here entirely on state law definitions, when he is unwilling to do just that in the "new property" context. There, he has argued, the state should not be able to create "new property" expectations and then "avoid all due process safeguards . . . merely by labelling them as not constituting 'property.'"[199] To the degree that he is suggesting that the meaning and extent of private property rights can be altered, but not abolished, by government, however, he is surely correct.

Justice Brennan was on more solid ground when he reminded Justice Scalia that the Nollans voluntarily subjected themselves to the easement condition by applying for permission to develop a new and larger house. Had they continued to use the property in its existing state (the bungalow), the commission could not have unilaterally imposed the condition.[200] Justice Scalia faulted this view and appeared to support some inherent private right to develop property: "the right to build on one's own property—even though its exercise can be subjected to legitimate permitting requirements—cannot remotely be described as a 'governmental benefit.'"[201] Justice Brennan poked fun at the majority for promoting "some privileged natural rights status" for real estate development.[202]

Sometimes, in an attempt to influence future interpretations of a Court opinion by lower courts, dissents will give their own spin to the majority's meaning. This risky strategy can backfire, however, if it invites the majority to respond directly to the dissent's characterization and to make its point even clearer and more rigid. Justice Brennan attempted to color the Scalia opinion and precipitated a direct counterpunch. He suggested that "the Commission should have little difficulty in the future in utilizing its expertise to demonstrate a specific connection between provisions for access and burdens on access produced by new development."[203] Thus, he advised, "alerted to the Court's apparently more demanding requirement, [the commission] need only make clear that a provision for public access directly responds to a particular type of burden on access created by a new development."[204] Not so, retorted Justice Scalia: "We do not share Justice Brennan's confidence" that the commission will be able to "avoid the effect of today's decision."[205] He continued, "We view the Fifth Amendment's property clause to be more than a pleading requirement, and compliance with it to be more than an exercise in cleverness and imagination."[206] The endless regression of point-counterpoint in judicial opinions is assured.[207]

The *Nollan* case has a strange epilogue. Addressing the public audience as well as his judicial colleagues, Justice Stevens wrote a dissent that hardly mentioned Justice Scalia's majority and instead attacked Justice Brennan's dissent in the 1981 *San Diego Gas & Electric Co.* case.[208] Claiming that Justice Brennan's positions in *Nollan* and *First English* (the majority decision joined by Justice Brennan that adopted his *San Diego Gas & Electric Co.* rule about damages for regulatory takings) created an untenable alchemy for land use regulation, he expressed the hope that Justice Brennan would one day see the light.[209]

Justice Brennan in his dissent barely acknowledged the Stevens dissent. He agreed that government "should be afforded considerable latitude in regulating private development, without fear that their regulatory efforts will often be found to constitute a taking."[210] But, of course, should government regulations cross the constitutional line and effect a taking, then compensation must be paid.

Justice Brennan's Own "Mount Laurel" Opinion

In the 1975 *Warth v. Seldin*[211] case, Justice Brennan had a chance to intimate his views on a question coincidentally addressed the same year by his judicial alma mater, the New Jersey Supreme Court, in its well-known *Southern Burlington County NAACP v. Township of Mount Laurel*[212] decision. In *Warth*, several low-income minority persons, several low-income housing advocacy groups and a builders association brought suit against the Rochester, N.Y., suburb of Penfield, alleging that the town's zoning ordinance excluded low- and moderate-income persons from living there in violation of their constitutional rights.[213] The Court held that each of the parties lacked standing—a constitutional and judge-made rule about when litigants have the right to bring a legal case—to challenge Penfield's ordinance[214] and, therefore, declined to consider the merits of their claims.

Observing that the Court's opinion "tosses out of court almost every conceivable kind of plaintiff who could be injured by the activity claimed to be unconstitutional," Justice Brennan's dissent accused the majority of holding an "indefensible hostility to the claim on the merits."[215] He heard "overtones of outmoded notions of pleading and of justiciability" in the majority's application of standing.[216] Technical door-closing rules, improperly used, can deny justice as easily as an unfavorable decision on the merits.[217] In a clever sentence, Justice Brennan summarized the inherent illogic of the majority's position:

> In effect, the Court tells the low-income minority and building company plaintiffs they will not be permitted to prove what they have alleged—that they could and would build and live in the town if changes were made in the zoning ordinance and its application—because they have not succeeded in breaching, before the suit was filed, the very barriers which are the subject of the suit.[218]

Even as the majority declined to address the merits, Justice Brennan decried the alleged conduct of the town: "[T]he portrait which emerges from the allegations and affidavits is one of total, purposeful, intransigent exclusion of certain classes of people from the town, pursuant to a conscious scheme never deviated from."[219] Although civil-procedure scholars may read *Warth* as a civil-procedure case, Justice Brennan predicted that others will view it as "revealing hostility to breaking down even unconstitutional zoning barriers that frustrate the deep human yearning of low-income and minority groups for decent housing they can afford in decent surroundings."[220]

Subsequent Supreme Court decisions confirmed his worst suspicions. For example, in *Village of Arlington Heights v. Metropolitan Housing Development Corp.*,[221] the Court imposed a stringent evidentiary standard that prevented a nonprofit housing corporation from proving that Arlington Heights, Ill., a Chicago suburb, had declined to rezone a parcel of land for the development of low-income housing because of racial discriminatory motives.[222] With the heyday of expansive Supreme Court interpretations of the Bill of Rights now past, Justice Brennan encouraged parties to turn to state constitutions for vindication of private rights.[223] Indeed, his favorite state court did just that in the *Mount Laurel* case, finding in the New Jersey state constitution a local government obligation to provide housing for a fair share of a region's low- and moderate-income families.[224] It was the constitution of New Jersey, not the United States, that prevented suburbs from zoning out the poor. The subtext of Justice Brennan's *Warth* dissent made clear he would be a happy member of the *Mount Laurel* majority.

A Matter of Family

By restricting the use, shape and size of buildings placed on the land, traditional land use controls indirectly, but fundamentally, affect the personal lives of individuals. For example, a zoning ordinance may prohibit apartments accessory to a house in a single-family district, thereby making it difficult for a family to provide housing for an elderly relative. An ordinance may bar additions to a house, thereby preventing a family from building a new workroom or recreation room. Local ordinances may forbid home offices, thereby restricting the range of job possibilities.

Sometimes, local regulations expressly and directly interfere with fundamental personal choices associated with the use of property. One of the most notorious—and unbelievable—examples was challenged in *Moore v. City of East Cleveland*,[225] where the Court grappled with a regulation used to stop a grandmother from sharing her house with one of her grandsons. Zoning ordinances commonly classify residential districts as single- and multifamily, but the definition of what constitutes a family is frequently left unclear. The city of East Cleveland, Ohio, limited occupancy in dwelling units to a single family and defined family in a narrow way.[226] One peculiar effect of the definition was to make it illegal for Inez Moore, a 63-year-old grandmother, to live with two grandsons who were first cousins rather than brothers.[227] The ordinance would have allowed her to live with one of her grandsons or with both of them had they been brothers.[228]

Justice Brennan joined Justice Lewis Powell's plurality opinion[229] holding that the ordinance, as applied, unconstitutionally abridged the freedom of personal choice in matters of family life, one of the liberties deemed to be afforded protection by the due process clause of the fourteenth amendment.[230] The plurality traced a series of controversial Supreme Court decisions giving substantive content to the due process clause and concluded that the "Constitution protects the sanctity of the family precisely because the institution of the family is deeply rooted in this Nation's history and tradition."[231] Weighed against the family, the city's arguments that it needed to mitigate overcrowding, traffic and parking, and ease a financial crunch on the school system, must fail.[232] In the most compelling of the three dissenting opinions,[233] Justice White attacked the plurality for its judicial activism in creating substantive rights not articulated more clearly by the Constitution.[234] For him, this role was best played by the legislature, not the Court.

Justice Brennan's concurring opinion chose not to address this major constitutional debate and instead focused on human and class issues implicated by the ordinance. His opening remark is forthright:

> [T]he Constitution is not powerless to prevent East Cleveland from prosecuting as a criminal and jailing a 63-year-old grandmother for refusing to expel from her home her now 10-year-old grandson who has lived with her and been brought up by her since his mother's death when he was less than a year old.[235]

He fairly bristled at what he termed the "cultural myopia" of the law.[236] Filled with "Brandeis brief" facts,[237] his opinion exhibited a sensitivity and understanding of differing family patterns in the United States. As in many other contexts, Justice Brennan was careful to ensure that preferences of the majority, codified into law, would not be imposed upon individuals by the government when exercise of fundamental rights was at stake.[238] For him, the Court's primary constitutional mission, in contrast to the legislative and executive branches, was the protection of the minority against the excesses of the majority.[239] Thus, if the nuclear family is found in much of white suburbia, he mused, the Constitution does not allow the government to impose that particular model on the rest of us.[240] He emphasized the practical importance of the extended family that "provided generations of early Americans with social services and economic and emotional support in times of hardship, and was the beachhead for successive waves of immigrants who populated our cities. . . ."[241] Even today, he continued, the extended family "remains not merely still a pervasive living pattern, but under the goad of brutal economic necessity, a prominent pattern—virtually a means of survival—for large numbers of the poor and deprived minorities of our society."[242]

The majesty of the Constitution sometimes is reduced to an everyday reality: for poor and minority families, "compelled pooling of scant resources requires compelled sharing of a household."[243] In sum, using his judicial prerogative to write separately after joining the plurality, Justice Brennan cast additional light on the class effects of an unusual land use regulation. Undaunted by the dangers of a "bully pulpit" judiciary, he seized an opportunity to bring public attention to the plight of needy groups of Americans.

PART II
THE STATE COURT YEARS: 1949 TO 1956

Typical single-family neighborhood in Englewood Cliffs, N.J., a town in which a developer wanted to build multifamily housing. From Guaclides v. Borough of Englewood Cliffs.

(Jerold S. Kayden)

4 THE CENTRALITY OF SOUND LAND USE PLANNING

New Jersey Palisades, whose rocky outcroppings overlooking the Hudson River increased the costs of housing development. From Guaclides v. Borough of Englewood Cliffs.

(Jerold S. Kayden)

Justice Brennan's state court apprenticeship gave him an intimate familiarity with the concerns of local communities and property owners, as well as with the evolving techniques of planning and zoning. New Jersey was growing, and small-town residents were worried that a way of life would be lost forever. With increased housing demand, owners of vacant land were sitting on potential gold mines. The conflict between preservation and development inevitably led to the courtroom and the argot of land use jurisprudence. Zoning amendments and bylaws, state enabling acts, cumulative uses, comprehensive planning, variances and special permits became second nature to Justice Brennan because these instruments surfaced again and again in the New Jersey courts. The judicial knowledge and skills necessary for the lofty constitutional land use debates of the U.S. Supreme Court were honed in the minor leagues of local disputes.

In the five cases discussed in this chapter, Justice Brennan adumbrates an approach generously deferential to the goals of New Jersey's communities, but only so long as communities demonstrate a commitment to sound and comprehensive planning mandated by state legislation. His philosophy is most clearly articulated in his major and only New Jersey land use dissent. The *Katobimar* "Shopping Center" case of 1955 involved a town's attempt to exclude commercial establishments such as shopping centers from its light industrial districts, an idea so novel and distinct from earlier methods of zoning that most "right-thinking" people would have rejected it. And that is exactly what a majority of the New Jersey Supreme Court justices did. In their minds, the accepted wisdom encompassed an ascending ladder of uses in which higher ones (here, a shopping center) could automatically enter lower districts (the proposed light industrial district). Ever receptive to new planning ideas, Justice Brennan endorsed the model of industrial parks concentrating exclusively on that use. He argued eloquently for a change in judicial philosophy that would embrace innovative zoning techniques pressed to serve modern challenges.

The 1954 *Birkfield* "Orange Plan" case highlighted the importance of comprehensive planning to Justice Brennan. For him, the clear evidence of the town's determination to follow its master plan was sufficient to rebut the property owner's claim of unequal treatment, the usual constitutional attack on a zoning classification. And again, in the 1951 *Guaclides* "Palisades" case, the presence of a plan placed a great burden on the challenger (not carried in that case) to show that the ordinance was arbitrary, unreasonable and capricious.

The large shadow cast by the *Birkfield* and *Guaclides* cases was their intimation of exclusionary zoning. The spectacle of a community composed predominantly of single-family residential neighborhoods and enjoying the public right to exclude multifamily units from its boundaries did not offend Justice Brennan, his fellow judges, the state legislature, local property owners and even central-city residents. Given the prevailing mores of the era, none had second thoughts when the decision characterized the exclusion of all but single-family dwellings as a "balanced and well-ordered scheme" of land uses. Only when excluded low-income and minority families years later challenged such zoning principles did realization and anger occur.

Dedication to the zoning plan and the single-family district are major themes in the 1953 *Conlon* "Bank" and the 1952 *Casper* "Boarding House" cases. *Conlon* involved an overly permissive commercial zone mapped in a residential area to allow a bank, and Justice Brennan invalidated the amendment. In the *Casper* case, he approved the denial of a boarding-house license to the owner of a 28-room house, where proof of city efforts to enforce applicable zoning indicated dedication to a plan.

The Shopping Center Case: Katobimar Realty Co. v. Webster

Is it irrational for a community to exclude shopping centers from light industrial areas? How should courts determine whether that decision is a legitimate one? These questions form the backdrop to Justice Brennan's most important—and his only dissenting—New Jersey land use opinion.

The borough of New Providence enacted its original zoning ordinance in 1933, dividing the community into several zoning districts. A districts were limited to single-family houses, B districts to uses permissible in A plus two-family dwellings, C districts to uses permissible in A plus laboratories, and D districts to uses permissible in A, B and C plus business, institutional and industrial uses. The ordinance generally followed the so-called cumulative or pyramid zoning model, where high uses, such as single-family residences, were allowed in low-use districts, such as commercial areas. Low uses, however, were not allowed in high-use districts. The top of the pyramid was exclusively single-family housing, the bottom of the pyramid was open to all uses.

In 1951 New Providence diverged somewhat from its earlier cumulative approach by carving out from some B and D districts a new industrial district allowing light industry and prohibiting residential and heavy industrial uses. The borough further diverged from the cumulative model in 1954, when it barred all retail commercial uses from its new industrial district. That same year, the Katobimar Realty Company sought to develop a shopping center of nine retail stores on a five-acre parcel of land in an industrial district. Robert Webster, the borough's building inspector, denied the company's application for a permit, because the zoning did not allow the proposed use. Indeed, evidence suggested that the borough adopted the 1954 retail commercial ban in industrial districts as a response to the company's proposed development. Katobimar brought suit, alleging that the 1954 zoning amendment was unreasonable, arbitrary and capricious, that the amendment deprived it of property without due process of law and that the amendment violated the state zoning act. The trial court upheld the ordinance, and Katobimar appealed.

Writing for a closely divided four-to-three New Jersey Supreme Court, Justice Harry Heher reversed the judgment of the trial court. After discussing general statutory and constitutional rules governing the exercise of zoning and the basic model of cumulative zoning, the majority turned to the specific facts of this case. While observing that the "motivation for the amendment is not the subject of a finding" by the trial court, the majority was clearly troubled by it: Justice Heher was suspicious that New Providence had not seen fit to exclude retail commercial uses from the industrial district in 1951, when that zoning classification was first adopted, three years before the shopping center proposal.

At base, the majority simply could not see any reason for the exclusion of retail businesses: "It is difficult to perceive a rational distinction referable to the fulfillment of the statutory zoning considerations, all or any of them, between the contemplated shopping center and the uses permissible in the limited industrial district now before us." The majority appeared to take judicial notice of land use relationships: "The projected business center and light industrial uses are not incompatible in nature; they are generally, so far as zoning policy goes, wholly congruous uses, and if in special circumstances a distinction may reasonably be made to serve an overriding public interest, such showing is not made here." Justice Heher added, "This is not a question of 'liberal' zoning, but of zoning comporting with the constitutional rights of private property and the equal protection of the laws."

In dissent, Justice Brennan took the majority to task for its crimped reading of the constitutional and statutory strictures governing zoning.

JUSTICE BRENNAN

New Jersey has witnessed a marked and salutary change in the judicial attitude toward municipal zoning over the past decade. Long overdue recognition of the legitimate aspirations of the community to further its proper social, economic and political progress, and of the propriety of requiring individual landowners to defer to the greater public good, have replaced the narrow concepts held by former courts. Present-day decisions rightly give maximum play to the philosophy underlying our constitutional and statutory zoning provisions that localities may decide for themselves what zoning best serves and furthers the local public welfare, subject only to the rule of reason forbidding arbitrary and capricious action. Mr. Justice Jacobs summed up the basic approach of those cases in his opinion in the *Pierro* case [where an ordinance excluded motels, but allowed boarding and rooming houses in its residential zones]:

> It must always be remembered that the duty of selecting particular uses which are congruous in residential zones [only residential zones were involved] was vested by the Legislature in the municipal officials rather than in the courts. Once the selections were made and duly embodied in the comprehensive zoning ordinance of 1939 they became presumptively valid and they are not to be nullified except upon an affirmative showing that the action taken by the municipal officials was unreasonable, arbitrary or capricious. * * *
> * * * We are satisfied that at long last conscientious municipal officials have been sufficiently empowered to adopt reasonable zoning measures designed towards preserving the wholesome and attractive characteristics of their communities and the values of taxpayers' properties.

The instant decision not only departs from the policy of the cited cases in its application of the law to the facts but, of graver concern, does so in language, substantially *in haec verba*, which did not command majority support in *Pierro* and appears only in the *Pierro* dissent. Local governing bodies and their advisors must surely be troubled to know which—the *Pierro* majority opinion or the *Pierro* dissent—expresses the prevailing view in this court. And the bewilderment will be the greater because this opinion is filed but a few weeks after *Pierro* was decided.

The prohibition of retail commercial uses in the non-nuisance industrial district was not a 1954 innovation. The local officials believed that the prohibition was accomplished in a 1951 amendment, before plaintiffs acquired their lands. Plaintiffs also thought this was the case, because when they first sought approval of their project they sought a zone change. It was only when the effectiveness of the 1951 amendment to accomplish the purpose was questioned that the more explicit 1954 amendment was adopted.

The motivation for the prohibition was the desire to attract non-nuisance industries to the borough to increase tax ratables and support the expanded school needs and greater municipal services incident to the rapid residential growth of the community. The borough emerged after World War II from a primarily rural and farm economy into a fast growing suburban community of modest homes. From its 1950 population of 3,500 it has grown to a 1955 population of 6,000. It was feared, and with good reason, that taxes to be realized on modest residential properties would be insufficient to support the mounting cost of schooling and borough government without undue hardship to the individual home owner.

Faced with that situation, the governing body intelligently and responsibly gave consideration to ways and means to increase tax revenues without impairment of the essentially residential character of the borough. They hit upon a program of attracting new non-nuisance industries, thereby augmenting ratables without incurring heavy additional expenses for municipal service.

Many of the post-war industrial developments are "industrial parks" where operations are limited to non-nuisance types carried on in attractive buildings on large acreages beautifully landscaped and compatible in appearance with fine residential areas. Every motorist of our State has seen and admired these desirable improvements which dot our landscape and vastly enhance its appearance. It was such a development that the borough fathers envisaged. The plan has been a marked success, as the photographs in evidence demonstrate.

This type of program as part of a comprehensive zoning plan for communities of the character of New Providence is customarily recommended by professional planners. There was expert evidence that not only are residences incompatible in such a zone but that general retail and commercial business should also be recognized as incompatible with a well planned district designed for non-nuisance industries. Numerous disadvantages from such an intermixture are referred to in the evidence.

The choice of the 130-acre area for the limited industrial use district was cautiously and purposefully made. The boundaries are a railroad line on the south, and brooks on the east, north and west, thus making a natural separation point between the zone and the surrounding territory. Its proximity to the railroad affords spur lines where needed. The topography is vacant and level, free from trees, stones and the like, and it is accessible to a sewer line. It is also a considerable distance from the primary residence and business centers.

The area formed part of a larger area comprising the Business Zone created by the original 1933 zoning ordinance. For the almost two decades until 1951 no one located a business there. This was another reason which satisfied the governing body that the highest and best use of the land could be realized only by zoning the segment selected exclusively for limited industrial uses as part of the program to attract such business to the borough.

The 1951 ordinance also excluded future residential construction in the new district. There was evidence that this is now customary in many zoning ordinances. Reference was made to such regulations in New York, Berkeley Heights, West Orange, Somerville, Summit and Springfield Township.

And the pattern was not new to New Providence. The C Zone created by the 1933 ordinance was a laboratory zone limited to "laboratories devoted to research, design and for experimentation; and fabrication incident thereto." The ordinance barred retail commercial structures and any business or industrial use other than a laboratory. The zone was highly successful in attracting substantial research enterprises. The expert opinion evidence was that a paramount factor in the success of the zone was the prohibition of commercial uses, and that for like reasons the ban was essential to assure the success of the limited non-nuisance industrial zone.

Upon this set of facts I find it impossible to square the majority's holding with the sustaining in *Duffcon* of an ordinance excluding all industry, or in *Wayne Township* of an ordinance barring houses of less than 768 square feet for one-story buildings, or in *Bedminster Township* of an ordinance fixing a maximum five-acre requirement, or in *Englewood Cliffs* of an ordinance excluding apartment houses from almost the entire borough, or, particularly, in *Pierro* of an ordinance excluding motels although the ordinance allowed boarding and rooming houses. Commercial shopping centers are not wholly banned from New Providence. Provision is made for them in the business districts contiguous to residential areas, where they rightly belong. In forbidding them in the district in question, the conclusion is inescapable that New Providence evolved a sound long-range policy designed to achieve a well balanced local economy and in nowise exceeded the zoning authority acknowledged in the cited cases.

The majority, using substantially the identical language of the *Pierro* dissent, *viz.*, "The essence of zoning is territorial division in keeping with the character of the lands and structures and their peculiar suitability for particular uses and uniformity of use within the division," jumps from that base to the conclusion that as a matter of law, "Generally, the higher uses are allowable in the less limited use districts, normally so when account is taken of the nature and design of the inherent limitations of the zoning process." We may grant that zoning practice has been to allow the higher uses in districts zoned for lesser uses, but it escapes me how that practice is raised to a limitation in law upon the scope of municipal powers granted under the constitution and the zoning statutes.

The limitation is not to be found in either constitution or statute and, in the nature of things, there is not sound reason why the congruity of uses should be made dependent upon considerations of the place of particular uses, up or down, in the scale of uses. The majority admit this in conceding that higher uses may on occasions be excluded from zones limited to lesser uses, but, other than by saying so, they offer no standard by which to guide municipal officials to know when the local situation will be deemed exceptional by the majority. If well-conceived and carefully thought out zoning plans such as this, so obviously and peculiarly appropriate to further the well-being of the community of New Providence, are to be struck down in this fashion, a grievous blow will be dealt the forward progress of zoning as an instrument for the enhancement of the overall social and economic welfare of our municipalities. ▬

The Orange Plan Case: Birkfield Realty Co. v. Board of Commissioners

One of the most common complaints of landowners—and people in general—is unequal treatment. When owners see their neighbors allowed to do something, then they understandably believe that they should be allowed the same freedom. Witnessing surrounding land use changes, the owners of Birkfield Realty Company thought they should be able to build an apartment building. Viewing evolution of the area from a different perspective, the city of Orange thought otherwise. The parties turned to the courts for conflict resolution.

Orange enacted its first zoning ordinance in 1922, classifying much land to the south of Central Avenue, an east-west road, as Residence A, suitable for single-family houses. Birkfield Realty Company owned land zoned Residence A several blocks south of Central Avenue and fronting South Center Street, a north-south road. Since 1922 the Orange Board of Commissioners had rezoned certain lots near Birkfield's property from Residence A to Residence C, a classification allowing construction of multifamily apartment projects. Specifically, the board rezoned to multifamily two parcels to the north (in 1928 and 1947) and one area (as late as 1940) and one parcel (1945) to the east of Birkfield's property.

In 1950 Birkfield applied to the city to rezone its land from Residence A to Residence C to permit construction of garden apartments. The company argued that the changes made to the zoning around its property

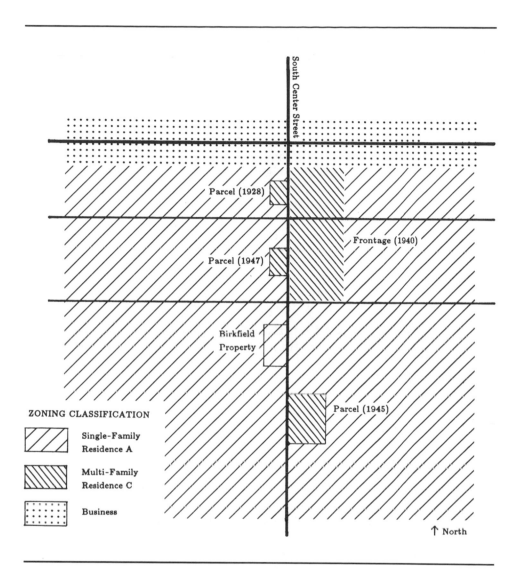

since 1922 had effectively destroyed the master plan underlying the city's zoning, thereby making it unreasonable to deny the requested change.

In rejecting Birkfield's application, the city relied on the very master plan proclaimed by the company to have been effectively nullified by the several post-1922 rezonings. In a 1947 version of its master plan, three years before Birkfield's multifamily proposal, the Orange Planning Board had made certain zoning recommendations affecting an area that included Birkfield's property. Although the plan suggested rezoning to multifamily much of the frontage along South Center Street, south of Central Avenue, it tantalizingly stopped several hundred feet short of the company's property. The purpose of the rezoning was to fill in multifamily zones between some of the earlier rezonings that had sporadically occurred since 1922. Specifically, on Birkfield's side of South Center Street, the rezoning would extend as far south as a property 300 feet to the north of Birkfield's land. Across the street, the rezoning would extend slightly south of the company's land to include a parcel previously rezoned multifamily in 1945. Birkfield's land, and the area to the south, would remain single-family. Although recommended in 1947, the rezonings had not occurred when Birkfield filed its rezoning application in 1950.

Claiming that Orange's refusal to rezone its property was unreasonable, arbitrary and capricious, and that the zoning ordinance as applied was unconstitutional, Birkfield brought suit. The trial court ruled for the city, and Birkfield appealed to the appellate division of the Superior Court of New Jersey. Justice Brennan wrote an opinion affirming the judgment of the trial court. Having grown up in neighboring Newark, he spoke knowingly about the actual physical setting of Orange and approvingly of that city's attempt to implement its master plan.

JUSTICE BRENNAN

In the circumstances we are not persuaded that plaintiff has successfully overcome the presumption that the zoning ordinance is altogether reasonable in its application to plaintiff's tract. The refusal by the governing body to permit still another encroachment to do violence to the existing zoning ordinance will not be viewed as arbitrary or capricious when, as here, [it is] grounded in a determination to adhere to and to further an approved and adopted zoning program essential to the larger plan for the physical development of the municipality and plainly designed and reasonably adapted to conserve and promote the public health, safety, morals and general welfare of the city. "Municipal planning, in a word, is the accommodation, through unity in construction, of the variant interests seeking expression in the local physical life to the interest of the community as a social unit. Planning is a science and an art concerned with land economics and land policies in terms of social and economic betterment. The control essential to planning is exercised through government ownership or regulation of the use of the locus."

The attainment of planning objectives cannot be achieved overnight, particularly in a long-settled community like Orange, founded in 1664, where the immediate effort must be in large part a struggle to preserve "such beneficial features as may have survived the period of spontaneous and uncontrolled growth" of the city. The regulatory power has, of course, its limits. We do not find that they have been over-reached in this case. The Legislature has expressly declared that proposed amendments to zoning ordinances shall first be submitted to the planning board, where it exists, for approval, disapproval or suggestions, and that that board shall have a reasonable time, not less than 30 days, for consideration and report, and in the event of an unfavorable report by the planning board, the amendments shall not become effective except by a favorable vote of two-thirds of the governing body. The legislative intent plainly accords important, although, of course, not decisive, weight to the recommendations of the planning board concerning zoning ordinance amendments when based upon legitimate considerations of public interest and such reasonable supervision and regulation as may be essential for the common good and welfare.

The total area of the City of Orange is only two and two-tenths square miles. About one-half, or a little more, of that area lies north of Central Avenue. That half is a striking example of the baneful consequences of planless growth and haphazard development. Orange is predominantly a residential community. Nevertheless, the north half of the city has only four small and widely separated sections presently zoned for single-family dwellings. It is zoned almost completely for business, industrial, two-family and multi-family uses.

South of Central Avenue, on the other hand, the south half of the city is not only almost entirely zoned for single-family residences but is presently built up almost entirely with single-family homes. The exceptions are confined to three sides of its perimeter (the fourth side is the South Orange line), back of the west side of the full length of Lincoln Avenue on the west, where apartment, commercial and industrial structures and two-family houses have been allowed, and along the Central Avenue frontage and the mentioned multi-family structures on South Center Street within a short distance south of Central Avenue. The section of approximately one-quarter square mile in area within that perimeter is one of the attractive single-family residential "oases" of Essex County. Many of the homes were built decades ago, but a large number have been built since the end of World War II. Considerable building activity of new one-family homes is now going on in several parts of the section, notably in the immediate vicinity of plaintiff's tract, indeed just to its rear which abuts on lots facing on a new street, Adrianne Court, upon which several substantial homes are being erected.

The planning board from its study of the community concluded that "in a city such as Orange, where there exists little vacant land, where the population growth has remained on the decline, it is most important to protect those areas and investments that are good, while encouraging new constructions in those areas in need of rejuvenation." Consistent with that general policy, which can hardly be characterized as unreasonable or arbitrary, the board adopted a subordinate policy applicable specially to the quarter-square mile section, which includes plaintiff's tract, namely,

> It will be the policy of the Planning Board to preserve the one family zone bordered by the South Orange line, Lincoln Avenue, Lighthipe Place, the rear lines of properties on the south side of Reynolds Terrace, and Center Street to the South Orange line. It may also be stated that despite repeated requests the Board contemplates no zoning variance at this time for land located on the west side of Center Street, between Highland Avenue and Fuller Terrace based upon the character of fine homes still standing in this area.

Plaintiff's tract is "on the west side of Center Street between Highland Avenue and Fuller Terrace." Lighthipe Place and "the rear line of properties on the south side of Reynolds Terrace" (which latter line includes the southerly boundary line of the garden apartments at 341–361 South Center Street) form a line starting a few hundred feet north of plaintiff's tract, which line roughly parallels Central Avenue and extends from South Center Street on the east about one-third mile to Lincoln Avenue on the west.

A large measure of discretion is necessarily vested in the governing body to determine the effect upon the general public interest and welfare of the exercise of its authority under [state enabling legislation] to amend the zoning ordinance as desired by the plaintiff. An exception in favor of plaintiff's lands might reasonably be considered by the governing body to be a threat to the whole carefully developed zoning program which is the first essential and an integral part of the master plan for the future development of the city. In the circumstances, whatever might be the merit in plaintiff's allegations, but for the existence of that approved program, certainly the fact that the ordinance had been amended in the several instances mentioned before the adoption of the program does not make the refusal to do so in this instance arbitrary and capricious. "If that were so, one variation would sustain if it did not compel others, and thus the general regulation would eventually be nullified." That refusal escapes the taint of unreasonable and capricious action when grounded as it was upon the governing body's determination, adopted upon the planning board's recommendation, to adhere to the comprehensive zoning program which called a halt to further encroachment in the single-family zone and affects plaintiff's tract in common with all others in the quarter square mile area which is the core of that zone. There is no reason to doubt that the general revision of the zoning ordinance necessary to implement the whole program will be enacted in due time. The delineation of the boundaries of the multi-family zone along South Center Street is desirable if not essential in the general interest as well as the interest of owners and prospective purchasers of lands to be affected by the change and not presently zoned for multi-family structures.

Plaintiff argues finally that "the only reason for the denial of plaintiff's application in this case is the objections of some of the neighbors." The city commission held a public hearing on plaintiff's application and heard the protests of property owners in the immediate neighborhood and received some protest petitions. The commissioner who moved that the application be rejected gave the objections received as a reason for his motion. The formal resolution adopted two weeks later, however, grounded the commission's action on the deviation from the master plan entailed in favorable action as well as upon consideration of the effect of the structure upon immediately adjacent single-family properties and a finding that the structure in that location would increase traffic congestion and cause a hazardous condition on South Center Street.

It is true that the advantage or detriment to neighboring land owners may not be the sole criterion which guides governing bodies in zoning matters. We are satisfied, however, that the city commission did not deny plaintiff's application because it viewed the desires of the neighboring property owners as determinative, but rather primarily because the granting of the application would be an unwarranted departure from the approved comprehensive zoning plan.

The Palisades Case:
Guaclides v.
Borough of Englewood Cliffs

Today, this case may sound like exclusionary zoning. Faced with a proposal to develop multifamily housing, a suburban community rezoned much of its area to preclude multifamily development. It continued, however, to allow such development in a location lacking adequate sewer facilities. In this 1951 case, the issue of exclusionary zoning was not even mentioned by any of the parties, let alone by the judges. Today's view of the case would be an anachronism.

Perched atop the rocky Palisades west of the Hudson River, the borough of Englewood Cliffs in 1950 was a small residential community of single-family homes. While many of its Bergen County municipal neighbors had experienced substantial growth in population and housing after the 1932 opening of the George Washington Bridge and the end of World War II, the population of Englewood Cliffs had remained stable at around 900 residents since 1932. Indeed, until 1950, when five new homes were built, the annual rate of new construction never exceeded two homes. A major explanation for the lack of growth was the geological impediment of rock outcroppings throughout the town. Where standard costs of developing a 7,000-square-foot lot typically would range from $600 to $700, and never exceed $1,000, costs on lots with rock outcroppings would range from $3,000 to $4,000. Although the original 1932 zoning ordinance permitted multifamily housing in several areas of the community, no multifamily projects had ever been developed.

Theodore and Mary Guaclides bought a 17-acre tract of land in Englewood Cliffs in 1945 and a two-acre lot for their own home in 1949. That same year, they agreed to sell 13 acres of the 17-acre parcel to a builder proposing to construct a garden apartment complex. Because the 17 acres were zoned for multifamily housing, the garden apartment development was a use permitted as a matter of right. After town residents protested by petition, the borough council amended the zoning ordinance to reclassify all multifamily zoning districts, including the one covering the Guaclideses' 17-acre parcel, to single-family housing requiring a minimum 7,000-square-foot lot. The only area exempted from this change was located in the northern part of Englewood Cliffs, an area lacking sewage facilities presumably necessary to service new development.

The Guaclideses challenged the zoning change as unreasonable, arbitrary and capricious. They lost in the trial court and appealed. In his first land use opinion as an appellate judge, Justice Brennan upheld the rezoning by Englewood Cliffs, in part by relying on its comprehensive nature.

JUSTICE BRENNAN

The obvious purpose and effect of the amending ordinance is to preserve the character of the borough as predominantly a community of single-family homes. We concur with the trial court's finding that in the circumstances shown by this record plaintiffs have not sustained their allegation that the ordinance is arbitrary, unreasonable and capricious in its effect.

There is a presumption that the regulation is reasonable, and the burden is upon plaintiffs to establish the contrary. The rule is that even "if the validity of the action be fairly debatable, the legislative judgment prevails."

Plaintiffs argue that the ordinance does not conform to the statutory requisites. We are unable to agree. The ordinance evinces, as required by that statute, (1) a comprehensive plan, (2) designed for one of the purposes enumerated in the section (in this instance, to "promote * * * the general welfare"), and (3) "made with reasonable consideration, among other things, to the character of the district and its peculiar suitability for particular uses, and with a view of conserving the value of property and encouraging the most appropriate use of land throughout such municipality."

The plan is clearly comprehensive, embracing, as it does, changes in 13 specified areas, and not just in the two where plaintiffs' tracts are located, and restricting virtually the entire community to structures of the specified single-family type, except where incidental and necessary commercial and business structures are allowed along defined areas bordering on named streets, and a small industrial zone, and except, too, the area in the north end reserved for multi-family structures. We find nothing in the ordinance to support plaintiffs' argument that the plan manifests an attempt at "spot" zoning aimed only at plaintiffs' tracts and intended as a discriminatory and arbitrary classification of their properties, as was held as to ordinances in the factual settings presented in [other cases]. These cases are plainly distinguishable. In each the regulation in the situation shown had the purpose and effect of imposing a discriminatory restriction not applicable to lands similarly situated and usually in the immediate neighborhood. The ordinance in the instant case applies to all lands throughout the borough previously zoned for multi-family dwellings, except those in the reserved north area, and becomes and is effective at a time when no apartment house exists anywhere in the community and when plaintiffs' 17-acre tract in common with like tracts in the immediate vicinity are undeveloped, or where built upon, are sites of single-family houses.

The design of the ordinance to promote the general welfare of the borough is evident. "Use zoning for single family dwellings serves the general prosperity and welfare." Although it is true that the general welfare clause of the statute cannot be invoked to prohibit a use solely because such use is "repugnant to the sentiments or desires of a particular class residing in the immediate neighborhood," nonetheless, when, as here, the design is "to promote the common good of the whole of the people of such community," the statutory requisite in this particular is fully met.

A community has broad powers reasonably to achieve the purposes to be served by zoning "to provide a balanced and well-ordered scheme for all activity deemed essential to the particular municipality." It has been held that a municipality predominantly residential in character has the power wholly to exclude from its borders industrial enterprises or activities, or to impose limitations on the extent thereof, for the purpose of preserving its residential character, and is not required merely to restrict such enterprises or activities to particular zones or areas, at least when, although separated therefrom but in the same geographical region, there is present a concentration of industry in an area peculiarly adapted to industrial development and sufficiently large to accommodate such development for years to come. And, equally here, the familiar restraints limiting the exercise of the police power will not be deemed to be flouted by the legislation of this borough enacted to preserve the long-standing character of the affected areas as predominantly districts of single-family homes and excluding multi-family structures therefrom, particularly as there is not and never has been any apartment type building in such areas and the ordinance permits their construction elsewhere in the borough.

Plaintiffs argue, however, that the restriction upon use is confiscatory as applied to their 17-acre tract, contending that the evidence showed the use of that tract for single-family homes is not economically feasible but is possible only at prohibitive cost. The evidence does not have so broad a reach. Plaintiffs' proofs showed only that the high cost of installing improvements for single-family houses makes the site unattractive to builders and promoters of housing projects for profit. There is no showing that individuals desiring to build homes for their own occupancy and willing and able to pay the premium cost would or will not do so. Hundreds of homes have been built in the borough and the inference is clear that their owners did not consider the higher improvement cost an insurmountable obstacle. The restriction enacted by the ordinance may well have the effect of attracting to the borough more persons desiring to build their own homes in a municipality where the intent to preserve its character as a community of single-family houses has been so definitely evidenced. A zoning ordinance does not contravene constitutional limitations merely because the restricted use may not be the most profitable use to which the property can be devoted. The restriction imposed by this ordinance is reasonably adapted to the needs of this borough and its effect in the circumstances is not a taking of property in the constitutional sense. "All property is held in subordination to the police power; and the correlative restrictions upon individual rights—either of person or of property—are incidents of the social order, deemed a negligible loss compared with the resultant advantages to the community as a whole, if not, indeed, fully recompensed by the common benefits."

The statutory test is not, as plaintiffs apparently believe, whether the design of the ordinance encourages the most appropriate use of plaintiffs' lands, but whether it encourages "the most appropriate use of land throughout the municipality," considering the character of the district and its peculiar suitability for particular uses and with a view to conserving the value of property for such uses. The legislative judgment implicit in this ordinance is that the most appropriate use of substantially all of the lands throughout the borough, including plaintiffs' tracts, is for single-family dwellings and that their value should be conserved for such use. Nothing in the circumstances shown by the record justifies judicial interference with this judgment of the borough council.

Plaintiffs argue finally that the ordinance must be struck down because the proofs show it was hurriedly adopted for [the] specific purpose of preventing their vendee from carrying out its known plan to construct the apartment building. Doubtless the filing of vendee's plot plan brought the issue to a head. It is evident, however, that the ordinance is in every respect valid, and, in such case, the law prevailing at the time of the filing of the plot plan is an immaterial consideration. Manifestly the ordinance would not be invalid merely because of the circumstance that the vendee's action gave incentive to its passage. [The cases] relied on by plaintiffs do not support plaintiffs' proposition. The effect of the ordinance in each of those cases was such as to require in any event a finding in the particular factual circumstances presented that the municipal action was arbitrary and capricious. Plainly the mention of the proof of precipitate municipal action is to be read in the entire context of each opinion, not as intended to lay down a rule that by itself such proof establishes the invalidity of the pertinent ordinance, but merely that such proof tended to confirm the finding that the ordinance in the situation shown evidenced arbitrary and capricious regulation designed to forestall the legitimate plans of the property owner for the use of the affected property. ▄▄▄

The Bank Case:
Conlon v. Board of Public Works

Attitudes about zoning depend on whose ox is being gored. A change to more restrictive zoning traditionally is challenged by the newly restricted property owner. A change to less restrictive zoning is attacked by the neighbors of the owner enjoying fewer restrictions. If residents counted on a neighborhood of single-family houses, they are unhappy with the possible intrusion of business uses. Expectations are driven as much by regulations affecting other land as those affecting one's own.

The city of Paterson rezoned from residential to business a single 17,000-square-foot parcel vacant for more than 40 years. Although several small retail stores were across the street, the lot was located within "perhaps the finest residential section of the municipality."The intention of the Board of Public Works, the city's zoning agency, was to allow for construction of a "professional type of building," although the zone change allowed many other types of business uses not desired by the board. The owner made plans to sell the lot for development of a branch bank.

The trial court ruled against the city of Paterson. Writing for a six-to-one New Jersey Supreme Court majority, Justice Brennan agreed that the city rezoning was improper because it did not further a comprehensive plan.

JUSTICE BRENNAN

Appellants defend the ordinance upon the ground that the restriction of the lot to use for a single-family dwelling is so arbitrary and unreasonable by rea-

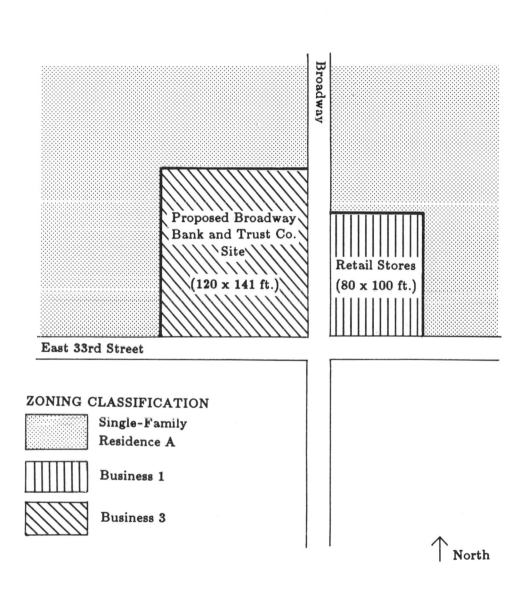

ZONING CLASSIFICATION

Single-Family
Residence A

Business 1

Business 3

son of circumstances peculiar to it and not applicable to other lots of the district as to make the restriction invalid in its application to the lot, and argue therefore that the "municipality may itself recognize that the zoning ordinance is arbitrary and invalid as to the particular parcel of land and may satisfy its statutory and constitutional obligation by amending its zoning ordinance and thereby giving the property the treatment which the statute and Constitution required."

But [the New Jersey Zoning Act] requires that "Such regulations shall be in accordance with a comprehensive plan" designed to promote the specified statutory purposes related generally to the health, safety and welfare of the community. It is true that the mere fact that the ordinance affects only a single lot does not show that it is deficient in this statutory requirement. The validity or invalidity of the ordinance depends upon more than the size of the lot or the fact that the lot is surrounded by uses of another character than those for which the lot is zoned. However, when the change of zone is not made with the purpose or effect of establishing or furthering a comprehensive zoning scheme calculated to achieve the statutory objectives but is designed merely to relieve the lot of the burden of the restriction of the general regulation by reason of conditions alleged to cause such regulation to bear with particular harshness upon it, the ordinance is invalid as not being "in accordance with a comprehensive plan" and as granting "in effect, a special exception or variance from the restrictive residential regulation, thereby circumventing the board of adjustment to which is committed by our Zoning Act the quasi-judicial duty of passing upon such matters, at least initially, in accordance with prescribed standards, * * * ."

The Law Division was clearly right in setting aside the instant ordinance. There was proof that the lot, vacant for more than 40 years, is not and is unlikely to be attractive as the site for a single family home. The city planning board in 1949 took into account the special conditions of the location which produce this result. The board concluded that another use should be sanctioned but because of the character of the neighborhood that such other use should be limited to a "professional type of building or its equivalent." It was against this background that the owner contracted to sell the lot to the Broadway Bank and Trust Company which desired a location for a branch bank. The plans for the branch bank were submitted to the planning board, which, in purported compliance with its function under [the New Jersey Zoning Act] to approve or disapprove proposed amending ordinances, approved the instant ordinance but carefully stated in its letter of November 9, 1951 that the approval was for the purpose of permitting "The Broadway Bank and Trust Company to build a branch bank with off street parking."

The technical assistant to the planning board testified at the public hearing on the ordinance before the Board of Public Works and disclosed that the branch bank project was considered by the planning board to be a "neighborhood type" use. However, there are many uses allowable in a Business 3 zone not of the "neighborhood type" which the municipal officials frankly acknowledged would be most undesirable in this neighborhood. Several objectors at the public hearing pointed out the danger that the lot might be put to one of the undesirable uses if for any reason the branch bank was not built. Indeed, the owner's expert witness testified that his opinion of the desirability of rezoning the lot was based upon the location there of the branch bank and said he would change his opinion "according to what structure would be in question" if the proposal related "to any other type of business allowed under a Business 3 Zone." The chairman of the Board of Public Works answered the objectors by saying that the ordinance might be repealed

"If for example something should happen and the bank or other structure applied for could not be erected by the applicant."

We fail to see even a debatable basis upon which to support a conclusion that this ordinance is in accordance with a comprehensive plan. It very clearly appears that the ordinance was not passed to permit all of the uses allowable in a Business 3 zone, which necessarily would be in view if the ordinance was purposed to establish or further a comprehensive zoning plan. To the contrary, the record brings us to the inescapable conclusion that the ordinance was adopted only to relieve the lot of the difficulties special to it and to permit the construction of the branch bank as not inharmonious with the residential character of the district. Indeed the implication is very plain that the ordinance would not have been adopted except upon the understanding that the branch bank would be built.

The action of the Board of Public Works in adopting the ordinance thus in fact constitutes an unlawful usurpation of the jurisdiction exclusively reserved by the Zoning Act to the local board of adjustment to grant, or recommend to the governing body the grant of, a variance, as amended. Subdivision (c) of that section authorizes the local board to grant a variance from the general regulation for a specific piece of property where, by reason of the exceptional narrowness, shallowness or shape at the time of the enactment of the general regulation or by reason of exceptional topographical conditions or other extraordinary and exceptional situation or condition of such piece of property, the strict application of the general regulation would result in peculiar and exceptional practical difficulties to, or exceptional and undue hardship upon, the owner of the property. Subdivision (d) authorizes the local board to recommend to the governing body of the municipality the granting of a variance in particular cases and for special reasons.

That the Zoning Act denies to a municipality the power by amending ordinance to grant a variance is emphasized by the 1948 and 1949 amendments to [the Act]. Those amendments introduced a new criterion governing the action of local boards of adjustment in passing upon applications for variances under both subdivisions (c) and (d). They provide that "No relief may be granted or action taken * * * unless * * * relief can be granted without substantial detriment to the public good and will not substantially impair the intent and purpose of the zone plan and zoning ordinance." In this way the Legislature made it plain that, though the owner proves his right to a variance by reason of the special situation of his property, the relief must be in terms of authorizing a specific variant use determined by the local board not to be unreasonable in the particular environment.

In arguing that the ordinance merely recognizes that the general regulation is arbitrary and invalid in its application to the lot, the defendants suggest that the owner could on that ground have successfully maintained a direct action to annul the zoning ordinance as applied to the lot without first asking the local board of adjustment to grant, or to recommend, a variance according to the statute. This might be so if the challenge were upon grounds which render the general ordinance invalid in its entirety even though the owner sought to have the ordinance declared invalid only as to his property. However, when, as here, the zoning ordinance is not claimed to be invalid in its entirety but only to be arbitrary and unreasonable in its application to the owner's land, and relief in that circumstance may be obtained from a local board of adjustment, the trial court should ordinarily decline to adjudicate an attack upon the ordinance until after the owner has exhausted his remedy to seek relief from the local board of adjustment. When the owner succeeds, by direct attack, in annihilating the zoning ordinance as to his property, the consequences to the general zoning plan may, of course, be more damaging than a change of zone, since the property is then subject to no restrictions whatever. Such a result is plainly undesirable, particularly now that the 1948 and 1949 amendments to [the Act] require that the local boards take into account the effect of a proposed variance upon the neighborhood scheme and approve only such as may be allowed without substantial impairment of the zone plan and zoning ordinance. The owner is not prejudiced by the requirement that he first exhaust his remedy before the local board since he may have a judicial determination of his contention that the regulation is arbitrary in its application to his land upon review of the action of the local board if he is aggrieved thereby.

One other argument by defendants should be noted. They point out that there are retail stores on a plot 80 x 100 feet on the northwest corner of the intersection opposite the lot in question and refer to the fact that the planning experts who testified agreed that "uniformity of treatment of both sides of the street is a proper goal in zoning." Apart from the fact that the ordinance was not adopted pursuant to a plan for extending the business zone, that small plot had stores upon it when it was constituted a Business 1 zone by the original zoning ordinance, adopted in 1921. Those uses might thus have continued as non-conforming uses. The significant fact, however, is that neither the zone nor the uses have been enlarged beyond this small plot. No business other than this has been permitted to invade the Residence A zone. Zoning one side of a street for purposes different from those prevailing on the other side is not per se illegal, and, while doubtless better reasoned planning theories favor the same use zoning on both sides of a street, in this instance there was testimony by plaintiff's expert that if this area was to be opened to additional business proper planning in the circumstances would require "a more extensive change which would probably mean going west on Broadway for at least one block." ▬

The Boarding House Case:
Casper v. City of Long Branch

One of the most common conflicts between local residents and municipal governments involves the use of private homes in single-family residential zoning districts. Zoning ordinances are replete with provisions restricting home offices, accessory or in-law apartments, and subdivisions into two or more units. Overworked zoning inspectors and underoccupied prying neighbors (the private attorneys general) look for business door bells and identifying plaques, extra kitchens and other evidence of illegal property use.

Owners naturally believe that they should be able to use their houses for whatever purposes they choose, as long as they do not disturb others. Sometimes, their livelihood depends upon illegal uses, and boarding houses are a logical extension of renting out illegally one or two rooms. Ann Casper apparently did more than take in a few boarders, however. Indeed, she sought a rooming-house license for a 28-room, 13-bath house she owned at 936 Ocean Avenue in the city of Long Branch. Because the house was located in a single-family residential zone, the city of Long Branch declined to grant her a license. There were indications that Long Branch and Casper had had previous run-ins over her attempt to operate her rooming house.

Casper sued for issuance of a license and lost in the trial court. Writing for the appellate division of the New Jersey Superior Court, Justice Brennan agreed with the city, citing its vigilant enforcement actions as evidence of its interest in maintaining the integrity of its zoning.

JUSTICE BRENNAN

Plaintiff's argument is that the refusal to issue her a permit was arbitrary and capricious because residences or structures at 907, 919, 1015, and 1139 Ocean Avenue, and a building at the rear of plaintiff's lot and another around the corner, are either used as boarding houses or are subdivided into apartments, and there is a 75-room hotel, the Leelands, across the street. However, these few exceptions do not show that the overall scheme or character of the neighborhood is other than single family residential. They may have existed, so far as appears, before the zoning ordinance was adopted. We will not assume the contrary and it is established that the existence of non-conforming uses in a relatively small portion of the area does not prove that the refusal to permit another is in any real sense arbitrary or unreasonable. There is no proof that the uses resulted from variances allowed by the municipality; rather, there is evidence of alert activity by the municipality to prosecute violations (for example, this plaintiff, and the owner at 907 Ocean Avenue, with many others), reasonably justifying the inference that the city is determined to maintain the integrity of the zoning scheme. So, plaintiff cannot succeed even if the cited few uses constitute violations, or indeed, even if they result from ill-advised or illegal variances. The refusal to issue the permit is not to be characterized as unreasonable and capricious when the proofs do not show that the general scheme has been so far shattered as to require the conclusion that the ordinance no longer subserves the objectives which underlie zoning, and there is also evidence of the determination of the city to avert a general breakdown by vigilant efforts to detect and stamp out violations and to call a halt to further encroachments.

This situation is in nowise comparable to the situations presented in [cases] cited by plaintiff. In those cases the municipalities attempted by ordinance to restrict properties to residential use after substantially all other properties in the vicinity had been converted for industrial or commercial purposes. The evidence in this record more persuasively points to the uses in question as isolated exceptions in a district otherwise almost entirely made up of substantial single-family residences. ■

5 THE THREAT OF LAND USE EXCEPTIONS

Quarry site in North Haledon, N.J., which the operator attempted to expand as a nonconforming use. From Struyk v. Samuel Braen's Sons.

(Jerold S. Kayden)

The movement of people from city to suburb during the late 1940s and 1950s threatened the cherished small-town character of many New Jersey communities. Horse farms, quarries and gravel pit operations, minding their own business in resplendent isolation, suddenly found themselves cheek-by-jowl with new residences. Standing between old values and new realities was the venerable zoning plan, designed for the slower-paced real estate conditions of the 1920s and 1930s. Frustrated by old bylaws restricting most land to less profitable single-family development, property owners attempted a circumvention through the end runs of variances and expansions of nonconforming uses. Incompatibilities created the stuff of lawsuits.

The field of variances has been one of considerable confusion right from its beginning. Dispensed by a board of appeals or a similarly named local administrative agency separate and distinct from the zoning authority, a variance allows a landowner to diverge from the applicable zoning rules enforcing use, shape and bulk. Eligibility depends on proof of special and unique circumstances relating to the physical conditions of the owner's land, as well as proof of economic hardship. Drafters of the 1924 model state zoning enabling act believed that, without the variance safety valve, zoning could not muster enough public support to be adopted. After all, if blindly applied, the essential broad-brush uniformity of zoning—everyone treated equally—could never ensure fairness in all cases. In similar fashion, the doctrine of nonconforming uses, allowing the continuation of past uses subsequently made illegal by adoption of a new ordinance, would leaven zoning's natural rigidity.

Of course, indiscriminate granting of variances and nonconforming uses could unravel the general contours of the zoning plan. Unfortunately, the tug of individual sympathies in urgent cases and the pull of political and financial connections in others expanded the role played by these twin devices. The exceptions swallowed the rule, as if Jonah had swallowed the whale.

With the four cases described in this chapter, Justice Brennan exhibited a keen awareness of the corrosive tendencies of variances and nonconforming uses on local planning and zoning efforts. In the *Leimann* "Garden Apartments" case of 1952, he reversed the trial court and overturned the issuance of a variance for a garden apartment development, emphasizing both the owner's failure to satisfy the variance criteria and the danger that a variance for such a large parcel (9.5 acres) could nullify the entire scheme of the ordinance. For similar reasons, in the *Rexon* "Machine Shop" case that same year, he approved the denial of a variance that would have allowed a machine shop in a residential area. The *Struyk* "Quarry" case of 1951 illustrated the same willingness to favor the general zoning scheme and view with suspicion deviations from it, this time in the context of a nonconforming use, a quarry. Reversing the trial court, Justice Brennan found that the quarry use was being expanded rather than maintained and, thus, the expansion was ineligible for special treatment. And in the 1952 *Cobble Close Farm* "Manure Barn" case, an amusing demonstration of the sort of noisome details arising in the august chambers of the judiciary, Justice Brennan made clear that self-inflicted harms such as unreasonable expectations do not justify issuance of variances. Otherwise, owners creating their own hardship would be rewarded, not penalized, for their behavior and zoning would become a sieve.

The Garden Apartments Case:
Leimann v. Board of Adjustment

Good real estate developers are creative, combining land, money and imagination to build housing, offices and other structures needed by people. Government regulations, if not appreciated, are at least accepted by all as a necessary component of doing business. Indeed, skillful dealings with the public sector may result in larger profits. Conversely, unjustified expectations and unrealistic reliance on favorable government action can be quite dangerous.

One of the trickiest—but potentially most lucrative—strategies used by successful developers is buying land under one zoning classification, then applying to the local government to have it changed to a less restrictive category. Other things being equal, land zoned for a density of 10 units to the acre is more valuable than land zoned at five units per acre. To accomplish their entrepreneurial goals, developers frequently need political savvy and powerful connections, both frequent enemies of sound and comprehensive planning. The principal technical routes include applications for zoning amendments or variances.

In the *Leimann* case, intending to develop an eight-building garden apartment complex of 140 units, several property owners in Cranford merged two vacant parcels totaling more than nine acres. The smaller parcel, more than three acres in size, had south frontage on Lincoln Avenue. The remaining six-acre parcel shared a common boundary with the first parcel but had no frontage on Lincoln Avenue or other streets. To provide access to the back, the owners deeded to Cranford and the county park commission strips of land along the west and north borders of the combined parcels for an access road, which was never constructed by the government.

Because the land was zoned Residence A (single-family dwellings), the owners needed a zoning amendment or a variance to move forward with their multifamily scheme. Zoning amendments, usually recommended by town planning boards and voted on by elected officials, are granted only when legitimate land use planning reasons support the change. Variances, approved by a specially appointed local body known as the board of adjustment or appeals, are granted only when unique topographical or other physical circumstances create undue hardship for the landowner. In reality, rezonings and variances have been frequently issued for reasons, political or otherwise, having nothing to do with the legal criteria set forth in state zoning acts and local ordinances.

Here, the owners elected to apply for, and received, a variance. Ronald Leimann, a neighbor, challenged the issuance of the variance but lost

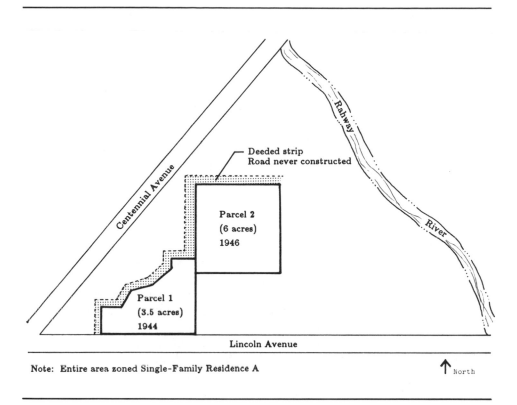

Deeded strip
Road never constructed

Parcel 2
(6 acres)
1946

Parcel 1
(3.5 acres)
1944

Centennial Avenue

Rahway

River

Lincoln Avenue

Note: Entire area zoned Single-Family Residence A

↑ North

in the trial court. In a five-to-two New Jersey Supreme Court decision, Justice Brennan reversed the trial court and overturned the issuance of the variance. As a general matter, it is not hard to understand his basic suspicion of variances. After all, they are inherently noncomprehensive, they can undermine sound planning, and they are issued by nonplanning bodies.

JUSTICE BRENNAN

It is basic to the fundamental purpose of zoning that the power of a local board to grant variances should be exercised sparingly and only in exceptional circumstances, and ordinarily only when relief can be granted "without substantial detriment to the public good and will not substantially impair the intent and purpose of the zone plan and zoning ordinance," provided always the proofs reasonably establish that strict application of the zoning ordinance results in an unnecessary and unjust interference with the rights of private property in the light of a situation peculiar to the particular property among properties generally of the district. The power must be exercised consonant with the duty laid upon the local board to protect the integrity of the general scheme from substantial impairment. A grant of variance which has the effect of frustrating the general scheme and is tantamount to an [sic] usurpation of the legislative power reserved to the governing body of the municipality to amend or revise the plan cannot be sustained. Subdivision (c) [of the New Jersey Zoning Act] confines the permissible exercise of the power to the allowance of relief in favor of the owner of a specific piece of property where by reason of exceptional narrowness, shallowness or shape at the time of the enactment of the regulation, or by reason of exceptional topographic conditions or other extraordinary and exceptional situation or condition of such piece of property, the strict application of the regulation would result in undue hardship upon the owner, and relief can be granted without substantial detriment to the public good and without substantially impairing the intent and purpose of the regulation.

The instant variance is wholly lacking in a reasonable basis and was plainly beyond the local board's power to grant. We consider it significant that the determination contains no express finding that the relief could be granted without substantial detriment to the public good and without substantial impairment of the intent and purpose of the zone plan. Subdivision (c) cannot be interpreted to contemplate that a 9½-acre tract may be considered "a specific piece of property" subject to the power of the local board to authorize a variance when, so far as appears, development of the zone has not been of single-family dwellings upon large tracts, or even partly so, but has emphasized the construction of such dwellings upon moderate sized lots. Determination of whether a given piece of property is "a specific piece of property" within the meaning of the statute properly the subject of consideration for a variance should take into account its size in relation to the sizes generally of pieces of property in the zone devoted to the permitted use. We regard such an interpretation of subdivision (c) as required by the statutory policy to control and limit variances within narrow limits in keeping with the spirit, intent and general purpose of zoning to divide communities into appropriate districts according to the suitability of each for particular uses and to ordain uniformity of use within each district. The variance in the circumstances here has the effect not simply of substantially impairing the intent and purpose of the Cranford zoning ordinance: the grant for so large an area as 9½ acres in a district where single-family dwellings are built usually on moderate sized lots virtually shatters, if indeed it does not wholly nullify, the general scheme of the zone.

Moreover, viewing the tract in the setting of its environment, the proofs are entirely insufficient to support the finding of unnecessary hardship to the owners upon the ground of its exceptional shape. Mere irregularity in contour is not the test. The statute contemplates proof that the property because of its shape cannot reasonably be put to the permitted use in the manner of properties generally in the district. Certainly it may not be said that the 3½-acre parcel with its frontage of 423 feet on Lincoln Avenue cannot be subdivided into lots of sizes comparable to the sizes of lots generally in the district. Nor was the six acre tract shown to be any less suitable for single-family residences upon like-sized lots except as access to it has been made difficult because the proposed street has not been constructed. There was testimony that the owners have been unsuccessful "on many occasions" in their efforts "to convey, or sell the property" for single-family residences "by reason of the peculiar set up of the property." The set up, however, is of the owners' own making. This is the case both as to the resultant irregular shape of the whole produced by the assembling of the two parcels, and as to the difficulty of access to the rear consequent upon the deeding of the border strip and the failure of the authorities to construct the road. When the condition said to require a variance is of his own making, an owner is generally denied relief. Furthermore, except as the shape of a specific piece of property existed "at the time of enactment of the regulation," its shape is not a basis for a finding that the use restriction results in peculiar and exceptional practical difficulty to, or exceptional and undue hardship upon, the owner. Here the inference from the proofs is clear that the assembling of the parcels resulting in the purported exceptional shape of the subject property was effected after the enactment of the zoning ordinance. The 3½-acre parcel was purchased from Cranford Trust Company in 1944. In 1943 the trust company sought a variance to permit construction of a garden type apartment upon the parcel. One of the defendants vigorously opposed the application upon the ground, among others, that the contemplated project would depreciate the property values in the neighborhood, and the application was denied.

Nor is the owners' difficulty of access to the rear of the property, created by their conveyance of the border strip and by the failure of the public authorities to construct the road, sufficient basis to support the variance as being rested upon "other extraordinary and exceptional situation or condition of such piece of property." The arrangement for the road was made in contemplation of the development of the land. If development for single family dwellings is not feasible without the road, the owners may pursue their remedy upon the alleged agreement to obtain its performance. Plainly a situation or condition is not to be deemed extraordinary and exceptional within the statutory intendment when the owners who brought it about have the means of correcting it. ▬

The Machine Shop Case:
Rexon v. Board of Adjustment

Conflict between land uses is the inevitable by-product of a technologically advancing world. For centuries, the English common law doctrine of nuisance dealt with smaller problems of incompatibility. Its Latin phrase *Sic utere tuo ut alienum non laedas*, loosely translated "Use your property in such a way as not to injure another," was the guiding light for equity court judges. The Industrial Revolution made for larger incompatibility problems. Nuisance law, inadequate to the task, nevertheless proved a comfortingly familiar analogy to judges when they reviewed and approved zoning's division of land into separate use districts.

As new residences spread over the countryside and developed as suburban enclaves, industrial uses became less desirable neighbors. G. Frederick Rexon owned and operated a machine shop in the borough of Haddonfield, a predominantly residential town in which no significant industrial activity existed. The shop was located on a 10,000-square-foot lot in the middle of a square block surrounded on all sides by other properties. As such, the lot lacked frontage on the four streets defining the overall block (Clement to the north, Mechanic to the east, Kings Highway East to the south and Tanner to the west). Indeed, when Rexon purchased his property, the only road access was a driveway from Kings Highway East. By subsequently buying a house on Tanner Street, however, he was able to create additional access from Tanner Street.

Years before Rexon's ownership, the lot contained a dairy, stable and several outbuildings. In 1944 the Atlas Instrument Company acquired it and built a small one-story cement block structure used in connection with its own machine shop business on Tanner Street. In 1948 Rexon, an employee of Atlas, bought the lot from the company to begin his own machine shop business.

The original zoning for the overall block was two-thirds retail and mercantile, including Rexon's parcel, and one-third residential. While a 1944 zoning amendment had allowed the Atlas Instrument Company to operate its small machine shop on Tanner Street, another 1944 amendment provided, "Any use or purpose which will create or which is likely in the opinion of the Board of Adjustment to create a nuisance or conditions of haz-

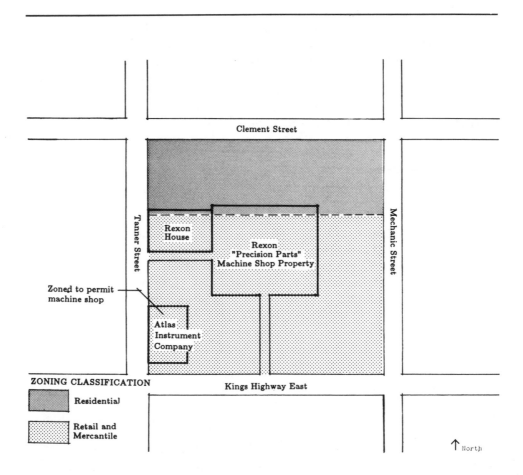

ard, smoke, fumes, noise, odor or dust detrimental to the health, safety or general welfare of the community shall not be permitted."

In 1950 Rexon removed the remaining farm structures and enlarged the cement block building to accommodate grinders, milling machines, lathes, saws and two fixed-arc welding machines. His business had grown substantially, employing 40 persons at a weekly payroll of between $3,000 and $3,500. Under the 1944 zoning amendment, he required a variance for his machine shop activities.

Following hearings, the board of adjustment denied the application, finding that the shop "created a condition disturbing to the residents" of the neighborhood and "produced loud noises caused by the pounding of metals and the handling of metallic materials, and in addition thereto, bright flashings of light caused by the operation of the electric arc welding machines." Concluded the board, "[T]he disturbances and conditions created . . . [were] such as to disturb the rest of the residents and the peaceful enjoyment of the residents." The board also found that "there is no exceptional narrowness or shallowness, or shape of the particular premises, or any exceptional applicable conditions or situations, whereby the strict application of the terms of the Zoning Ordinance would result in peculiar or practical difficulties to or exceptional or undue hardships upon the petitioner," and that "no relief can be granted under the petition . . . without substantial detriment to the public good and without substantially impairing the intent and purpose of the Zoning Plan and Zoning Ordinance."

Rexon sued the board to require issuance of the variance and also claimed that application of the zoning to his property worked an arbitrary and capricious interference with his rights, amounting to a confiscation. He cited difficulties of access to his parcel that make "the land in question . . . so peculiarly situated as to make it unique."

The trial court upheld the board's denial of the variance, and Rexon appealed. Writing for a unanimous New Jersey Supreme Court, Justice Brennan agreed with the board's denial of the variance. Citing his own *Leimann* opinion, involving the merged parcels for a proposed garden apartment project, he once again demonstrated skepticism about variances. His reading of the New Jersey Zoning Act indicated that variances were appropriate only in limited circumstances where the property owner has unique problems not of his or her own making.

JUSTICE BRENNAN

The Legislature has directed that variances under [the New Jersey Zoning Act] shall not be had except upon a showing of undue hardship to the owner upon one or more of the grounds specified in that subsection and further, both as to that subsection and generally as to variances and exceptions under [the Act], unless relief can be granted "without substantial detriment to the public good and will not substantially impair the intent and purpose of the zone plan and zoning ordinance." The scope of a local board's authority under subsection (c) has been considered in several recent opinions of this court and need not be elaborated upon here.

The action of a board of adjustment in denying a variance is presumptively correct and the person assailing the action has the burden to prove otherwise. On judicial review the proper issue is whether the board acted reasonably upon the showing made before it and its denial will be sustained in the absence of an affirmative showing that it was unreasonable, arbitrary or capricious. In the instant case the Law Division sustained the local board's action as reasonable in light of the proofs, and we reach the same conclusion after our own examination of the record.

Plaintiff premises his claim of undue hardship upon the statutory element of "other extraordinary and exceptional situation or condition of such piece of property," arguing that because the property is not readily accessible to the public a conclusion of undue hardship upon him is compelled. The condition of limited accessibility has obtained, however, since the property became a detached piece in 1927, many years before the adoption of the zoning ordinance. As the abutting lots surrounding the piece were built upon, the value of the piece, even before the adoption of the zoning ordinance, apparently lay largely in its utility as an appendage to one of them. Such was its value to Atlas Instrument Company when it bought the lot in 1944. And there was substantial testimony that the structures upon the lot are adaptable for use by adjoining mercantile establishments. Plaintiff's own expert witness acknowledged that the building thereon "definitely is of such a character it could be used as a storehouse, or a building of similar nature * * * adaptable to any business in that area surrounding that property." The borough's expert witness also testified that "with very little expenditure of money, it could be utilized for a storage building or a warehouse as an adjunct to some of the businesses on Kings Highway East." We cannot say that in this posture of the proofs the local board's action was unreasonable and arbitrary. A situation or condition of a piece of property is not to be deemed extraordinary and exceptional and to impose undue hardship upon the owner within the intendment of [the Act] if, viewed in the setting of its environment, the property may reasonably be adapted to a permitted use. We concur with the holding of the Law Division that there was substantial evidence before the local board opposed to plaintiff's contention that the lot has no practical utility except for the purposes of his business. A zoning ordinance does not contravene constitutional limitations merely because the restricted use may not be the most profitable use to which the property can be devoted.

The fact situation in the instant case is wholly different from that passed upon in *Schaible*, upon which plaintiff relies. That case arose under subdivision (d) of [the Act] and turned upon a finding that "as things now are, prosecutors are deprived of any practical economic use of their property."

Moreover, the *Schaible* case was decided before the amendments of 1948 and 1949 to [the Act] introduced the requirement that relief is not to be granted thereunder unless it may be done without substantial detriment to the public good and without substantial impairment of the intent and purpose of the zoning plan. The evidence pointing to a serious threat to the health and well-being of the citizens of this residential community from the continuance of plaintiff's factory operation fully supports the local board's finding that a variance could not be granted without substantial detriment to the public good and without substantially impairing the general regulation. True, the Atlas Instrument Company for several years has operated its machine shop on the Tanner Street lot under the 1944 amendment to the zoning ordinance which sanctioned that use. The municipal action in that regard may have been improper as tantamount to spot zoning, but, so far as appears, the propriety of the action was not challenged and apparently the business has been operated in a manner which has not occasioned complaints by citizens. However, plaintiff can get no comfort from that municipal action even assuming the action was improper. "If that were so, one variation would sustain if it did not compel others, and thus the general regulation would eventually be nullified." ▬

The Quarry Case:
Struyk v. Samuel Braen's Sons

The *Leimann* "Garden Apartments" and *Rexon* "Machine Shop" cases show how variances can undercut the intent and effect of land use plans and are not justified when the landowners themselves create or know in advance the very circumstances of hardship they are subsequently trying to escape. The second of the potent, albeit necessary, evils faced by planners and jurists is the nonconforming use, a legal land use made illegal when new zoning no longer authorizes such use in its current location. Nonconforming uses are, nevertheless, allowed to continue in the interests of justice, although zoning laws require that they terminate after some reasonable period of years. While variances and nonconforming uses can create havoc with comprehensive planning, zoning would be too harsh a task master without such obeisance to fairness.

Samuel Braen's Sons operated a private quarry in the borough of North Haledon for more than 40 years, well before the borough enacted its zoning ordinance in 1941. One year after the ordinance was adopted, the company acquired a residentially zoned adjoining 7.5-acre vacant parcel (the Blasberg tract) in anticipation of expanding its quarry operations. In 1947 the company stripped away the top soil and dirt of the Blasberg tract, exposing rock, and three years later began quarrying operations.

North Haledon, through building inspector Neil Struyk, obtained a conviction by jury against Samuel Braen's Sons for conducting quarrying activities on the Blasberg tract in violation of the applicable residential zoning classification. However, the trial court judge set aside the conviction and entered a judgment of acquittal on the ground that the Blasberg tract was already being worked as a quarry in 1941, when North Haledon enacted its zoning ordinance, and that the additional quarry area therefore qualified as a nonconforming use.

The borough appealed to the appellate division of the New Jersey

Superior Court, and Justice Brennan wrote the opinion reversing the judgment of the trial court. Displaying his consistent concern for the integrity of planning, he found that this was expansion, not maintenance, of a nonconforming use, and thus an unjustified exception to the zoning. As in the *Leimann* and *Rexon* cases, this owner also created or knew about his own problem, and fairness did not demand that government solve it.

JUSTICE BRENNAN

The trial court set aside the conviction and entered a judgment of acquittal upon a finding that the Blasberg tract was being worked as a quarry when the ordinance was passed. This finding is based on testimony that defendant was permitted by the previous owner for some 25 years before the passage of the ordinance to truck across the tract shovels, drills and other equipment employed in working the pit of the original quarry, and evidence that before 1950 defendant "did clean up a lot of loose rocks." Clearly such proof was wholly insufficient to support a finding that quarrying of the Blasberg tract was in fact being conducted at the time the ordinance became effective.

Quarrying is usually the digging out of stone or slate from an open excavation. Assuming that a stripping operation necessary to the proper and convenient use of the pit may constitute quarrying, there was no proof here of any stripping preparatory to the working of a pit on the Blasberg tract prior to 1947. The cleaning up of loose rock and the hauling of equipment both prior and subsequent to the passage of the ordinance were solely incidents to the working of the original quarry. Defendant's president frankly admitted that until 1950 "I would not say we did any quarrying" on the Blasberg tract.

The use at the time the ordinance was adopted established the non-conforming use which defendant was entitled to continue. The policy of the law is to restrict rather than to increase non-conforming uses. They may not be enlarged or radically modified. The quarrying of the Blasberg tract which added blasting and other operations to cut and dig rock therefrom represented a substantial change from the preexisting non-conforming use and violated the ordinance. The permitted continuance of a non-conforming use is the continuance of the same use and not of some other kind of use. Defendant acquired the tract subject to the zoning ordinance and with full knowledge of the restrictions imposed thereunder, and it seems obvious its efforts to extend its activities into forbidden territory is in effect an attempt to circumvent the prohibition of which it was fully aware. Plainly, the judgment appealed from cannot be sustained for the reason given by the County Court.

However, defendant argues other reasons here, raised but not passed upon in the County Court. At the oral argument both sides expressed the desire that this court determine them; and we shall therefore do so and shall not remand for their disposition in the County Court.

First, defendant contends that the quarrying of the Blasberg tract is merely the extension to that property of its presently existing non-conforming use on the original quarry property, and relies on [the *Lamb* case]. It was held in the *Lamb* case that the owner of a ten-acre lot from which on one acre it was excavating sand and gravel when the zoning ordinance was adopted was not guilty of a nonconforming use of land by extending its excavation thereafter to other portions of the tract, for it was not to be supposed "a land owner would be entitled to continue a previous nonconforming use only on the precise spot where it was being done." Such is not the situation here. Defendant acquired the Blasberg tract after the zoning ordinance was passed and the extent of any non-conforming use which may be continued thereon is to be measured solely by the non-conforming use, if any, being made of it at the time the ordinance became effective.

Defendant contends further that the provisions of the zoning ordinance limiting the use of the tract to residential purposes are unreasonable with regard to the character of the district and its peculiar suitability for particular uses and that the ordinance is therefore unconstitutional as applied to the Blasberg tract. True, a distinction has been recognized between the effect of a zoning ordinance prohibiting a manufacturing or commercial business in a residential district which may be conducted in another locality with equal profit and advantage, and an effect which deprives the owner of land of the natural products thereof and of the right to remove or work them. However, this distinction becomes one of degree of hardship in view of the modern trend in the law of zoning which recognizes that a community has broad powers reasonably to achieve the purposes to be served by zoning to provide a balanced and well ordered scheme for all activity deemed essential to the particular community. There is a presumption that the ordinance is reasonable and the burden was upon defendant to establish the contrary. Our examination of the record does not persuade us that defendant successfully overcame the presumption. There was expert testimony on behalf of defendant that the tract was unsuitable for the construction of residences because of its rockbase; but North Haledon is a small residential community and there was other evidence that the general area abutting the Blasberg tract is in a stage of development of residential properties and that a roadway is being cut through which will provide access to the tract if developed for residential purposes. Debatable questions in this regard should be resolved in favor of upholding the legislative judgment, and defendant has not proved it is unreasonable to expect that the tract can be developed for residences.

Defendant next argues that the zoning ordinance is unconstitutional because it makes no provisions for manufacturing or industrial uses within the borough other than such as are connected with retail business. Here again sufficient proof to overcome the presumption of the validity of the ordinance was not supplied. North Haledon is almost exclusively a residential community, and though there was evidence that some areas, including the Blasberg tract, are adaptable to industrial development, the record is lacking in persuasive evidence that, as argued by defendant, "there is precious little industrial space in the surrounding area," that is, in the entire region of which North Haledon is a part. The expert for defendant admitted the existence in neighboring municipalities of areas available for industrial development. [The *Duffcon* case] is authority that a municipality predominantly residential in character has the power wholly to exclude from within its borders industrial enterprises or activities, or to impose limitations upon the extent thereof, for the purpose of preserving its residential character, and is not required merely to restrict such enterprises or activities to particular zones or areas of the municipality, when, although separated therefrom but in the same geographical region, there are areas adapted to and sufficiently large to accommodate industrial development. Defendant's proofs do not establish that such areas are lacking in the region which includes North Haledon.

Defendant's last point is that there was an irregularity in connection with the passage of the zoning ordinance which renders its enactment invalid. The argument goes solely to the alleged failure of the municipal records to evidence compliance with [the New Jersey Zoning Act], requiring that the governing body shall not adopt a zoning ordinance until the zoning commission shall make a preliminary report and thereafter hold public hearings thereon before submitting its final report. The testimony shows that public hearings were held by the zoning commissioners but that the reports made to the governing body were oral. That the zoning ordinance was presented to the mayor and council by the zoning commission, given the proper preliminary and final hearings, duly advertised, passed and signed by the mayor, is not questioned. Assuming that the statute contemplates the making of written reports which are to be filed with the municipal records, the irregularity cannot at this late date be invoked to invalidate the ordinance. The ordinance has been in effect for ten years and "public policy forbids an attack based upon informalities and irregularities in the procedure which led to the adoption of the ordinance, when it has been accepted as a valid enactment for a long period of time, and property owners affected by it have conformed to its provisions, and have fixed their status accordingly." ▬

The Manure Barn Case:
Cobble Close Farm v.
Board of Adjustment

Landowners sometimes act as if zoning laws did not exist. They purchase property and make plans without regard to whether the ordinance forbids their proposed development. Perhaps they are acting on wishful thinking, or perhaps they believe they can obtain a rezoning or a variance.

Cobble Close Farm, a developer, acquired a 23-acre parcel in Middletown and planned to convert several of the existing farm structures into attached family residences totaling nine units. Because the proposed development was located in a single-family zoning district forbidding attached multifamily developments, the building inspector refused to issue a permit. Cobble Close Farm asked the local board of adjustment to overturn the inspector's decision and to grant a variance from the applicable zoning. The board declined both requests.

Cobble Close Farm sued the board and inspector, charging that the ordinance should not apply to its property and that it was entitled to a

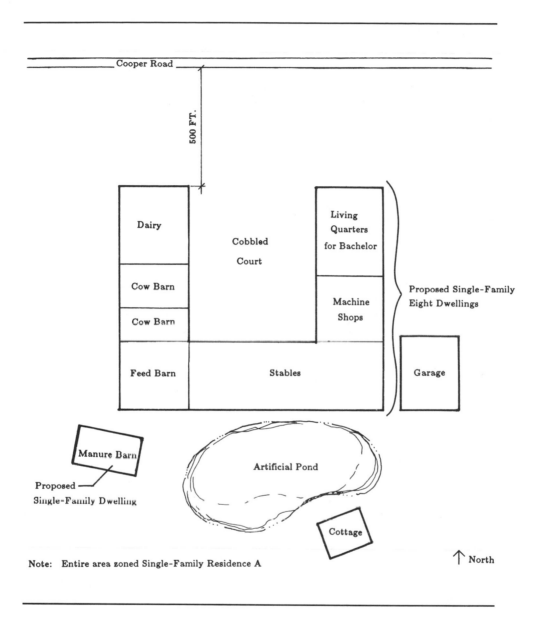

Cooper Road

500 FT.

Dairy

Cobbled Court

Living Quarters for Bachelor

Cow Barn

Machine Shops

Proposed Single-Family Eight Dwellings

Cow Barn

Feed Barn

Stables

Garage

Manure Barn

Proposed — Single-Family Dwelling

Artificial Pond

Cottage

Note: Entire area zoned Single-Family Residence A

↑ North

variance. The developer claimed that the town had acted in an arbitrary and capricious fashion. The trial court upheld the local decisions, and Cobble Close Farm appealed.

Writing for a unanimous New Jersey Supreme Court, Justice Brennan affirmed the judgment of the trial court. He found that the zoning clearly prohibited the proposed development and that no variance was warranted, because Cobble Close Farm knew the zoning rules when it purchased the property. Once again, variances are not to be granted when landowners create the circumstances from which they seek relief.

JUSTICE BRENNAN

This is a zoning case. We certified of our own motion the appeal of plaintiff to the Appellate Division from the judgment entered in the Law Division against the plaintiff corporation and in favor of the defendants, Board of Adjustment of the Township of Middletown and David Simpson, Building Inspector of said Township.

Herbert N. Straus and Therese Kuhn Straus, his wife, for many years maintained a country estate of 70 acres in Middletown Township with acreage on both sides of Cooper Road, the mansion house being on the larger part north of the road. On the 23-acre parcel south of the road Mr. and Mrs. Straus built a group of accessory buildings—a dairy, cow barns, stables, machinery shops, manure barn, a large garage, living quarters for bachelor workmen of the estate, and a cottage containing the workmen's dining room and commodious living quarters for other persons in their employ. All of the buildings except the manure barn, the garage and the cottage are grouped in the form of a square around a cobbled court. The garage is close by the group. The cottage stands apart from the group across an artificial pond and is connected to the group by an arched stone colonnade running along the pond. The manure barn is a distance removed from the group. The buildings are of expensive construction, "elaborate," with cast stone walls, tile roofs and floors, mullioned windows, oak panelling, "an architectural showplace," "a thing of beauty." The evidence discloses that the replacement cost of the buildings would approximate $417,000 and that their present sound value after allowance for depreciation is about $292,000.

After Mr. Straus' death the mansion house and the acreage on the north side of Cooper Road were sold. Later, on December 6, 1949, plaintiff's president and his wife acquired at public auction the 23-acre parcel with the accessory buildings for the sum of $28,000, taking title on March 6, 1950 in the name of plaintiff corporation which they organized as their nominee for the purpose. The president and his wife took up residence in the cottage. Plaintiff corporation has invested an additional $20,000 in improvements, but whether to the cottage alone or to the buildings generally does not appear.

The instant controversy grows out of plaintiff's desire to convert the manure barn into a one-family dwelling and the group of buildings around the cobbled court into eight one-family residences. The trial court found that the plans for the eight residences would result in "multiple family units having a common roof, common walls and a common heating plant." The plan is not for residences on separate lots. No subdivision of the 23-acre parcel was made. The plan proposes that a dairy building and a portion of a cow barn connected with it would make up one residence; the remaining portion of that cow barn, all of another cow barn and a two-story feed barn would make the second; the horse barn and a portion of the machinery barn would provide the third; another portion of the machinery barn would supply the fourth, and still another portion of the same machinery barn would provide the fifth; and that the building formerly used as quarters for bachelor employees, which is under one roof, would make up into three residences.

GOVERNORS STATE UNIVERSITY
UNIVERSITY PARK
IL 60466

The township zoning ordinance expressly forbids multi-family units, and it is plain that a consummation of plaintiff's plan would violate that regulation.

The defendant building inspector denied plaintiff a building permit for the proposed alterations because the structures as so altered would not comply with the requirements of the zoning ordinance. Plaintiff appealed to the board of adjustment and also applied to that board for a variance from the provisions of the ordinance. The board sustained the action of the building inspector and denied the variance. The judgment entered in the Law Division sustained the board of adjustment as to both determinations.

The conveyance to plaintiff was made expressly subject to the township's zoning ordinance. The ordinance was originally adopted in 1935 and was substantially amended and revised in 1949, about two months before the auction sale.

Middletown is a sprawling community of great area and is predominantly residential. All but a small portion of the township is zoned for residential purposes. There are five residence districts, A to E, inclusive. The provisions applicable to structures in Zone A, wherein plaintiff's property is located, are designed to make that zone "the highest type zone in the township," and it is primarily a district of substantial homes on sizeable plots. The zone is in the southeast section of the township, running along the Navesink River for some two and one half miles and extending back from the river up to a mile in some places. Cooper Road runs east and west, paralleling the river, and bisects the westerly half of Zone A.

The zoning ordinance provides that no building in the zone may be "erected, altered or used" (1) on a plot of land containing an area less than one acre; (2) and having a frontage of less than 150 feet "on the road or street"; (3) all buildings must be set back at least 75 feet from the "curb line" and if no "curb line" from the "street line," and not less than 15 feet from any rear "lot" line and not less than 15 feet from any side "lot" line; (4) the ground floor of the building may not contain less than 1,500 square feet; (5) other than barns, stables, garages and greenhouses accessory to the residence on a "lot" no structure may be used for any purpose "other than for a one family dwelling for strictly residential purposes"; (6) not more than one dwelling shall be constructed on one "lot" except that living quarters may be provided in accessory structures for persons "employed in domestic service upon the premises."

The residents of Zone A take a live interest in the maintenance of the zoning standards and the preservation of the character of the district. There are two community organizations, Blossom Cove Road Association and Riverside Drive Protective Association, which took an active part in the proceedings below in opposition to the relief sought by plaintiff from the board of adjustment.

Plaintiff argues first that the ordinance has no application to its property. The contention is that the interconnected structures surrounding the cobbled court are buildings "fronting on a private court 500 feet from the

GOVERNORS STATE UNIVERSITY
UNIVERSITY PARK
IL 60466

public road" and that the manure barn is a structure on "plaintiff's right of way," and that "neither they nor the proposed dwellings are erected on 'lots' and do not front upon any 'street' or 'road' and there is no 'curb line,' 'street line,' or 'lot line' from which setbacks may be measured," and therefore that the buildings are not within the prohibition of the ordinance against the erection, alteration or use of buildings on a "plot of land containing an area less than one acre and having a frontage of less than 150 feet on the road or street." We find no merit in this argument. The "lot" of land within the meaning given that word by the ordinance is plaintiff's parcel of 23 acres. The ordinance expressly defines a "lot" as "a parcel of land, the location, dimensions and boundaries of which are determined by the latest official record * * * ." The frontage, setback and side line requirements are thus to be measured from the boundaries of the 23-acre parcel.

And because the 23-acre parcel is a "lot" under the ordinance, the prohibition against more than one dwelling on a "lot" except for accessory living quarters for persons in domestic service on the premises precludes plaintiff's alteration of any of the structures for the residential uses proposed while the cottage is maintained as a residence and the parcel remains undivided. It is urged that the cottage is not a "main residence" within the meaning of the ordinance because it was not such but in accessory use to the Straus mansion when the 23-acre parcel was part of the larger estate. This argument is plainly specious. Upon the separation of plaintiff's parcel from the larger tract, and the use of the cottage as a residence, the cottage became the "main building on the same lot" in contemplation of the ordinance and the other buildings "subordinate and accessory to the main building on the same lot."

Plaintiff next argues that if the ordinance is applicable to its buildings, to require it to comply therewith results in an arbitrary and capricious interference with its right of enjoyment and use of the property, compelling an adjudication either that the ordinance is invalid as applied to plaintiff's property or that the local board of adjustment should have granted plaintiff a variance from the terms of the ordinance upon grounds of undue hardship. In view of this court's decision in *Lionshead Lake, Inc. v. Township of Wayne* (1952), plaintiff abandoned at the oral argument the contention made on its brief that the minimum ground floor area limitation, considered with the plot area and setback requirements, was invalid as an attempt to control the minimum cost of homes and as having no relation to zoning purposes.

Plaintiff is met with the presumption that the zoning ordinance is altogether reasonable in its application to the property and the burden was upon it to establish the contrary. We are not persuaded that plaintiff successfully overcame the presumption. The gist of the argument is that the application of the ordinance would "make the buildings unusable for any purpose and they would continue to deteriorate from disuse until, eventually, they would have to be destroyed and an architectural show place would be lost to the Township," a result allegedly "not permissible in view of the purpose of the statute, to conserve the value of property, and of the zoning ordinance to conserve the value of buildings."

But it is not the fact that the "buildings are unusable for any purpose" allowed by the ordinance. They may still be used for the purposes for which they were originally designed, even though they are doubtless more elaborate in construction and equipment than would normally be necessary in accessory use to the cottage as the main residence on the property. The ordinance expressly authorizes the use of the buildings as a "stable, garage, playhouse, barn, greenhouse or building used for living quarters for help, which is subordinate and accessory to a main building on the same lot." In addition, "farm purposes" and the keeping of farm animals are permitted uses on a tract of this size, and plainly the buildings are adaptable to such uses. Significantly, plaintiff was formed, among other purposes, "to operate farms, to raise and sell the products thereof, and to purchase, raise and sell domestic animals."

Thus, as the buildings may reasonably be devoted to uses permitted by the zoning ordinance there is no basis for the claim that a requirement upon plaintiff to confine the uses of the structures to permissible uses makes the ordinance arbitrary and capricious in its application to plaintiff's property. That the buildings are of picturesque and unique architectural design and of expensive construction may make them particularly adaptable for more profitable non-permitted uses, namely, for conversion to residences, but a zoning ordinance does not contravene constitutional limitations merely because permissive uses thereunder may not be the most profitable uses to which the buildings can be devoted. Zoning regulations are not to be formulated or applied with a design to encourage the most appropriate use of *plaintiff's property* but rather "with reasonable consideration, among other things, to the character of the district and its peculiar suitability for particular uses, and with a view of conserving the value of property and encouraging the most appropriate use of land throughout such municipality."

Nor did the Law Division fall into error in sustaining the local board's denial of a variance. In the proceeding before the Law Division the board's action was properly considered to be presumptively correct and the plaintiff had the burden to prove otherwise. The trial court rightly found that the board acted reasonably upon the showing made before it and that plaintiff had failed affirmatively to show that the action of the board was unreasonable, arbitrary or capricious. In that circumstance the action of the board was properly sustained.

[The New Jersey Zoning Act] confines the permissible exercise by local boards of adjustment of the power to grant variances to the allowance of relief in favor of the owner of a specific piece of property where by reason of exceptional narrowness, shallowness or shape at the time of the enactment of the regulation, or by reason of exceptional topographical conditions or other extraordinary and exceptional situations or conditions of such piece of property the strict application of the regulation would result in undue hardship upon the owner, and relief can be granted without substantial detriment to the public good and without substantially impairing the intent and purpose of the regulation [citing *Leimann*]. The local board's determination that no ground for relief within these limitations was established by plaintiff was in nowise arbitrary in the circumstances shown. The alleged hardship is obviously not the result of any peculiarity inherent in the property itself. The situation is the consequence of the acquisition by plaintiff of the portion of the larger Straus estate and the use of the cottage as the main residence, with full knowledge of the limitations of the ordinance in such case upon the uses of the buildings sought to be converted. Mr. and Mrs. Straus could not have done what plaintiff seeks to do and plaintiff is not to have relief from a situation of its own making. Plaintiff's acquisition of the parcel and its president's use of the cottage as the main residence thereon, plaintiff knowing that the ordinance barred the use as residences of any of the other buildings in that circumstance, if not conclusive against the existence of undue hardship, plainly weighs heavily against the claim that hardship actually ensued.

Plaintiff sought to have the local board suggest what other uses than accessory uses would be approved by it. The board refused to deal with anything except the actual state of facts presented by plaintiff's proposal. This was quite proper. It is not the duty of the board, nor of the court, to search out and list the uses which the board could approve by way of variance from the permitted uses.

Plaintiff next argues that the participation of Mr. J. Marshall Booker, a member of the local board, during some of the proceedings before the board denied plaintiff due process of law. Mr. Booker is president of Blossom Cove Road Association and was present on September 27, 1950 at a meeting of the members of that association which voted to oppose plaintiff's effort to obtain approval of the conversion plans. At the outset of the first hearing before the board of adjustment on January 20, 1951, plaintiff filed a challenge for Mr. Booker's recusement upon the ground that he had prejudged the case. Plaintiff was not permitted by the board to complete its examination under oath of Mr. Booker in support of the challenge. Mr. Booker sat with the board for the remainder of the hearing on that day and later viewed the premises with other members of the board. The hearing was adjourned for one week until January 27. Before the taking of testimony was resumed Mr. Booker voluntarily withdrew from further participation in the proceedings. He took no part whatever in the deliberations or vote upon the decision. The trial court found no evidence that the decision of the members of the board who did take part therein was in any manner influenced by Mr. Booker. Upon our independent review of the record we reach the same conclusion. This is therefore not a case for the application of the principle that a determination of a quasi-judicial body should be set aside when infected with the taint of self-interest of one of the quasi-judges.

The third count of the complaint filed in the Law Division sought a judgment declaring that the provision of the zoning ordinance prohibiting the erection or use of any building in any residential zone for a "hospital, dispensary, asylum, children's home, orphanage, nursery or private school" is invalid and operates to deprive plaintiff of its property without due process of law in violation of the Fourteenth Amendment of the United States Constitution. The Law Division did not deal with this claim for relief in its findings of fact and conclusions of law, other than as may be inferred from its general finding that the ordinance offends no constitutional provisions, state or federal. But plaintiff was not in any event entitled to be heard upon this count of its complaint. The municipality is not a party to the complaint and was not given the opportunity to defend against this attack upon the validity of its ordinance. ▬

6 DISCRETION, COMPETITION AND PUBLIC USE

Surviving billboard in Raritan, N.J., where a local ordinance prohibited billboards. From **United Advertising Corp. v. Borough of Raritan.**
(Jerold S. Kayden)

Municipal governments operate under a profusion of rules set forth by state statutes, city ordinances and regulations, judicial opinions and local custom. No matter how detailed the rules, however, day-to-day governance necessarily entails a considerable exercise in flexibility and judgment. Land use regulations can cause millions of dollars of gains and losses to property owners or otherwise impinge on equally important nonfinancial private rights. With such high stakes, discretionary land use decision making is especially vulnerable to political and financial pressures from within and without city hall.

For example, a community arrogates to itself the discretionary right to decide who can open a business or erect a billboard. A city runs for profit a parking facility or selects one private operator over another. Justified by vague pronouncements about the public interest, these exercises in discretionary government power may actually reflect protectionist or anticompetitive sentiment. If existing local businesses wield disproportionate influence over local officials, such businesses may improperly win public assistance for private gain. The weeding out of inefficiency by the free market—tolerated if not championed by small-town chambers of commerce—is distorted by improper government preference for some private parties over others. Of course, all zoning ordinances to some degree conflict with the public policy expressed by antitrust laws. Surprising as this statement may seem at first, it becomes clear when local land use regulations are tightened. The more bite on a single property owner—the less commercial use permitted, for example—the greater the value of remaining land that is mapped commercial.

The exercise of standardless discretion, with no clear justification other than protectionism, troubled Justice Brennan in the *Weiner* "Auction Store" case of 1954. In overturning the licensing scheme for local businesses, he made a quick allusion to the fact that the license for the proposed auction store was denied apparently to protect existing auction stores. Unnecessary as it is to the formal holding of the case, this suspicion may very well be the speck that determined the entire outcome.

The 1952 *United Advertising* "Billboard" case involved a local ban on off-site billboards, the typical free-standing structures advertising products ranging from cigarettes to tanning lotion. The bylaw did allow, however, on-site business signs identifying products and services offered on the premises. In passing, Justice Brennan observed that no evidence suggested that the law was meant to protect the local enclave of business properties. He accepted the accumulated wisdom that billboards, as unique land use nuisances, may be heavily regulated. In 1952, it must be recalled, the protections of the first amendment had not yet been extended by the Supreme Court to advertising messages carried on billboards.

In the *Camden* "Parking Garage" case of 1954, Justice Brennan did not fetter the city government with needless restrictions on how best to provide parking in its central business district. Relying on the private sector, even if it made money on public property, was no violation of the constitutional norms for "publicness" of governmental action.

The 1951 *Tice* "Amusement Park" case must be Justice Bren-
nan's least significant land use opinion, at least from a legal viewpoint. Here,
he gave the go-ahead to a business endeavor blocked by the local government
because of its stingy interpretation of the zoning ordinance.

The Auction Store Case:
Weiner v. Borough of Stratford

Called on to determine whether local action is arbitrary and capricious,
courts have demanded that ordinances spell out standards to guide the exercise of municipal discretion. It is the lack of standards in the *Weiner* case
that bothered Justice Brennan. Roy Weiner planned to open an auction store
in Stratford. Although the zoning permitted such use, another local ordinance stated that no person may "engage in or carry on any business, trade or
calling" unless he or she obtains a license, for an annual fee, from the borough clerk. The license procedure required that new business applications
first be made to the planning board. The planning board in turn would forward factual findings and a recommendation to the borough council, which
would then "decide on granting or denying the license." There were no
objective standards in the law indicating when a license would or would not
be issued. In Weiner's case, the planning board recommended against
approval of his application and the borough council denied his license. He
sued the borough to have the ordinance declared invalid, but the trial court
ruled in favor of Stratford. In a unanimous New Jersey Supreme Court decision, Justice Brennan reversed the judgment of the trial court and decided for
Weiner.

Justice Brennan first addressed the issue of whether the local
ordinance and license fee were authorized by state legislation. While localities may regulate businesses, he observed, license fees must bear some pro-
portionate relationship to that cost of regulation. Otherwise, he noted, the
fee becomes a disguised and unauthorized measure to raise revenue for the
municipal budget. With today's profusion of subdivision exactions, linkage
charges and impact fees demanded of developers by local governments, this
concern has modern currency. Justice Brennan found Stratford's local ordinance "singularly wanting in regulatory features" and believed that the fee
was designed to raise revenue for the local budget. Because no evidence in
the record allowed for a determination of the relationship of license fee to
regulatory cost, however, he declined to make a final ruling on this issue.

Instead, Justice Brennan spotlighted the unguided municipal
discretion, speculating that Stratford had probably exercised it for the impermissible goal of protecting competing local businesses.

JUSTICE BRENNAN

The borough correctly argues that a municipality has power to enact a licensing and regulatory ordinance as a police measure, referring us [to state stat-
utes] under which the municipality has a broad grant of police powers to

enact ordinances not prohibited by or inconsistent with the Federal or State Constitutions or other statutes, and which are deemed by the municipality to be "necessary and proper for the good government, order and protection of persons and property, and for the preservation of the public health, safety and welfare of the municipality and its inhabitants." However, unless the provisions of a licensing and regulatory ordinance vesting discretion in licensing officials to grant or deny a license provide adequate standards to govern the deliberations of the officials having the discretionary power, the provisions must be struck down as utterly void. This principle has been too long firmly settled to require elaboration. The reasons underlying the principle are summarized in [McQuillin, a treatise on municipal corporations] as follows:

> The fundamental rules that a municipal legislative body cannot * * * vest arbitrary or unrestrained power or discretion in * * * itself, and that all ordinances must set a standard or prescribe a rule to govern in all cases coming within the operation of the ordinance and not leave its application or enforcement to ungoverned discretion, caprice or whim are fully applicable to the administration and enforcement of ordinances requiring licenses or permits and imposing license or permit fees or taxes. Accordingly, an ordinance requiring a license or permit, or imposing a license fee or tax, should provide all of the terms under which the license or permit is to be issued and prescribe a uniform rule applicable to all of the class to which it is intended to apply, * * * . * * * ungoverned discretion in officials, * * *, in the enforcement of ordinances, makes possible, if not probable, abusive discrimination in violation of the constitutional guaranty of due process and equal protection of the law, and also violates the requisite of reasonableness pertaining to all ordinances. The requirement of definite standards and conditions for the guidance of authorities in the execution of discretionary power in licensing sometimes is called the "ordinary business rule."

We search in vain for any general rule of action or standard of conduct in this ordinance governing the borough council in its determination whether to grant or deny the application for a license to conduct a new business. Plaintiff also attacks the planning board's part in the procedure as outside any function of such bodies authorized by [state statute], but we pass that question. At all events, the complete absence of any standards guiding the determination of the borough council, the body with the power of ultimate decision, renders the new business provision wholly invalid.

This very record illustrates the error into which officials will fall when the ordinance does not provide the proper standards to control the exercise of their discretion. It appears that while some point was made of increased traffic hazards which it was thought would be created by an auction store operation, the true reason for denial of the license to the plaintiff was more probably that ascribed by the borough clerk to the planning board, namely, "that in the interest of the people of Stratford, a public auction is not needed as it would affect a number of business establishments which have been serving the town over a number of years." This is a "subversion of competition * * * not in the public interest"; the police power "must be directed to a legitimate end, i.e., the protection of a basic interest of society rather than the mere advantage of particular individuals." ▬▬

The New Jersey Billboard Case:
United Advertising Corp. v.
Borough of Raritan

For decades, billboard companies have consistently—and effectively—battled advocates of environmental and scenic beauty. Like tobacco companies, billboard interests appear to enjoy a disproportionate influence over government policy. If the majority wants to rid the landscape of these ugly eyesores, complain exasperated residents, why does government fail to act? One explanation is the truism that, in a representative democracy, well-organized and financially robust minority interests will frequently triumph over poorly organized majority interests.

A critical indicator of a powerful business lobby is the quality and quantity of its legal response to government regulation. For every major billboard ban enacted by local communities, a legal challenge is probably initiated by billboard interests. The arsenal accompanying each side has changed, however, as legal doctrines have evolved. In the 1930s, 1940s and 1950s, aesthetic justifications were considered taboo by courts, outside the ambit of the state's police power to promote health, safety, morals and the general welfare. Thus, communities fell over themselves in asserting safety (traffic), and even moral (guess what takes place under billboards), justifications for their regulations. The "aesthetics-plus" doctrine (aesthetics plus a traditional traffic or moral reason) to sustain aesthetic regulation was born.

In the 1960s and 1970s, two developments (one political, one legal) gave new weapons to antibillboard interests, even as a third development strengthened the billboard forces. Lady Bird Johnson lent her considerable influence to eliminating billboards along interstate highways, and environmental groups became strong participants on the political scene. Courts finally endorsed aesthetics as an acceptable public purpose. At the same time, commercial speech (including billboard messages) received recognition by the Supreme Court as a protected interest under the Constitution's first amendment. Justice Brennan's two brushes with billboard regulation, one in 1952, the other in 1981, reflect these historical developments.

The New Jersey Billboard Act of 1930 imposed state permitting requirements and fees on the billboard industry. In 1942 the state legislature amended the act and, among other things, deleted a section barring issuance of state billboard permits "in a place where the same is or shall be prohibited by any municipal ordinance."

In 1951 the borough of Raritan adopted zoning regulations prohibiting off-site billboards—billboards directing attention to businesses and services not offered at the billboard site—within nine districts. The regulations also required removal within two years of pre-existing billboards newly prohibited by the ordinance, unless the local board of adjustment authorized their continuation. United Advertising Corporation owned two billboards licensed under the amended state billboard act but newly prohibited by Raritan's ordinance. One of the billboards was located in a business district, the other in an industrial district.

United sued the borough, claiming that the 1942 amendment to the state billboard act meant that municipalities could no longer regulate billboards. United also alleged that Raritan's law unconstitutionally discriminated, because it permitted billboards directing attention to on-site businesses while prohibiting all other advertising billboards.

The trial court agreed with United on its first claim, concluding that "the repealing statute abolished the right of the municipality to legislate on the subject of billboards." In a five-to-one New Jersey Supreme Court decision, Justice Brennan reversed the trial court's interpretation of the state law changes. Reaching United's claim that Raritan's law unconstitutionally discriminated, Justice Brennan found no such infirmity: in an era before commercial speech enjoyed first amendment protection, the company's assertion was doomed from the start.

JUSTICE BRENNAN

We do not agree that such significance is to be attached to the omission of the [1930] clause from the 1942 act. The purpose of the clause in the 1930 law was obviously to make clear the legislative intent that the municipal power to control by zoning ordinance the location of billboards as structures, conferred by the [New Jersey Zoning Act], which followed the 1927 zoning amendment to the 1844 Constitution, was not to be considered withdrawn or in anywise curtailed by the 1930 law. But this was wholly precautionary. Without the clause the 1930 act was not to be construed as having the effect of superceding municipal power in the field. The exercise of the municipal zoning power to control the location of billboards within the community would not prevent or interfere with the realization of the objectives which the 1930 law was purposed to attain. The same is true of the 1942 statute. Each imposes annual fees "in lieu of all other taxes, license fees or excises for outdoor advertising," for licenses entitling the holder to carry on the business of outdoor advertising, and for permits for each "billboard, building, structure or other object for the display of outdoor advertising." The excess of moneys over the costs of administration is proportionately distributable under each statute "to and among the municipalities in which billboards, buildings, structures or other objects used for outdoor advertising purposes and for which permits have been granted are located."

Each statute also contains regulatory provisions governing the grants by the State of permits to locate billboards. Those in the 1930 law forbade the location of a billboard within 500 feet of a highway intersection or railroad crossing where obstruction of or interference with the view of a vehicle or train might result, prohibited location of a billboard upon a public highway, park or other public property without the prior permission of the public body having control thereover, and enjoined against the issuance of a permit for a location which in the judgment of the state authority would be injurious to property in the vicinity, or injuriously affect any public interest.

The 1942 statute incorporates the substance of these restrictions, sets a limit upon the size of billboards and adds more prohibitions: against the simulation of an official sign by an advertising sign, against location where the view of an existing sign would be obstructed, or where, in proximity with existing signs, there would be constituted a traffic hazard on an adjacent highway or where the public health, safety or morals would be endangered.

Plainly the regulatory provisions of both laws "were obviously intended to supplement, not supplant, the powers of a municipality to deal with the problem of" billboards. They are wholly negative restrictions which with complete consistency are made fully applicable as regulations governing the location of outdoor advertising billboards and other structures where no municipal prohibition against such location prevents. Thus, as there is no express statement in the 1942 law that the municipal zoning power shall be abrogated as to billboards, and an intent that the law be given that effect not appearing by necessary or unmistakable implication admitting of no other reasonable explanation, indeed the contrary implication more reasonably appearing, it follows that the omission from the 1942 statute of the essentially surplus clause in the 1930 act is no support for the conclusion reached by the trial judge. Too, it must be remembered that the borough's zoning ordinance was passed after the amendments of the Zoning Act by [other provisions], made to conform the statute to the Zoning Article of the 1947 Constitution, and that in determining the scope of the zoning power under the 1948 amendments we are enjoined to apply the mandate of the 1947 Constitution that laws concerning municipalities shall be liberally construed in their favor. The broad powers continued in the 1948 act are not to be deemed abridged by other laws in the absence of most cogent evidence of legislative intent to abridge them.

Plaintiff's complaint, however, alleges another ground, not passed upon below, which it urges to support its contention that the prohibitory provisions of the ordinance are invalid. The ordinance, while excluding advertising signs in all districts, permits signs directing attention to businesses on the premises. This distinction, it is argued, constitutes unlawful discrimination. We see no merit in the point.

The business sign is in actuality a part of the business itself, just as the structure housing the business is a part of it, and the authority to conduct the business in a district carries with it the right to maintain a business sign on the premises subject to reasonable regulations in that regard as in the case of this ordinance. Plaintiff's placements of its advertising signs, on the other hand, are made pursuant to the conduct of the business of outdoor advertising itself, and in effect what the ordinance provides is that this business shall not to that extent be allowed in the borough. It has long been settled that the unique nature of outdoor advertising and the nuisances fostered by billboards and similar outdoor structures located by persons in the business of outdoor advertising, justify the separate classification of such structures for the purposes of governmental regulation and restriction.

And as such separate classification offends no constitutional provision, there also exists no invidious discrimination in the provisions of the ordinance barring plaintiff's signs in the business and industrial zones while allowing therein manufacturing plants, junk yards, coal and coke yards and other uses suggested by plaintiff as also having undesirable attributes. It is enough that outdoor advertising has characteristic features which have long been deemed sufficient to sustain regulations or prohibitions peculiarly applicable to it.

Nor is there anything in the ordinance to support plaintiff's argument that the distinction made by the ordinance is designed "to protect local business and to put plaintiff out of business." To the contrary, the scheme of the ordinance makes it very evident that the municipality has strictly regulated all signs to confine their use to the reasonable requirements of signs incident to and part of businesses authorized on the premises. It forbids any sign whatever with an area in excess of three square feet except as a zoning permit is obtained for its use. No sign of any sort may be placed, inscribed or supported upon the roof or upon any structure which extends above the roof of any building. In residence districts, except for temporary "for rent" and "for sale" signs on property, only a professional person may have a business sign and it must be non-illuminated and not exceed three square feet in area. In the two business districts and in the Industrial M-1 District a business may have a sign only if it is either non-illuminated and not more than 20 square feet in area and in no case exceeding the aggregate of 10% of the wall surface, including window and door area on which it is displayed, or is a non-flashing sign not exceeding ten square feet in area and not exceeding in the aggregate 5% of the wall surface. Flashing signs are prohibited in the Industrial M-2 Districts, and business signs may not exceed more than 40 square feet in area and cannot be erected less than 200 feet from a street or highway or a residence district. Plainly, the municipal purpose is directed toward minimizing the abuses and hazards incident to the use of signs and to confine their use within the reasonable requirements of businesses permitted to be conducted at the places of their location.

Plaintiff urges further that there is an unconstitutional abridgement of the guaranties of freedom of speech and freedom of the press in a distinction which permits a business man to use a sign to advertise his business upon the premises, although "he may not use that same sign to urge the public to purchase an automobile or a particular brand of ice cream or any other lawful article of commerce, at a store he owns across the street." The short answer to this is that these guaranties impose no such restraint upon governmental regulation of purely commercial advertising [citing *Valentine v. Chrestensen*].

There is, however, substantial merit in plaintiff's challenge to the validity of the provision of the ordinance requiring the removal of nonconforming signs within two years of the effective date of the ordinance unless permission to continue individual signs for further periods is first obtained from the local board of adjustment. This section of the ordinance is plainly contrary to the express provision of the zoning statute, that "any nonconforming use or structure existing at the time of the passage of an ordinance may be continued upon the lot or in the building so occupied and any such structure may be restored or repaired in the event of partial destruction thereof." It is beyond the power of a municipality to limit by zoning ordinance the right expressly given the owner by this statute indefinitely to continue a nonconforming use. The section is, however, clearly separable from the balance of the ordinance and may be declared invalid without effecting the other provisions of the ordinance. ▬▬

The Parking Garage Case: Camden Plaza Parking, Inc. v. City of Camden

City downtowns never seem to have enough parking. Public and private lots and garages attempt, but fail, to keep pace with the public's endless affection for the automobile. Because economic vitality of central business districts depends on the availability of sufficient parking, local governments and specially designated public agencies have involved themselves in providing it. Sometimes, they have built and operated facilities themselves. Other times, they have turned to the private sector to do so on public land. In an age of increasing privatization of public services, it is interesting to recall the conceptual concerns held by courts as they were asked to approve private use of publicly owned land in the 1940s and 1950s.

The city of Camden had a parking problem in its central business district. A 1953 study commissioned by the city revealed an existing deficiency of 250 off-street parking spaces and an expected deficiency of 1,000 additional spaces following the opening of a proposed new department store near the municipally owned City Hall Plaza. The plaza itself was used as an open-air, off-street parking lot, operated partly by Camden and partly by a private firm under lease from Camden. The parking study recommended that the city construct a new 1,400-space, multistory garage on City Hall Plaza to accommodate the 175 spaces already provided on the plaza, the current need for 250 spaces and the anticipated need for 1,000 spaces.

Not wanting to finance and construct the new garage itself, Camden elected to offer for private bid a 50-year lease on the plaza, with the highest bidder building and operating the garage at its expense. Actual title to City Hall Plaza would remain with Camden. Nedmac Associates, Inc. (Camden spelled backwards), one of two private companies responding to public advertisements, won the bidding contest. The losing company, Camden Plaza Parking, Inc., sued on the basis of alleged irregularities in the bidding process and lost in the trial court. Two Camden taxpayers who opposed the parking garage deal also sued and lost.

Both the company and the taxpayers appealed. In a six-to-one New Jersey Supreme Court decision, Justice Brennan found that provision of parking was clearly a public use and that technicalities about who actually operated the garage did not change that essential public nature. Whatever the broad arguments about public versus private, however, state legislation did not authorize the city to lease municipally owned land to private persons for the garage. Only specially created parking authorities were legislatively authorized to enter into such agreements, found Justice Brennan, so Camden's actions were invalid.

Justice Brennan

Action by a municipality to relieve traffic congestion through the establishment of off-street public parking facilities is the exercise of a public and essential governmental function, and publicly-owned lands used for such purposes are devoted to a public use. The parking crisis in the modern day threatens the very welfare of the community, and statutes and court decisions recognize that public lands employed by public bodies for public off-street parking are devoted to a public purpose. "It is only in recent years that the matter of the provision or operation of such off-street parking facilities by municipal corporations has attained such prominence" and "One important question met with rather generally in the cases on the present subject is that as to whether the provision of off-street parking facilities by a municipality is a 'public purpose,' 'public use,' 'municipal purpose' or the like, as distinguished from a private purpose or use. * * * . * * * the greater amount of the authority—particularly that found in the later cases—supports the view that the provision by a municipal corporation of off-street parking facilities for use by the general public is a public or municipal purpose as distinguished from a private one, at least when the primary object of the parking project is to alleviate traffic congestion and thereby promote the usability of the municipal streets for the movement of traffic." And the land and facility do not cease to be used for a public purpose when leased to private operators for operation as a public parking facility. The public character of the use in the instant case is expressly recognized in the municipal resolution of March 11, 1954 which contains findings that the development of the city-owned tract as an off-street parking facility in the mode proposed in the resolution is necessary "in order to promote the public safety, convenience and welfare and in the best interest of the public."

But municipalities have only such powers as are given them by the Legislature and in authorizing municipalities to provide public off-street parking facilities the Legislature has not seen fit to authorize the leasing of municipal land to a private person to construct and operate a public parking facility thereon. There is legislation which permits a municipality itself to operate off-street parking facilities and to charge parking fees. And under [state legislation], a municipality may undertake, as a local improvement, the work of providing facilities for the parking of motor vehicles by the acquisition, by purchase or lease, and improvement of real property and by the construction of buildings and structures. But the only statutory authority whereby municipally-owned lands may be leased to private persons to construct and operate a public off-street parking facility is that which is given a parking authority created under the Parking Authority Law of 1948. The plan under consideration here, however, does not involve a parking authority; the City of Camden has not created a parking authority under that law. We note that the Parking Authority Law expressly authorizes "any public body * * * upon such terms, with or without consideration, as it may determine" to "(a) * * * Dedicate, sell, convey, or lease any of its property to a parking authority" and that under [other provisions] an authority is empowered "to take over or lease, or manage, any parking project or undertaking constructed or owned by any county or municipality."

A lease arrangement substantially like that involved here was sustained by the Supreme Judicial Court of Massachusetts, but under a statute which expressly authorized the City of Boston to lease to a private corporation a portion of the subsurface of Boston Common and the Public Garden to be used as a site for an underground parking garage for use by the public. The court found that Boston did not, as claimed by objectors, originally take the land under any trust which prevented the expressly authorized lease, and that, although Boston after acquiring the land had dedicated the land to public use as a common, the Legislature, representing the general public, could properly authorize the city to vary the public use. And in [a New York case], the right of parking authorities to lease to a private individual, for operation as a parking place, a certain municipal park in Coney Island was sustained but only because the court was able to find distinctive circumstances, namely, that such use could properly be deemed an incidental use of an adjacent greater park much patronized by the public. Neither decision is a helpful precedent upon the case made in the record before us.

The city argues that statutory authority for the proposed lease is to be found in [state legislation] providing that "Every municipality may lease for fixed and limited terms to any person any land or building of the municipality not presently needed for public use," or, Camden being a city of the second class of this state, in [state legislation] providing that "Every city of the second class of this state may lease to any person, partnership, corporation or association any land or building of the municipality not needed for public use for a fixed term not exceeding fifty (50) years." But, as is said above, the construction and operation of the proposed public-owned parking facility upon the publicly owned tract constitutes the use of the land a public use even though the facility is privately constructed and operated under lease from the city. These statutes are therefore inapplicable since the tract does not satisfy the description of land "not presently needed for public use" or "not needed for public use."

The city contends that City Hall Plaza is not held presently in a governmental capacity but in a proprietary function and, citing [a Kentucky case], argues that, like property purchased or condemned for a public purpose, but which has not been dedicated to such use, it therefore may be leased under the cited statutes because [it is] not actually in public use. Apart from the fact that the tract, in part at least, is and has for some time been in use as a public off-street parking lot, partially metered and partially operated by a private lessee, and thus has been and is devoted to a public use which the proposed multi-storied structure will merely substantially enlarge, the only municipally-owned lands which may be leased on the authority of [state legislation] are lands "not presently needed for public use" or "not needed for public use." The emphasis is on the need for the land for public use when its leasing is attempted. Here the city's own resolution of March 11, 1954 establishes unequivocally that the land is imperatively needed for use as a substantially enlarged public off-street parking facility. Thus the present need of the land for public use is conclusively demonstrated. ▬

The Amusement Park Case:
Tice v. Borough of Woodcliff Lake

Not all land use decisions turn on major constitutional or statutory issues. Many cases involve simple disputes about the meaning of technical words in the zoning text, the application of district regulations to specific property or the procedures under which building approvals are obtained. Of course, conceptual simplicity should not disguise the fact that, to the landowner, these questions can be of major importance. For example, a New York City developer erected a luxury apartment tower several stories higher than that authorized by the text of the zoning ordinance. The developer, however, claimed reliance on a zoning map that, unlike the text, contained some degree of ambiguity. In 1988 the highest state court in New York reconciled the clear and ambiguous zoning documents in favor of the city and against the developer. One possible solution: the developer must tear down the extra stories.

The *Tice* case presents nothing quite as dramatic, although its outcome was undoubtedly significant to the landowners. Roy and Frank Tice wanted to build a 400-by-85-foot public swimming pool, accompanied by bathhouses, a refreshment stand and picnic areas. The building inspector and zoning board of adjustment of the borough of Woodcliff Lake refused to issue a permit, because they defined the Tice project as an "amusement park" expressly prohibited by the text of the local zoning ordinance. They also claimed that the Tices in any event had not complied with procedural requirements of the zoning ordinance and building code.

The trial court sided with Woodcliff Lake, and the Tices appealed. Justice Brennan agreed with the Tices that their project was not an amusement park but found that other questions needed to be resolved in further court proceedings.

JUSTICE BRENNAN

We do not agree that the project contemplated the building of an "amusement park" within the common understanding of what an "amusement park" is. An essential attribute of an "amusement park" is the grouping together in one place of various amusements for pleasurable diversion. That attribute is not present here. Actually only one amusement was planned. The facilities for picnicking and refreshment were clearly to be provided, not as amusements of themselves, but as incidents to enhance the attraction of the pool to members of the public enjoying swimming as a pastime. The judgment cannot, therefore, be sustained.

Should this court return the case to the Law Division for further proceedings or, as urged by plaintiffs, with direction to enter judgment in plaintiffs' favor for the relief sought? The pleadings and pretrial order framed another issue which borough counsel urged at the trial should be decided "preliminarily" before coming to the question of "amusement park," but that issue was not determined in the trial court. The issue was whether "the plaintiffs have complied with the ordinances of the Borough relating to the issuance of such permit." The arguments in the briefs on this point are centered largely on the question whether the application and the crude drawings submitted with it comply with the provisions as to form and content detailed in the zoning ordinance and the companion building code.

Plaintiffs urge, on the authority of [the *Reimer*] case, that other reasons for the denial of the permit, even if valid, must be deemed to have been waived because, they contend, the only reason assigned by the borough for the refusal was that the project was an "amusement park" and, that reason being unsound in law, plaintiffs are entitled to relief in this court "ordering the issuance of the building permit applied for." In the *Reimer* case, Mr. Justice Katzenbach, sitting alone on an application for a writ of mandamus, held that where a municipality at the time of a refusal to grant a permit for the erection of garages made no objection that the application was not in writing and did not object to the sufficiency of the plans submitted, it could not raise either objection for the first time in opposition to the issuance of the writ "* * * as it was not a ground for the refusal. In effect it was waived."

Even if the factual situations were on all fours, which is not altogether free from doubt, we would not be constrained to follow the principle laid down by *Reimer*. To bar a municipality from raising in the law action other reasons justifying the denial of the permit merely because they were not assigned at the time it was denied would be attended by unfortunate and undesirable consequences. For example, are the plaintiffs to be licensed to erect structures departing from construction standards particularized in the building code? Such may be the logical effect of the holding in the *Reimer* case. We cannot subscribe to a principle which tends so easily to defeat the vital public interest in safety and health which underlie those standards. If the borough officials in fact grounded their action only on the belief the project was an "amusement park," may we not reasonably assume that they saw no occasion to give time to a close examination of the application and its supporting papers when in their view the proposed structures and use were in any event prohibited by the zoning ordinance? We fail to see why their omission is to have the consequence of foreclosing the borough to defend the plaintiffs' action in the Law Division on other substantial grounds merely because the borough officials thought there was no occasion to determine and specify those grounds when the permit was refused.

If the issue had not been pleaded and specified in the pretrial order as an issue for determination, but had been advanced for the first time in this court, doubtless a different question, which we need not discuss or decide, would be presented. It is plain, however, that the circumstances here require that this action be returned to the Law Division for trial of the issue framed by the parties.

As there must be further proceedings in the Law Division, we shall state our views of the effect to be given a new or amendatory zoning ordinance called to our attention at the oral argument. We were advised by counsel for the borough that prior to the trial below a new or amendatory ordinance was enacted by the borough prohibiting swimming pools as such in the district where plaintiffs' premises are located. A valid, applicable and subsisting ordinance precluding plaintiffs' planned project would be a bar in the Law Division to the relief sought by the plaintiffs. The decision determining the cause is controlled by the ordinance in effect at the time of the decision and not by the ordinance which was operative when the permit was sought.We denied the motion of counsel for the borough to supplement the record to put the new or amendatory ordinance in evidence as it was not pleaded or asserted in the pretrial order as a bar to plaintiffs' claimed relief (although enacted, we were informed, before the answer was filed), and plaintiffs have not had an opportunity to challenge its validity or its application in other respects to the issues presented. The new or amendatory ordinance may, however, be put in issue by appropriate steps in the Law Division to accomplish an amendment of the borough's answer and by the making of a new or amended pretrial order. ▬

PART III

THE SUPREME COURT YEARS: 1956 TO THE PRESENT

Supreme Court of the United States (1935, Cass Gilbert), Washington, D.C.
(Supreme Court Historical Society)

7 CHOOSING WHERE AND HOW TO LIVE

Grandmother Inez Moore and one of her grandsons at their home in East Cleveland, Ohio. From Moore v. City of East Cleveland.

(Jerold S. Kayden)

I n the elevated sanctum of the U.S. Supreme Court, it should come as no surprise that Justice Brennan faced weightier and more complex issues than those encountered in the New Jersey courts. After all, with its chary exercise of review, the Court necessarily considers only those land use cases presenting significant constitutional clashes between private and public rights. Justice Brennan's two opinions discussed in this chapter— the *Warth* "Exclusionary Zoning" and *Moore* "Grandmother" cases—amply demonstrate just how deeply land use regulations can cut into private rights and especially into those involving everyday choices about where and with whom we live.

With its subtext of race and class divisions, the *Warth* case raises disturbing allegations of the misuse of the zoning power. Large American cities are increasingly composed of ill-housed, undereducated and underemployed poor and minority residents. Whispers of a permanent underclass are today amplified by loud and raucous debates in think tanks, universities and government offices. In stark contrast to the inner cities, the surrounding suburbs remain predominantly white, well-off and moderately successful in fulfilling a widely held American dream. With suburbs experiencing higher employment growth than central cities, a suburban residential location becomes that much more critical.

When poor and minority urban dwellers attempt to move outside the city, they frequently find the door effectively closed by a lack of affordable housing. In the 1975 *Warth* case, several of these individuals accused a community of using zoning as an instrument of exclusion by imposing unnecessary restrictions on housing development to increase its price beyond the means of low-income families. In denying them judicial consideration on the merits of their claims, a majority of the Supreme Court applied the constitutional and judge-made rule of standing. Justice Brennan's strong dissenting opinion not only disputed the majority's interpretation of the rule but intimated his disapproval of exclusionary zoning techniques.

The *Moore* case in 1977 underscored the potentially far-reaching and intrusive power wielded by local governments. A grandmother was told that her 10-year-old grandson could no longer live with her, because he was not related to her within the meaning of the word "family" used in the local housing ordinance. The grandmother declined to comply and eventually triumphed through the intervention of the Supreme Court. Justice Brennan's concurring opinion is a powerful reminder that America's great strength lies in its tolerance and celebration of diversity. Preference by government for one model of family (nuclear) over another (extended) violates this tradition. His brief history lesson emphasizes the welcoming function of large families and ethnic neighborhoods that provided economic and spiritual safe haven to immigrants arriving in a strange new land.

The Exclusionary Zoning Case:
Warth v. Seldin

From the 1950s to the present, many American families have realized their dream of owning a house with a fence in the suburbs. Disturbingly, some communities have erected a symbolic fence along their borders to prevent poor and minority families from enjoying that same dream. One of the mechanisms commonly used to this end is zoning. At its worst, the ordinance becomes a tool of exclusion, with its technically benign trio of use, height and bulk restrictions perniciously adapted to make construction of affordable housing all but impossible.

Several tell-tale signs characterize the typical exclusionary zoning bylaw: residential districts for multifamily housing are nonexistent or mapped to virtually unbuildable areas of a town; residential districts require a minimum of several acres per lot for each house; dwelling units must meet large minimum interior room sizes. Each of these requirements succeeds in increasing the cost of housing, placing it beyond the reach of low-income individuals.

On the heels of several decades of judicial and legislative scrutiny, municipalities today rarely practice blatant exclusionary zoning. For example, it is unusual to find a minimum of 10 acres required for single-family lots throughout a community. Instead, local governments have learned that growth management techniques, including annual caps on the number of dwelling units allowed or long-term moratoria on all new construction, can effectively achieve the same exclusionary result. Legitimate justifications about matching municipal infrastructure such as sewers and schools with residential growth may in fact mask illegal desires to exclude low-income and minority families. Thus, the judicial task of ferreting out permissible from impermissible motivations is made that much more difficult.

The *Warth* case involved a classic allegation of exclusionary zoning. Residents in and near Rochester, N.Y., and local housing and building organizations sued the town of Penfield, a Rochester suburb, alleging that its zoning ordinance had the purpose and effect of excluding low- and moderate-income persons in violation of the first, ninth and fourteenth amendments of the U.S. Constitution. Each of the parties claimed different impacts from Penfield's exclusionary practices. The low-income minorities asserted that Penfield's practices forced them to live in less attractive environments. Several Rochester taxpayers, including Warth, claimed that Rochester had to impose higher taxes on them because of Penfield's actions, presumably because Rochester had to provide social services for a disproportionate share of low-income families.

The challenging organizations represented a variety of parties and interests. Metro-Act, a nonprofit organization, declared its mission "to alert ordinary citizens to problems of social concern . . . to inquire into the reasons for the critical housing shortage for low and moderate income persons in the Rochester area and to urge action on the part of citizens to alleviate the general housing shortage for low and moderate income persons." The Housing Council in the Monroe County Area, a nonprofit organization of 71 public and private organizations, described 17 of its members as interested or involved in low- and moderate-income housing in Penfield, with one member "stymied by its inability to secure the necessary approvals." The Rochester Home Builders Association assailed the Penfield ordinance because it deprived its members of potential profits. Thus, in the funny alliances that litigation can engender, private developers and poverty organizations worked hand-in-hand.

In their factual allegations, the challenging parties noted that 98 percent of the town's vacant land was zoned for single-family housing and that associated zoning requirements for lot size, setbacks, floor area and habitable space caused housing prices to be prohibitive for low- and moderate-income persons. They further observed that only .3 percent of land available for residential construction was allocated to multifamily uses and that density and other requirements made development on that land unaffordable. The individuals and organizations also claimed that Penfield's town, zoning and planning boards delayed action on and arbitrarily disapproved low-income housing proposals; refused to grant necessary variances, permits or tax abatements; failed to provide support services; and amended the zoning to make project approvals impossible. The plaintiffs therefore asked the federal district court to declare Penfield's zoning unconstitutional, to prevent the various boards from enforcing it, to order preparation of a new ordinance and to award $750,000 in damages. The district court declined this invitation and dismissed the complaint. The court of appeals affirmed, and the parties brought their case to the Supreme Court of the United States.

In its five-to-four decision, the Supreme Court agreed with the lower courts. The Court never considered the merits of the allegations made by the different parties. Instead, Justice Lewis F. Powell, Jr., joined by Chief Justice Warren E. Burger, and Justices Potter Stewart, Harry A. Blackmun and William H. Rehnquist, concluded that the parties lacked standing to bring their action. As the majority described, "In essence the question of standing is whether the litigant is entitled to have the court decide the merits of the dispute or of particular issues. This inquiry involves both constitutional limitations and prudential limitations on its exercise. . . . In both dimensions it is founded in concern about the proper—and properly limited—role of the courts in a democratic society."

The constitutional aspect of standing derives from article III of the Constitution, restricting the jurisdiction of the federal courts to actual cases and controversies between parties. The key question is whether the complaining party has alleged a sufficiently "personal stake" in the outcome of the case to warrant invocation of federal-court jurisdiction. The so-called prudential aspect of standing adds a further strainer of cases and emphasizes the personal nature of the injury suffered by the complaining party. By demanding that complainants demonstrate a link between actions of the accused and harms suffered by complainants, standing rules help to ensure that issues presented to the courts are sharpened by real and concrete adversarial situations.

Applying the rules of standing, the majority reviewed all parties and their respective claims. For example, with regard to the low-income minority individuals, Justice Powell wrote that "[w]e must assume, taking the allegations of the complaint as true, that Penfield's zoning ordinance and the pattern of enforcement by respondent officials have had the purpose and effect of excluding persons of low and moderate income, many of whom are members of racial or ethnic minority groups. We also assume, for purposes here, that such intentional exclusionary practices, if proved in a proper case, would be adjudged violative of the constitutional and statutory rights of the persons excluded."

Even under such assumptions, however, the Court declined to reach the substance of the case: "the fact that these petitioners share attributes common to persons who may have been excluded from residence in the town is an insufficient predicate for the conclusion that petitioners themselves have been excluded, or that [Penfield's] assertedly illegal actions have violated their rights." In short, "[p]etitioners must allege and show that they personally have been injured, not that injury has been suffered by other, unidentified members of the class to which they belong and which they purport to represent."

Not only should Warth and his coclaimants have shown their own injuries, they also should have linked those injuries to specific acts committed by Penfield. Thus, said Justice Powell, "[w]e may assume, as petitioners allege, that [Penfield's] actions have contributed, perhaps substantially, to the cost of housing in Penfield. But there remains the question whether petitioners' inability to locate suitable housing in Penfield reasonably can be said to have resulted, in any concretely demonstrable way, from [Penfield's] alleged constitutional and statutory infractions."

Setting the standing standard for these plaintiffs, the majority directed them to "allege facts from which it reasonably could be inferred that, absent [Penfield's] restrictive zoning practices, there is a substantial probability that they would have been able to purchase or lease in Penfield, and that, if the court affords the relief requested, the asserted inability of petitioners will be removed." Because the majority found the record "devoid of the necessary allegations," it dismissed the case.

The four dissenters—Justice Brennan and Justices William O. Douglas, Byron R. White and Thurgood Marshall—would have taken the case. In his typically forthright fashion, Justice Douglas wrote alone, "With all respect, I think that the Court reads the complaint and the record with antagonistic eyes." Justice Brennan, joined by Justices White and Marshall, was no more enthralled with the Court's decision and would have reached the merits.

JUSTICE BRENNAN

In this case, a wide range of plaintiffs, alleging various kinds of injuries, claimed to have been affected by the Penfield zoning ordinance, on its face and as applied, and by other practices of the defendant officials of Penfield. Alleging that as a result of these laws and practices low- and moderate-income and minority people have been excluded from Penfield, and that this exclusion is unconstitutional, plaintiffs sought injunctive, declaratory, and monetary relief. The Court today, in an opinion that purports to be a "standing" opinion but that actually, I believe, has overtones of outmoded notions of pleading and of justiciability, refuses to find that any of the variously situated plaintiffs can clear numerous hurdles, some constructed here for the first time, necessary to establish "standing." While the Court gives lip service to the principle, oft repeated in recent years, that "standing in no way depends on the merits of the plaintiff's contention that particular conduct is illegal," in fact the opinion, which tosses out of court almost every conceivable kind of plaintiff who could be injured by the activity claimed to be unconstitutional, can be explained only by an indefensible hostility to the claim on the merits. I can appreciate the Court's reluctance to adjudicate the complex and difficult legal questions involved in determining the constitutionality of practices which assertedly limit residence in a particular municipality to those who are white and relatively well off, and I also understand that the merits of this case could involve grave sociological and political ramifications. But courts cannot refuse to hear a case on the merits merely because they would prefer not to, and it is quite clear, when the record is viewed with dispassion, that at least three of the groups of plaintiffs have made allegations, and supported them with affidavits and documentary evidence, sufficient to survive a motion to dismiss for lack of standing.

Before considering the three groups I believe clearly to have standing—the low-income, minority plaintiffs, Rochester Home Builders Association, Inc., and the Housing Council in the Monroe County Area, Inc.—it will be helpful to review the picture painted by the allegations as a whole, in order better to comprehend the interwoven interests of the various plaintiffs. Indeed, one glaring defect of the Court's opinion is that it views each set of plaintiffs as if it were prosecuting a separate lawsuit, refusing to recognize that the interests are intertwined, and that the standing of any one group must take into account its position vis-à-vis the others. For example, the Court says that the low-income minority plaintiffs have not alleged facts sufficient to show that but for the exclusionary practices claimed, they would be able to reside in Penfield. The Court then intimates that such a causal relationship could be shown only if "the initial focus [is] on a particular project." Later, the Court objects to the ability of the Housing Council to prosecute the suit on behalf of its member, Penfield Better Homes Corp., despite the fact that Better Homes had displayed an interest in a particular project, because that project was no longer live. Thus, we must suppose that even if the low-income plaintiffs had alleged a desire to live in the Better Homes project, that allegation would be insufficient because it appears that that particular project might never be built. The rights of low-income minority plaintiffs who desire to live in a locality, then, seem to turn on the willingness of a third party to litigate the legality of preclusion of a particular project, despite the fact that the third party may have no economic incentive to incur the costs of litigation with regard to one project, and despite the fact that the low-income minority plaintiffs' interest is not to live in a particular project but to live somewhere in the town in a dwelling they can afford.

Accepting, as we must, the various allegations and affidavits as true, the following picture emerges: The Penfield zoning ordinance, by virtue of regulations concerning "lot area, set backs, . . . population density, density of use, units per acre, floor area, sewer requirements, traffic flow, ingress and egress [and] street location," makes "practically and economically impossible the construction of sufficient numbers of low and moderate income" housing. The purpose of this ordinance was to preclude low and moderate income people and nonwhites from living in Penfield, and, particularly because of refusals to grant zoning variances and building permits and by using special permit procedures and other devices, the defendants succeeded in keeping "low and moderate income persons . . . and non-white persons . . . from residing within . . . Penfield."

As a result of these practices, various of the plaintiffs were affected in different ways. For example, plaintiffs Ortiz, Reyes, Sinkler, and Broadnax, persons of low or moderate income and members of minority groups, alleged that "as a result" of respondents' exclusionary scheme, they could not live in Penfield, although they desired and attempted to do so, and consequently incurred greater commuting cost, lived in substandard housing, and had fewer services for their families and poorer schools for their children than if they had lived in Penfield. Members of the Rochester Home Builders Association were prevented from constructing homes for low- and moderate-income people in Penfield, harming them economically. And Penfield Better Homes, a member of the Housing Council, was frustrated in its attempt to build moderate-income housing.

Thus, the portrait which emerges from the allegations and affidavits is one of total, purposeful, intransigent exclusion of certain classes of people from the town, pursuant to a conscious scheme never deviated from. Because of this scheme, those interested in building homes for the excluded groups were faced with insurmountable difficulties, and those of the excluded groups seeking homes in the locality quickly learned that their attempts were futile. Yet, the Court turns the very success of the allegedly unconstitutional scheme into a barrier to a lawsuit seeking its invalidation. In effect, the Court tells the low-income minority and building company plaintiffs they will not be permitted to prove what they have alleged—that they could and would build and live in the town if changes were made in the zoning ordinance and its application—because they have not succeeded in breaching, before the suit was filed, the very barriers which are the subject of the suit.

As recounted above, plaintiffs Ortiz, Broadnax, Reyes, and Sinkler alleged that "as a result" of respondents' exclusionary practices, they were unable, despite attempts, to find the housing they desired in Penfield, and consequently have incurred high commuting expenses, received poorer municipal services, and, in some instances, have been relegated to live in substandard housing. The Court does not, as it could not, suggest that the injuries, if proved, would be insufficient to give petitioners the requisite "personal stake in the outcome of the controversy as to assure the concrete adverseness which sharpens the presentation of issues." Rather, it is abundantly clear that the harm alleged satisfies the "injury in fact, economic or otherwise," requirement which is prerequisite to standing in federal court. The harms claimed—consisting of out-of-pocket losses as well as denial of specifically enumerated services available in Penfield but not in these petitioners' present communities—are obviously more palpable and concrete than those held sufficient to sustain standing in other cases.

Instead, the Court insists that these petitioners' allegations are insufficient to show that the harms suffered were caused by respondents' allegedly unconstitutional practices, because "their inability to reside in Penfield [may be] the consequence of the economics of the area housing market, rather than of respondents' assertedly illegal acts."

True, this Court has held that to maintain standing, a plaintiff must not only allege an injury but must also assert a " 'direct' relationship between the alleged injury and the claim sought to be adjudicated," that is, "[t]he party who invokes [judicial] power must be able to show . . . that he has sustained or is immediately in danger of sustaining some direct injury as the result of [a statute's] enforcement." But as the allegations recited above show, these petitioners have alleged precisely what our cases require—that because of the exclusionary practices of respondents, they cannot live in Penfield and have suffered harm.

Thus, the Court's real holding is not that these petitioners have not alleged an injury resulting from respondents' action, but that they are not to be allowed to prove one, because "realization of petitioners' desire to live in Penfield always has depended on the efforts and willingness of third parties to build low- and moderate-cost housing," and "the record is devoid of any indication that . . . [any] projects, would have satisfied petitioners' needs at prices they could afford."

Certainly, this is not the sort of demonstration that can or should be required of petitioners at this preliminary stage. In [another Supreme Court case], a similar challenge was made: it was claimed that the allegations were vague, and that the causation theory asserted was untrue. We said: "If . . . these allegations were in fact untrue, then the appellants should have moved for summary judgment on the standing issue and demonstrated to the District Court that the allegations were sham and raised no genuine issue of fact. We cannot say . . . that the appellees could not prove their allegations which, if proved, would place them squarely among those persons injured in fact."

Here, the very fact that, as the Court stresses, these petitioners' claim rests in part upon proving the intentions and capabilities of third parties to build in Penfield suitable housing which they can afford, coupled with the exclusionary character of the claim on the merits, makes it particularly inappropriate to assume that these petitioners' lack of specificity reflects a fatal weakness in their theory of causation. Obviously they cannot be expected, prior to discovery and trial, to know the future plans of building companies, the precise details of the housing market in Penfield, or everything which has transpired in 15 years of application of the Penfield zoning ordinance, including every housing plan suggested and refused. To require them to allege such facts is to require them to prove their case on paper in order to get into court at all, reverting to the form of fact pleading long abjured in the federal courts. This Court has not required such unachievable specificity in standing cases in the past, and the fact that it does so now can only be explained by an indefensible determination by the Court to close the doors of the federal courts to claims of this kind. Understandably, today's decision will be read as revealing hostility to breaking down even unconstitutional zoning barriers that frustrate the deep human yearning of low-income and minority groups for decent housing they can afford in decent surroundings.

Two of the petitioners are organizations among whose members are building concerns. Both of these organizations, Home Builders and Housing Council, alleged that these concerns have attempted to build in Penfield low- and moderate-income housing, but have been stymied by the zoning ordinance and refusal to grant individual relief therefrom.

Specifically, Home Builders, a trade association of concerns engaged in constructing and maintaining residential housing in the Rochester area, alleged that "[d]uring the past 15 years, over 80% of the private housing units constructed in the Town of Penfield have been constructed by [its] members." Because of respondents' refusal to grant relief from Penfield's restrictive housing statutes, members of Home Builders could not proceed with planned low- and moderate-income housing projects, and thereby lost profits.

Housing Council numbers among its members at least 17 groups involved in the development and construction of low- and middle-income housing. In particular, one member, Penfield Better Homes, "is and has been actively attempting to develop moderate income housing in . . . Penfield," but has been unable to secure the necessary approvals.

The Court finds that these two organizations lack standing to seek prospective relief for basically the same reasons: none of their members is, as far as the allegations show, currently involved in developing a particular project. Thus, Home Builders has "failed to show the existence of any injury to its members of sufficient immediacy and ripeness to warrant judicial intervention," while "the controversy between respondents and Better Homes, however vigorous it may once have been, [has not] remained a live, concrete dispute."

Again, the Court ignores the thrust of the complaints and asks petitioners to allege the impossible. According to the allegations, the building concerns' experience in the past with Penfield officials has shown any plans for low- and moderate-income housing to be futile for, again according to the allegations, the respondents are engaged in a purposeful, conscious scheme to exclude such housing. Particularly with regard to a low- or moderate-income project, the cost of litigating, with respect to any particular project, the legality of a refusal to approve it may well be prohibitive. And the merits of the exclusion of this or that project is [sic] not at the heart of the complaint; the claim is that respondents will not approve any project which will provide residences for low- and moderate-income people.

When this sort of pattern-and-practice claim is at the heart of the controversy, allegations of past injury, which members of both of these organizations have clearly made, and of a future intent, if the barriers are cleared, again to develop suitable housing for Penfield, should be more than sufficient. The past experiences, if proved at trial, will give credibility and substance to the claim of interest in future building activity in Penfield. These parties, if their allegations are proved, certainly have the requisite personal stake in the outcome of this controversy, and the Court's conclusion otherwise is only a conclusion that this controversy may not be litigated in a federal court. ▬▬

The Grandmother Case:
Moore v. City of East Cleveland

When people first hear the facts of *Moore v. City of East Cleveland*, they have trouble believing that the incident actually transpired. A municipality told a 63-year-old grandmother that she must throw her 10-year-old grandson out of her home or face jail. Neither the grandmother nor the grandson had done anything improper, other than to reside in the same house. Standing up for her family, the feisty grandmother refused to knuckle under, was convicted by a trial court, fined $25 and sentenced to five days in jail. Claiming that her constitutional rights had been violated, she pursued her case all the way to the Supreme Court of the United States and won. The Court's reputation as a forum of last resort for all Americans is enhanced.

What is fascinating about the *Moore* case is how few complaints it elicits from unschooled critics of judicial activism. Even as they vigorously attack Supreme Court decisions upholding a right to birth control devices or to an abortion, they simultaneously applaud a judicial intervention affirming a right to family. Yet, each of these rights arises from the same wellspring, the due process clause, guaranteeing that government shall not "deprive any person of . . . liberty . . . without due process of law." In giving content to the word "liberty," the Court is forced to decide which private relationships and actions fall under its umbrella. Looking for an express right to family, let alone to birth control and abortion, in the Constitution is the wrong inquiry, because the framers did not—and could not—expressly enumerate every liberty deserving of protection for all time. Perhaps because its resolution may seem correct to the nonlawyer, the *Moore* case reveals that there is no easy litmus test for constitutional interpretation.

Inez Moore, the 63-year-old grandmother, lived with her son Dale and grandsons Dale, Jr., and John in her home in East Cleveland, Ohio. Dale, Jr., the son of Dale, moved in with his grandmother on the death of his mother. John was the child of another of Moore's sons. That the two grandsons were first cousins, not brothers, posed the issue.

East Cleveland's housing ordinance restricted the occupancy of each dwelling unit to members of a single family. In almost impenetrable language, the law defined family to include, among others, the nominal head of the household (in this case Inez Moore), the husband or wife of the nominal head and unmarried children of the nominal head but "not more than one

dependent married or unmarried child of the nominal head of the household
. . . and dependent children of such dependent child." As applied, the law
prohibited the living arrangement constituted by the Moore household.

In 1973 the city sent Moore a violation notice stating that grandson John was an "illegal occupant" under the terms of the law. After Moore
declined to turn John out of her home, the city filed criminal charges against
her. Although she claimed in trial court that the housing ordinance was
unconstitutional, the court found her guilty and sentenced her to five days in
jail and a $25 fine. The intermediate state appeals court affirmed, and the
Ohio Supreme Court denied review of her case.

The Supreme Court of the United States, in a five-to-four decision communicated by six separate opinions, reversed the state court judgment. There was no majority opinion. Justice Powell, joined by Justices
Brennan, Marshall and Blackmun, wrote the plurality opinion finding that
the housing ordinance deprived Moore of her liberty in violation of the due
process clause of the fourteenth amendment. Justice John Paul Stevens provided the fifth vote for overturning the ordinance but based his vote on a
ground different from that adopted by the plurality. Although he signed onto
the plurality, Justice Brennan, joined by Justice Marshall, wrote a concurring
opinion stating his own views on the matter.

The plurality asserted that the "the usual judicial deference to
the legislature is inappropriate" when government "undertakes such intrusive regulation of the family." Noting that " '[t]his Court has long recognized
that freedom of personal choice in matters of marriage and family life is one
of the liberties protected by the Due Process Clause of the Fourteenth
Amendment,' " Justice Powell cited a "host of cases" where the Court has
"consistently acknowledged a 'private realm of family life which the state
cannot enter.' " Owing to the eloquence of expression, Justice Powell quoted
from Justice John Harlan's dissenting opinion in *Poe v. Ullman* (1961) on the
meaning of the due process clause:

> Due process has not been reduced to any formula; its content cannot be deter-
> mined by reference to any code. The best that can be said is that through the
> course of this Court's decisions it has represented the balance which our Nation,
> built upon postulates of respect for the liberty of the individual, has struck
> between that liberty and the demands of organized society. If the supplying of
> content to this Constitutional concept has of necessity been a rational process, it
> certainly has not been one where judges have felt free to roam where unguided
> speculation might take them. The balance of which I speak is the balance struck
> by this country, having regard to what history teaches are the traditions from
> which it developed as well as the traditions from which it broke. That tradition is
> a living thing. A decision of this Court which radically departs from it could not
> long survive, while a decision which builds on what has survived is likely to be
> sound. . . . No formula could serve as a substitute, in this area, for judgment and
> restraint. . . . [T]he full scope of the liberty guaranteed by the Due Process Clause
> cannot be found in or limited by the precise terms of the specific guarantees else-
> where provided in the Constitution. This "liberty" is not a series of isolated
> points pricked out in terms of the taking of property; the freedom of speech,
> press, and religion; the right to keep and bear arms; the freedom from unreasona-

ble searches and seizures; and so on. It is a rational continuum which, broadly speaking, includes a freedom from all substantial arbitrary impositions and purposeless restraints, . . . and which also recognizes, what a reasonable and sensitive judgment must, that certain interests require particularly careful scrutiny of the state needs asserted to justify their abridgment.

In this case, then, Justice Powell and his three brethren concluded that the right of family, extending from grandmother to grandson, "require[s] particularly careful scrutiny of the state needs asserted to justify [its] abridgement." The city's asserted rationales of "preventing overcrowding, minimizing traffic and parking congestion, and avoiding an undue financial burden on East Cleveland's school system," were served "marginally, at best" by the housing restriction.

Justice Stevens did not find it necessary to apply a less deferential standard of review to invalidate East Cleveland's ordinance. For him, the law failed even under the minimum standard appropriate for the garden-variety zoning case, "[s]ince this ordinance has not been shown to have any 'substantial relation to the public health, safety, morals or general welfare' of the city of East Cleveland, and since it cuts so deeply into a fundamental right normally associated with the ownership of residential property—that of an owner to decide who may reside on his or her property. . . ."

The most surprising aspect of Justice Stevens's opinion was his choice of constitutional pegs on which to hang the ordinance: "East Cleveland's unprecedented ordinance constitutes a taking of property without due process and without just compensation." This formulation would surprise most land use law aficionados, because regulatory takings usually are found only when the owner is denied economically viable use of property (see Justice Brennan's *Penn Central* opinion for further elaboration) or when the law authorizes a public physical occupation of property. Perhaps Justice Stevens was simply being prescient: 10 years later in 1987, a regulatory taking was found in the *Nollan v. California Coastal Commission* case, without any claim of economic impact.

The dissenters also displayed a multiplicity of views, with Chief Justice Burger, Justice White and Justice Stewart (joined by Justice Rehnquist) each writing separately. Chief Justice Burger declined to reach the constitutional issue because, he decided, Inez Moore deliberately refused to seek the administrative remedy of a variance from the housing ordinance. Referring, as he frequently did throughout his tenure on the Court, to the "critical overburdening of federal courts," he suggested that Moore should be required to exhaust her administrative remedies before burdening the U.S. Supreme Court.

Justice Stewart, with Justice Rehnquist, found that Moore's claim fell outside the protection of the Constitution. Justice Stewart pigeonholed those "rare cases" where personal interests have been deemed "implicit in the concept of ordered liberty," such as the abortion case of *Roe v. Wade* (1973). Here, however, he concluded that "[t]he interest that [Moore] may have in permanently sharing a single kitchen and a suite of contiguous rooms with some of her relatives simply does not rise to that level. To equate this interest with the fundamental decisions to marry and to bear and raise children is to extend the limited substantive contours of the Due Process Clause beyond recognition."

In the most compelling of the dissents, Justice White joined the debate in terms most familiar to followers of the 1987 Senate hearings on Court of Appeals Judge Robert Bork's failed nomination to the U.S. Supreme Court. Justice White's concern was partially an institutional one:

> That the Court has ample precedent for the creation of new constitutional rights should not lead it to repeat the process at will. The Judiciary, including this Court, is the most vulnerable and comes nearest to illegitimacy when it deals with judge-made constitutional law having little or no cognizable roots in the language or even the design of the Constitution.

He saw a dangerous analogy to the so-called *Lochner* era, during which the Court freely struck down legislation regulating the workplace:

> Realizing that the present construction of the Due Process Clause represents a major judicial gloss on its terms, as well as on the anticipation of the Framers, and that much of the underpinning for the broad, substantive application of the Clause disappeared in the conflict between the Executive and the Judiciary in the 1930's and 1940's, the Court should be extremely reluctant to breathe still further substantive content into the Due Process Clause so as to strike down legislation adopted by a State or city to promote its welfare. Whenever the Judiciary does so, it unavoidably pre-empts for itself another part of the governance of the country without express constitutional authority.

Although he joined the plurality opinion, Justice Brennan also wrote separately to emphasize the importance of the extended family and the myopic view of family life implied by East Cleveland's ordinance. Indeed, Justice Brennan's own grandmother had lived in his home when he was growing up in Newark, N.J.

JUSTICE BRENNAN (selected notes included)

I join the plurality's opinion. I agree that the Constitution is not powerless to prevent East Cleveland from prosecuting as a criminal and jailing a 63-year-old grandmother for refusing to expel from her home her now 10-year-old grandson who has lived with her and been brought up by her since his mother's death when he was less than a year old. I do not question that a municipality may constitutionally zone to alleviate noise and traffic congestion and to prevent overcrowded and unsafe living conditions, in short to enact reasonable land-use restrictions in furtherance of the legitimate objectives East Cleveland claims for its ordinance. But the zoning power is not a license for local communities to enact senseless and arbitrary restrictions which cut deeply into private areas of protected family life. East Cleveland may not constitutionally define "family" as essentially confined to parents and the parents' own children. The plurality's opinion conclusively demonstrates that classifying family patterns in this eccentric way is not a rational means of achieving the ends East Cleveland claims for its ordinance, and further that the ordinance unconstitutionally abridges the "freedom of personal choice in matters of . . . family life [that] is one of the liberties protected by the Due Process Clause of the Fourteenth Amendment." I write only to underscore the cultural myopia of the arbitrary boundary drawn by the East Cleveland ordinance in the light of the tradition of the American home that has been a feature of our society since our beginning as a Nation—the "tradition" in the plurality's words, "of uncles, aunts, cousins, and especially grandparents sharing a household along with parents and children. . . ." The line drawn by this ordinance displays a depressing insensitivity toward the economic and emotional needs of a very large part of our society.

In today's America, the "nuclear family" is the pattern so often found in much of white suburbia. J. Vander Zanden, Sociology: A Systematic Approach 322 (3d ed. 1975). The Constitution cannot be interpreted, however, to tolerate the imposition by government upon the rest of us of white suburbia's preference in patterns of family living. The "extended family" that provided generations of early Americans with social services and economic and emotional support in times of hardship, and was the beachhead for successive waves of immigrants who populated our cities,[4] remains not merely still a pervasive living pattern, but under the goad of brutal economic necessity, a prominent pattern—virtually a means of survival—for large numbers of the poor and deprived minorities of our society. For them compelled pooling of scant resources requires compelled sharing of a household.[5]

The "extended" form is especially familiar among black families.[6] We may suppose that this reflects the truism that black citizens, like generations of white immigrants before them, have been victims of economic and other disadvantages that would worsen if they were compelled to abandon extended, for nuclear, living patterns.[7] Even in husband and wife households, 13% of black families compared with 3% of white families include relatives under 18 years old, in addition to the couple's own children. In black households whose head is an elderly woman, as in this case, the contrast is even more striking: 48% of such black households, compared with 10% of counterpart white households, include related minor children not offspring of the head of the household.[9]

I do not wish to be understood as implying that East Cleveland's enforcement of its ordinance is motivated by a racially discriminatory purpose: The record of this case would not support that implication. But the prominence of other than nuclear families among ethnic and racial minority groups, including our black citizens, surely demonstrates that the "extended family" pattern remains a vital tenet of our society.[10] It suffices that in prohibiting this pattern of family living as a means of achieving its objectives, appellee city has chosen a device that deeply intrudes into family associational rights that historically have been central, and today remain central, to a large proportion of our population.

Moreover, to sanction the drawing of the family line at the arbitrary boundary chosen by East Cleveland would surely conflict with prior decisions that protected "extended" family relationships. For the "private realm of family life which the state cannot enter," recognized as protected in *Prince v. Massachusetts*, was the relationship of aunt and niece. And in *Pierce v. Society of Sisters*, the protection held to have been unconstitutionally abridged was "the liberty of parents and guardians to direct the upbringing and education of children under their control." Indeed, *Village of Belle Terre v. Boraas*, the case primarily relied upon by the appellee, actually supports the Court's decision. The Belle Terre ordinance barred only unrelated individuals from constituting a family in a single-family zone. The village took special care in its brief to emphasize that its ordinance did not in any manner inhibit the choice of related individuals to constitute a family, whether in the "nuclear" or "extended" form. This was because the village perceived that choice as one it was constitutionally powerless to inhibit. Its brief stated: "Whether it be the extended family of a more leisurely age or the nuclear family of today the role of the family in raising and training successive generations of the species makes it more important, we dare say, than any other social or legal institution. . . . If any freedom not specifically mentioned in the Bill of Rights enjoys a 'preferred position' in the law it is most certainly the family." The cited decisions recognized, as the plurality recognizes today, that the choice of the "extended family" pattern is within the "freedom of personal choice in matters of . . . family life [that] is one of the liberties protected by the Due Process Clause of the Fourteenth Amendment."■

8 AESTHETICS AND FREEDOM OF SPEECH

Billboard advertisement in San Diego, where a city ban on billboards was challenged. From Metromedia, Inc. v. City of San Diego.
(Jerold S. Kayden)

W hether knowingly or not, individuals constantly express ideas through their use of land. Sometimes that expression is explicit and verbal, as in announcements delivered through billboards or posted signs. Sometimes that expression is subtle and nonverbal, as in the choice of an architectural style or an exterior paint color. In their pursuit of beauty, tourist dollars and other public goals, communities do not tolerate total freedom of expression when it comes to land use. Many towns prohibit or substantially restrict billboards. Planning departments commonly review architectural designs for proposed buildings. Zoning itself takes sides in matters of aesthetics. Recently, bending to the dictates of the postmodern architectural movement, San Francisco's ordinance effectively disallowed flat roofs on new skyscrapers while encouraging articulation and ornamentation. In an earlier time, New York City's 1961 zoning revision took its cue for height and setback rules from that apotheosis of modernism, the Seagram Building (1957, Ludwig Mies van der Rohe; with Philip Johnson) on Park Avenue.

Because the first amendment of the Constitution guarantees that government shall not abridge "freedom of speech," land use regulations affecting expression are regularly challenged in court. The three opinions of Justice Brennan discussed in this chapter—the *Metromedia*, *Vincent* and *Renton* cases—deal with the most common land use and free speech intersections. The three also are linked by application of Justice Brennan's theory of serious and comprehensive government efforts, designed to assure the reviewing court that government, indeed, values seriously its asserted justifications for restricting expression.

In the 1981 *Metromedia* "Billboards Revisited" case, the issue was San Diego's ban on billboards within city limits. The problem with billboards is that their very purpose—to communicate messages in as eye-catching and intrusive a way as possible—is inherently incompatible with the aesthetic goals of a city. Nonetheless, as Justice Brennan suggested in his concurring opinion, the first amendment's protection of speech may mean that otherwise noble goals may have to yield to this bedrock constitutional interest. In *Metromedia*, Justice Brennan flunked San Diego for its failure to demonstrate a comprehensive and serious effort addressing its aesthetic concerns.

The 1984 *Vincent* "Campaign Posters" case involved a poster ban on public property throughout Los Angeles. It raised the spectacle of a law, passed by the city council, that prevented candidates for that same body from posting signs supporting their election. In dissent and unpersuaded that Los Angeles was seriously pursuing an overall aesthetics goal, Justice Brennan was unwilling to tolerate this infringement on free speech rights.

The 1986 *Renton* "Erogenous Zoning" case presented a land use patronized by some and abhorred by others in communities across the country: adult entertainment businesses such as adult movie theaters and bookstores. Frustrated that something so inconvenient as the first amendment apparently precludes enactment of total bans on adult entertainment uses, local governments make protean efforts to achieve the same end in a constitutional way. Thus, zoning that concentrates or disperses such uses within the community is artfully employed. Justice Brennan dissented from the majority's approval of one city's approach, finding no evidence in the record to support the city's assertion that adult uses caused secondary "non-speech" related problems in local neighborhoods.

The Billboards Revisited Case:
Metromedia, Inc. v. City of San Diego

Almost 30 years after *United Advertising Corp. v. Borough of Raritan*, Justice Brennan had an opportunity to revisit the issue of billboard regulation. This time, however, the constitutional backdrop was different: commercial speech such as advertising messages was now entitled to first amendment protection. Thus, billboard regulations previously upheld under the deferential standard of review appropriate for non-speech-related land use restrictions received greater scrutiny. A comparison of Justice Brennan's opinions in *United Advertising* and *Metromedia* reveals the extent and impact of the change.

In order "to eliminate hazards to pedestrians and motorists brought about by distracting sign displays" and "to preserve and improve the appearance of the City," San Diego enacted a ban on all off-site billboards—signs publicizing goods, services and activities not offered at the site of the sign. The commonplace free-standing roadway billboard advertising a product, as well as billboards containing noncommmerical messages, were prohibited by the ordinance.

The law did not ban all signs within the city, however. On-site signs identifying or advertising the owner or occupant of a site were allowed. In addition, the ordinance provided 12 specific exemptions from the off-site ban, including government signs; bench signs at public bus stops; signs manufactured, transported or stored in San Diego, but not used for advertising; commemorative historical plaques; religious symbols; signs within shopping malls; for sale or lease signs; time, temperature and news signs; signs affixed to public transportation vehicles; signs affixed to moving commercial vehicles such as trucks; temporary subdivision directional signs; and temporary political campaign signs. Summarizing the law, and telegraphing one of its essential flaws, the Supreme Court's plurality opinion recounted that "[u]nder this scheme, onsite commercial advertising is permitted, but other commercial advertising and noncommercial communications using fixed-structure signs are everywhere forbidden unless permitted by one of the specified exceptions."

Metromedia and several other billboard companies owned 500 to 800 billboards in San Diego, located mostly in areas zoned commercial and industrial. Landowners leased their land to the billboard companies, which maintained the billboards. Messages were normally changed on a monthly basis, and advertisers typically contracted for use of several signs in locations throughout the city. While most billboards carried commercial messages, some were used to convey noncommercial political and social messages. Fair market value of the billboards ranged from $2,500 to $25,000 each. Metromedia and other companies sued San Diego to prevent enforcement of the ordinance. The state trial court ruled in favor of the companies, finding that the ordinance was an unconstitutional exercise of the city's police power as well as an unconstitutional abridgment of first amendment rights. The state intermediate appeals court agreed that the ordinance was an unconstitutional exercise of the police power. The California Supreme Court reversed the lower courts, ruling that the ordinance represented a proper exercise of the police power and did not violate the first amendment.

In disagreeing with California's highest court and overturning the San Diego ordinance, the U.S. Supreme Court in its six-to-three judgment issued no fewer than five separate opinions: one plurality, one concurring in the judgment, one concurring and dissenting at the same time and two dissenting. Justice White, joined by Justices Stewart, Marshall and Powell, wrote the plurality opinion striking down the ordinance on first amendment grounds. Justice White began his analysis, however, by discussing what was legitimate about the law. To the extent that it merely banned all off-site commercial billboards, he noted, it was constitutional because the city's goals of traffic safety and aesthetics were sufficiently substantial to justify such a ban. On the issue of aesthetics, Justice White observed,

> It is not speculative to recognize that billboards by their very nature, wherever located and however constructed, can be perceived as an "esthetic harm." . . . San Diego, like many States and other municipalities, has chosen to minimize the presence of such structures. . . . Such esthetic judgments are necessarily subjective, defying objective evaluation, and for that reason must be carefully scrutinized to determine if they are only a public rationalization of an impermissible purpose. But there is no claim in this case that San Diego has as an ulterior motive the suppression of speech, and the judgment involved here is not so unusual as to raise suspicions in itself.

For Justice White, then, the San Diego ordinance failed because it accorded preferential treatment to commercial speech (on-site identifying signs) over noncommercial speech (off-site signs carrying noncommercial messages), thereby inverting the first amendment's expressed preference for noncommercial speech. Furthermore, the ordinance's preference for certain types of noncommercial speech (commemorative plaques, government signs) over others placed the government in the impermissible role of choosing between categories of noncommercial speech. The plurality's bottom line emerged: a city may choose to allow some commercial signs and not others or even ban all commercial signs. If it is going to permit some commercial signs, however, it must permit all noncommercial signs. If it allows some noncommercial signs, then it must allow all noncommercial signs. Although the plurality opinion did not directly decide the issue, it suggested that a total ban on all commercial and noncommercial billboards was too heavy a burden on the overall exercise of first amendment rights.

Because Justice White's opinion garnered only three other votes—one short of a majority—it did not represent binding precedent for lower courts. Normally, one would look to the concurring opinion, in this case that of Justice Brennan, to divine the general leaning of a majority of the

Court. Justice Brennan's concurrence did create a majority for striking down the San Diego billboard ordinance on the ground that the city had not shown a serious enough interest in aesthetics to justify its ban on this important medium of expression. However, it was the dissents, and especially Justice Stevens's opinion, that illuminated the true inclination of the Court. For example, it was Justice Stevens, not Justice Brennan, who expressly agreed with Justice White that a ban on all off-site commercial billboards was constitutional.

Justice Stevens presented an interesting hypothetical example to highlight his views. What about graffiti? It has existed since the days of ancient Egypt and Greece and was "an inexpensive means of communicating political, commercial, and frivolous messages to large numbers of people; some creators of graffiti have no effective alternative means of communication." Although the language of the first amendment prohibiting any law "abridging the freedom of speech" may be "read to foreclose any law reducing the quantity of communication within a jurisdiction"—the sort of absolutist view championed by Justice Hugo Black—surely a municipality "has the right to decide that its interests in protecting property from damaging trespasses and in securing beautiful surroundings outweigh the countervailing interest in uninhibited expression by means of words and pictures in public places." Concluded Justice Stevens, "If the First Amendment categorically protected the marketplace of ideas from any quantitative restraint, a municipality could not outlaw graffiti." What impelled Justice Stevens to dissent from the plurality's overturning of the San Diego law was that, unlike the plurality, he was not troubled by the ordinance's various exceptions.

The other dissenters also would have upheld the ordinance. Inveighing against "the long arm and voracious appetite of federal power—this time judicial power—with a vengeance, reaching and absorbing traditional concepts of local authority," Chief Justice Burger concluded that the ordinance did not violate the first amendment. Justice Rehnquist, lamenting his contribution to the Court's "virtual Tower of Babel, from which no definitive principles can be clearly drawn," found the city's aesthetics interest, even in areas "as unsightly as the older parts of many of our major metropolitan areas," sufficient to justify the regulation.

Justice Brennan took this opportunity to revive his emphasis on comprehensiveness, which he had used in New Jersey, as a predicate for legitimate government land use regulation.

JUSTICE BRENNAN (selected notes included)

Believing that "a total prohibition of outdoor advertising is not before us," the plurality does not decide "whether such a ban would be consistent with the First Amendment." Instead, it concludes that San Diego may ban all billboards containing commercial speech messages without violating the First Amendment, thereby sending the signal to municipalities that bifurcated billboard regulations prohibiting commercial messages but allowing noncommercial messages would pass constitutional muster. I write separately because I believe this case in effect presents the total ban question, and because I believe the plurality's bifurcated approach itself raises serious First Amendment problems and relies on a distinction between commercial and noncommercial speech unanticipated by our prior cases.

As construed by the California Supreme Court, a billboard subject to San Diego's regulation is "a rigidly assembled sign, display or device permanently affixed to the ground or permanently attached to a building or other inherently permanent structure constituting, or used for the display of, a commercial or other advertisement to the public." San Diego's billboard regulation bans all commercial and noncommercial billboard advertising with a few limited exceptions. The largest of these exceptions is for on-premises identification signs, defined as "signs designating the name of the owner or occupant of the premises upon which such signs are placed, or identifying such premises; or signs advertising goods manufactured or produced or services rendered on the premises upon which such signs are placed." Other exceptions permit signs for governmental functions, signs on benches at bus stops, commemorative plaques for historical sites, religious symbol signs, for sale signs, time/weather/news public service signs, and temporary political campaign signs erected for no longer than 90 days and removed within 10 days after the election to which they pertain.

Let me first state the common ground that I share with the plurality. The plurality and I agree that billboards are a medium of communication warranting First Amendment protection. The plurality observes that "[b]illboards are a well-established medium of communication, used to convey a broad range of different kinds of messages." As the parties have stipulated, billboards in San Diego have been used

> to advertise national and local products, goods and services, new products being introduced to the consuming public, to publicize the "City in Motion" campaign of the City of San Diego, to communicate messages from candidates for municipal, state and national offices, including candidates for judicial office, to propose marriage, to seek employment, to encourage the use of seat belts, to denounce the United Nations, to seek support for Prisoners of War and Missing in Action, to promote the United Crusade and a variety of other charitable and socially-related endeavors and to provide directions to the traveling public.[4]

Although there are alternative channels for communication of messages appearing on billboards, such as newspapers, television, and radio, these alternatives have never dissuaded active and continued use of billboards as a medium of expression and appear to be less satisfactory. Indeed the parties expressly stipulated that "[m]any businesses and politicians and other persons rely upon outdoor advertising because other forms of advertising are insufficient, inappropriate and prohibitively expensive." Justice Black said it well when he stated the First Amendment's presumption that "all present instruments of communication, as well as others that inventive genius may bring into being, shall be free from governmental censorship or prohibition."

Where the plurality and I disagree is in the characterization of the San Diego ordinance and thus in the appropriate analytical framework to apply. The plurality believes that the question of a total ban is not presented in this case, because the ordinance contains exceptions to its general prohibition. In contrast, my view is that the practical effect of the San Diego ordinance is to eliminate the billboard as an effective medium of communication for the speaker who wants to express the sorts of messages described [in the record], and that the exceptions do not alter the overall character of the ban. Unlike the on-premises sign, the off-premises billboard "is, generally speaking, made available to 'all-comers,' in a fashion similar to newspaper or broadcasting advertising. It is a forum for the communication of messages to the public." Speakers in San Diego no longer have the opportunity to communicate their messages of general applicability to the public through billboards. None of the exceptions provides a practical alternative for the general commercial or noncommercial billboard advertiser. Indeed, unless the advertiser chooses to buy or lease premises in the city, or unless his message falls within one of the narrow exempted categories, he is foreclosed from announcing either commercial or noncommercial ideas through a billboard.

The characterization of the San Diego regulation as a total ban of a medium of communication has more than semantic implications, for it suggests a First Amendment analysis quite different from the plurality's. Instead of relying on the exceptions to the ban to invalidate the ordinance, I would apply the tests this Court has developed to analyze content-neutral prohibitions of particular media of communication. Most recently, in *Schad v. Mount Ephraim*, this Court assessed "the substantiality of the governmental interests asserted" and "whether those interests could be served by means that would be less intrusive on activity protected by the First Amendment," in striking down the borough's total ban on live commercial entertainment. *Schad* merely articulated an analysis applied in previous cases concerning total bans of media of expression. For example, in *Schneider v. State*, the Court struck down total bans on handbill leafletting because there were less restrictive alternatives to achieve the goal of prevention of litter, in fact alternatives that did not infringe at all on that important First Amendment privilege. In *Martin v. City of Struthers*, the Court invalidated a municipal ordinance that forbade persons from engaging in the time-honored activity of door-to-door solicitation.

Of course, as the plurality notes, "[e]ach method of communicating ideas is 'a law unto itself' and that law must reflect the 'differing natures, values, abuses and dangers' of each method." Similarly, in *Southeastern Promotions, Ltd. v. Conrad*, this Court observed: "Each medium of expression, of course, must be assessed for First Amendment purposes by standards suited to it, for each may present its own problems." It is obvious that billboards do present their own unique problems: they are large immobile structures that depend on eye-catching visibility for their value. At the same time, the special problems associated with billboards are not of a different genus than those associated with commercial live entertainment in the borough of Mount Ephraim, or with door-to-door literature distribution in the city of Struthers. In the case of billboards, I would hold that a city may totally ban them if it can show that a sufficiently substantial governmental interest is directly furthered by the total ban, and that any more narrowly drawn restriction, i.e., anything less than a total ban, would promote less well the achievement of that goal.

Applying that test to the instant case, I would invalidate the San Diego ordinance. The city has failed to provide adequate justification for its substantial restriction on protected activity. First, although I have no quarrel with the substantiality of the city's interest in traffic safety, the city has failed to come forward with evidence demonstrating that billboards actually impair traffic safety in San Diego. Indeed, the joint stipulation of facts is completely silent on this issue. Although the plurality hesitates "to disagree with the accumulated, common-sense judgments of local lawmakers and of the many reviewing courts that billboards are real and substantial hazards to traffic safety," I would not be so quick to accept legal conclusions in other cases as an adequate substitute for evidence in this case that banning billboards directly furthers traffic safety.[7] Moreover, the ordinance is not narrowly drawn to accomplish the traffic safety goal. Although it contains an exception for signs "not visible from any point on the boundary of the premises," billboards not visible from the street but nevertheless visible from the "boundary of the premises" are not exempted from the regulation's prohibition.

Second, I think that the city has failed to show that its asserted interest in aesthetics is sufficiently substantial in the commercial and industrial areas of San Diego. I do not doubt that "[i]t is within the power of the [city] to determine that the community should be beautiful," but that power may not be exercised in contravention of the First Amendment. This Court noted in *Schad* that "[t]he [city] has presented no evidence, and it is not immediately apparent as a matter of experience, that live entertainment poses problems . . . more significant than those associated with various permitted uses; nor does it appear that the [city] has arrived at a defensible conclusion that unusual problems are presented by live entertainment." Substitute the word "billboards" for the words "live entertainment," and that sentence would equally apply to this case.

It is no doubt true that the appearance of certain areas of the city would be enhanced by the elimination of billboards, but "it is not immediately apparent as a matter of experience" that their elimination in all other areas as well would have more than a negligible impact on aesthetics. The joint stipulation reveals that

> [s]ome sections of the City of San Diego are scenic, some blighted, some containing strips of vehicle related commercial uses, some contain new and attractive office buildings, some functional industrial development and some areas contain older but useful commercial establishments.

A billboard is not necessarily inconsistent with oil storage tanks, blighted areas, or strip development. Of course, it is not for a court to impose its own notion of beauty on San Diego. But before deferring to a city's judgment, a court must be convinced that the city is seriously and comprehensively addressing aesthetic concerns with respect to its environment. Here, San Diego has failed to demonstrate a comprehensive coordinated effort in its commercial and industrial areas to address other obvious contributors to an unattractive environment. In this sense the ordinance is underinclusive. Of course, this is not to say that the city must address all aesthetic problems at the same time, or none at all. Indeed, from a planning point of view, attacking the problem incrementally and sequentially may represent the most sensible solution. On the other hand, if billboards alone are banned and no further steps are contemplated or likely, the commitment of the city to improving its physical environment is placed in doubt. By showing a comprehensive commitment to making its physical environment in commercial and industrial areas more attractive, and by allowing only narrowly tailored exceptions, if any,[10] San Diego could demonstrate that its interest in creating an aesthetically pleasing environment is genuine and substantial. This is a requirement where, as here, there is an infringement of important constitutional consequence.

I have little doubt that some jurisdictions will easily carry the burden of proving the substantiality of their interest in aesthetics. For example, the parties acknowledge that a historical community such as Williamsburg, Va., should be able to prove that its interests in aesthetics and historical authenticity are sufficiently important that the First Amendment value attached to billboards must yield. And I would be surprised if the Federal Government had much trouble making the argument that billboards could be entirely banned in Yellowstone National Park, where their very existence would so obviously be inconsistent with the surrounding landscape. I express no view on whether San Diego or other large urban areas will be able to meet the burden. But San Diego failed to do so here, and for that reason I would strike down its ordinance.

The plurality's treatment of the commercial-noncommercial distinction in this case is mistaken in its factual analysis of the San Diego ordinance, and departs from this Court's precedents. In Part IV of its opinion, the plurality concludes that the San Diego ordinance is constitutional insofar as it regulates commercial speech. Under its view, a city with merely a reasonable justification could pick and choose between those commercial billboards it would allow and those it would not, or could totally ban all commercial billboards. In Part V, the plurality concludes, however, that the San Diego ordinance as a whole is unconstitutional because, *inter alia*, it affords a greater degree of protection to commercial than to noncommercial speech:

> The use of onsite billboards to carry commercial messages related to the commercial use of the premises is freely permitted, but the use of otherwise identical billboards to carry noncommercial messages is generally prohibited. . . . Insofar as the city tolerates billboards at all, it cannot choose to limit their content to commercial messages; the city may not conclude that the communication of commercial information concerning goods and services connected with a particular site is of greater value than the communication of noncommercial messages.

The plurality apparently reads the onsite premises exception as limited solely to commercial speech. I find no such limitation in the ordinance. As noted *supra*, the onsite exception allows "signs designating the name of the owner or occupant of the premises upon which such signs are placed, or identifying such premises; or signs advertising goods manufactured or produced or services rendered on the premises upon which such signs are placed." As I read the ordinance, the content of the sign depends strictly on the identity of the owner or occupant of the premises. If the occupant is a commercial enterprise, the substance of a permissible identifying sign would be commercial. If the occupant is an enterprise usually associated with noncommercial speech, the substance of the identifying sign would be noncommercial. Just as a supermarket or barbershop could identify itself by name, so too could a political campaign headquarters or a public interest group. I would also presume that, if a barbershop could advertise haircuts, a political campaign headquarters could advertise "Vote for Brown," or "Vote for Proposition 13."

More importantly, I cannot agree with the plurality's view that an ordinance totally banning commercial billboards but allowing noncommercial billboards would be constitutional.[13] For me, such an ordinance raises First Amendment problems at least as serious as those raised by a total ban, for it gives city officials the right—before approving a billboard—to determine whether the proposed message is "commercial" or "noncommercial." Of course the plurality is correct when it observes that "our cases have consistently distinguished between the constitutional protection afforded commercial as opposed to noncommercial speech," but it errs in assuming that a governmental unit may be put in the position in the first instance of deciding whether the proposed speech is commercial or noncommercial. In individual cases, this distinction is anything but clear. Because making such determinations would entail a substantial exercise of discretion by a city's official, it presents a real danger of curtailing noncommercial speech in the guise of regulating commercial speech.

In *Cantwell v. Connecticut*, the Court reviewed a statute prohibiting solicitation of money by religious groups unless such solicitation was approved in advance by the Secretary of the Public Welfare Council. The statute provided in relevant part:

> Upon application of any person in behalf of such [solicitation], the secretary shall determine whether such cause is a religious one . . . and conforms to reasonable standards of efficiency and integrity, and, if he shall so find, shall approve the same and issue to the authority in charge a certificate to that effect.

The Court held that conditioning the ability to solicit on a license, "the grant of which rests in the exercise of a determination by state authority as to what is a religious cause, is to lay a forbidden burden upon the exercise of liberty protected by the Constitution." Specifically rejecting the State's argument that arbitrary and capricious acts of a state officer would be subject to judicial review, the Court observed:

> Upon [the state official's] decision as to the nature of the cause, the right to solicit funds depends. . . . [T]he availability of a judicial remedy for abuses in the system of licensing still leaves that system one of previous restraint which, in the field of free speech and press, we have held inadmissible.

As Justice Frankfurter subsequently characterized *Cantwell*: "To determine whether a cause is, or is not, 'religious' opens too wide a field of personal judgment to be left to the mere discretion of an official."

According such wide discretion to city officials to control the free exercise of First Amendment rights is precisely what has consistently troubled this Court in a long line of cases. The plurality's bifurcated approach, I fear, will generate billboard ordinances providing the grist for future additions to this list, for it creates discretion where none previously existed.

It is one thing for a court to classify in specific cases whether commercial or noncommercial speech is involved, but quite another—and for me dispositively so—for a city to do so regularly for the purpose of deciding what messages may be communicated by way of billboards. Cities are equipped to make traditional police power decisions, not decisions based on the content of speech. I would be unhappy to see city officials dealing with the following series of billboards and deciding which ones to permit: the first billboard contains the message "Visit Joe's Ice Cream Shoppe"; the second, "Joe's Ice Cream Shoppe uses only the highest quality dairy products"; the third, "Because Joe thinks that dairy products are good for you, please shop at Joe's Shoppe"; and the fourth, "Joe says to support dairy price supports: they mean lower prices for you at his Shoppe." Or how about some San Diego Padres baseball fans—with no connection to the team—who together rent a billboard and communicate the message "Support the San Diego Padres, a great baseball team." May the city decide that a United Automobile Workers billboard with the message "Be a patriot—do not buy Japanese-manufactured cars" is "commercial" and therefore forbid it? What if the same sign is placed by Chrysler?[14]

I do not read our recent line of commercial cases as authorizing this sort of regular and immediate line-drawing by governmental entities. If anything, our cases recognize the difficulty in making a determination that speech is either "commercial" or "noncommercial." In *Virginia Pharmacy Board v. Virginia Citizens Consumer Council, Inc.*, after noting that "not all commercial messages contain . . . a very great public interest element," the Court suggested that "[t]here are few to which such an element, however, could not be added." The Court continued: "Our pharmacist, for example, could cast himself as a commentator on store-to-store disparities in drug prices, giving his own and those of a competitor as proof. We see little point in requiring him to do so, and little difference if he does not." In *Bigelow v. Virginia*, the Court observed that the advertisement of abortion services placed by a New York clinic in a Virginia weekly newspaper—although in part a commercial advertisement—was far more than that:

> Viewed in its entirety, the advertisement conveyed information of potential interest and value to a diverse audience—not only to readers possibly in need of the services offered, but also to those with a general curiosity about, or genuine interest in, the subject matter or the law of another State and its development, and to readers seeking reform in Virginia. The mere existence of the Women's Pavilion in New York City, with the possibility of its being typical of other organizations there, and the availability of the services offered, were not unnewsworthy.

"The line between ideological and nonideological speech is impossible to draw with accuracy." I have no doubt that those who seek to convey commercial messages will engage in the most imaginative of exercises to place themselves within the safe haven of noncommercial speech, while at the same time conveying their commercial message. Encouraging such behavior can only make the job of city officials—who already are inclined to ban billboards—that much more difficult and potentially intrusive upon legitimate noncommercial expression. ▬

The Campaign Posters Case: Members of City Council v. Taxpayers for Vincent

The *Vincent* case afforded Justice Brennan the chance, albeit in dissent, to discuss more expansively his concept of comprehensive and serious aesthetic efforts necessary to sustain government regulations impinging on first amendment free speech rights. The city of Los Angeles enacted a law barring persons from posting signs, painting or writing on public property such as utility poles, fire hydrants, trees and bridges. Roland Vincent was a candidate for election in March 1979 to the Los Angeles City Council. A group of his supporters, known as Taxpayers for Vincent, engaged a private company to make and post political signs for him. The company created 15-by-44-inch signs with the message "Roland Vincent—City Council" and attached them to utility poles around Los Angeles. The city's Bureau of Street Maintenance removed 48 of the signs and 1,159 other mostly commercial posters from public property during the first week of March 1979.

Taxpayers for Vincent and the private poster company sued the city, claiming that the poster law violated the first amendment's free speech clause. The federal district court rejected their claim, finding in general that the "large number of signs illegally posted . . . constitute a clutter and visual blight" and that the Vincent campaign posters in particular "would add somewhat to the blight and inevitably would encourage greatly increased posting in other unauthorized and unsightly places. . . ." The federal court of appeals reversed the district court, essentially adopting the test from Justice Brennan's *Metromedia* opinion that the city had failed to demonstrate a comprehensive effort aimed at eliminating other contributors to an unattractive environment. That court mistakenly read Justice Brennan's concurring opinion in *Metromedia* as the decisive fifth vote when it was actually Justice Stevens's opinion there, as well as those of the dissenters, who held the decisive views governing aesthetics laws.

In its six-to-three decision, the U.S. Supreme Court upheld the antiposter ordinance. To the careful reader of the Tower of Babel opinions in the *Metromedia* case, the *Vincent* Court alignment is hardly surprising. Justice Stevens, joined by Chief Justice Burger and Justices White, Powell, Rehnquist and the most recently appointed justice, Sandra Day O'Connor, wrote the majority opinion. In *Metromedia*, five of these six justices, one way or another, had agreed that the assertion by a municipality of an aesthetics interest was sufficient at least to justify a ban on commercial billboards. It was Justice Brennan, joined by Justice Blackmun, who had urged a greater showing by the municipality before crediting its aesthetics goal. Justice Stevens's *Vincent* majority picked up on this point, reciting how seven of the nine justices in *Metromedia* (excluding Justices Brennan and Blackmun) "explicity [sic] concluded that [the aesthetics] interest was sufficient to justify a prohibition of billboards," and that such justification was equally sufficient here. But the majority overstated its case: four of the seven justices to whom it referred—the ones in the *Metromedia* plurality opinion—concluded that the aesthetics interest was only sufficient to justify a prohibition of commercial billboards and not a prohibition of both commercial and noncommercial billboards. Indeed, in a footnote, the *Metromedia* plurality explicitly reserved the question whether "a total prohibition of outdoor advertising" would be permissible. If anything, that opinion suggested disapproval of a total ban by referring to a case overturning a total ban on live entertainment, another medium of expression protected by the first amendment.

The majority drew one other comparison with the *Metromedia* case: like billboards, "the substantive evil—visual blight—is not merely a possible byproduct of the activity, but is created by the medium of expression itself." In short, posited the majority, there is no way to eliminate the visual clutter of posters other than by banning them. And, in any event, "there is not even a hint of bias or censorship in the City's enactment or enforcement of this ordinance." Justice Stevens noted that "there is no claim that the ordinance was designed to suppress certain ideas that the City finds distasteful" or that the ordinance was applied to the Vincent supporters "because of the views that they express." Of course, it is at least ironic that the ordinance, enacted by the Los Angeles City Council, operated to ban the political posters of a candidate for that same body.

In striking a different balance between the candidate's interest in free speech and the city's interest in aesthetics, Justice Brennan elaborated on his ideas in *Metromedia.* And he picked up a third adherent, Justice Marshall (in addition to Justice Blackmun), for his point of view.

JUSTICE BRENNAN (selected note included)

The plurality opinion in *Metromedia, Inc. v. San Diego* concluded that the City of San Diego could, consistently with the First Amendment, restrict the commercial use of billboards in order to "preserve and improve the appearance of the City." Today, the Court sustains the constitutionality of Los Angeles' similarly motivated ban on the posting of political signs on public property. Because the Court's lenient approach towards the restriction of speech for reasons of aesthetics threatens seriously to undermine the protections of the First Amendment, I dissent.

The Court finds that the City's "interest [in eliminating visual clutter] is sufficiently substantial to justify the effect of the ordinance on appellees' expression" and that the effect of the ordinance on speech is "no greater than necessary to accomplish the City's purpose." These are the right questions to consider when analyzing the constitutionality of the challenged ordinance, but the answers that the Court provides reflect a startling insensitivity to the principles embodied in the First Amendment. In my view, the City of Los Angeles has not shown that its interest in eliminating "visual clutter" justifies its restriction of appellees' ability to communicate with the local electorate.

The Court recognizes that each medium for communicating ideas and information presents its own particular problems. Our analysis of the First Amendment concerns implicated by a given medium must therefore be sensitive to these particular problems and characteristics. The posting of signs is, of course, a time-honored means of communicating a broad range of ideas and information, particularly in our cities and towns. At the same time, the unfettered proliferation of signs on public fixtures may offend the public's legitimate desire to preserve an orderly and aesthetically pleasing urban environment. In this case, as in *Metromedia*, we are called upon to adjudge the constitutionality under the First Amendment of a local government's response to this recurring dilemma—namely, the clash between the public's aesthetic interest in controlling the use of billboards, signs, handbills, and other similar means of communication, and the First Amendment interest of those who wish to use these media to express their views, or to learn the views of others, on matters of importance to the community.

In deciding this First Amendment question, the critical importance of the posting of signs as a means of communication must not be overlooked. Use of this medium of communication is particularly valuable in part because it entails a relatively small expense in reaching a wide audience, allows flexibility in accommodating various formats, typographies, and graphics, and conveys its message in a manner that is easily read and understood by its reader or viewer. There may be alternative channels of communication, but the prevalence of a large number of signs in Los Angeles is a strong indication that, for many speakers, those alternatives are far less satisfactory.

Nevertheless, the City of Los Angeles asserts that ample alternative avenues of communication are available. The City notes that, although the posting of signs on public property is prohibited, the posting of signs on private property and the distribution of handbills are not. But there is no showing that either of these alternatives would serve appellees' needs nearly as well as would the posting of signs on public property. First, there is no proof that a sufficient number of private parties would allow the posting of signs on their property. Indeed, common sense suggests the contrary at least in some instances. A speaker with a message that is generally unpopular or simply unpopular among property owners is hardly likely to get his message across if forced to rely on this medium. It is difficult to believe, for example, that a group advocating an increase in the rate of a property tax would succeed in persuading private property owners to accept its signs.

Similarly, the adequacy of distributing handbills is dubious, despite certain advantages of handbills over signs. Particularly when the message to be carried is best expressed by a few words or a graphic image, a message on a sign will typically reach far more people than one on a handbill. The message on a posted sign remains to be seen by passersby as long as it is posted, while a handbill is typically read by a single reader and discarded. Thus, not only must handbills be printed in large quantity, but many hours must be spent distributing them. The average cost of communicating by handbill is therefore likely to be far higher than the average cost of communicating by poster. For that reason, signs posted on public property are doubtless "essential to the poorly financed causes of little people," and their prohibition constitutes a total ban on an important medium of communication. Because the City has completely banned the use of this particular medium of communication, and because, given the circumstances, there are no equivalent alternative media that provide an adequate substitute, the Court must examine with particular care the justifications that the City proffers for its ban.

As the Court acknowledges, when an ordinance significantly limits communicative activity, "the delicate and difficult task falls upon the courts to weigh the circumstances and to appraise the substantiality of the reasons advanced in support of the regulation." The Court's first task is to determine whether the ordinance is aimed at suppressing the content of speech, and if it is, whether a compelling state interest justifies the suppression. If the restriction is content-neutral, the court's task is to determine (1) whether the governmental objective advanced by the restriction is substantial, and (2) whether the restriction imposed on speech is no greater than is essential to further that objective. Unless both conditions are met the restriction must be invalidated.

My suggestion in *Metromedia* was that courts should exercise special care in addressing these questions when a purely aesthetic objective is asserted to justify a restriction of speech. Specifically, "before deferring to a city's judgment, a court must be convinced that the city is seriously and comprehensively addressing aesthetic concerns with respect to its environment." I adhere to that view. Its correctness—premised largely on my concern that aesthetic interests are easy for a city to assert and difficult for a court to evaluate—is, for me, reaffirmed by this case.

The fundamental problem in this kind of case is that a purely aesthetic state interest offered to justify a restriction on speech—that is, a governmental objective justified solely in terms like "proscribing intrusive and unpleasant formats for expression"—creates difficulties for a reviewing court in fulfilling its obligation to ensure that government regulation does not trespass upon protections secured by the First Amendment. The source of those difficulties is the unavoidable subjectivity of aesthetic judgments—the fact that "beauty is in the eye of the beholder." As a consequence of this subjectivity, laws defended on aesthetic grounds raise problems for judicial review that are not presented by laws defended on more objective grounds—such as national security, public health, or public safety. In practice, therefore, the inherent subjectivity of aesthetic judgments makes it all too easy for the government to fashion its justification for a law in a manner that impairs the ability of a reviewing court meaningfully to make the required inquiries.

Initially, a reviewing court faces substantial difficulties determining whether the actual objective is related to the suppression of speech. The asserted interest in aesthetics may be only a facade for content-based suppression. Of course, all would agree that the improvement and preservation of the aesthetic environment are important governmental functions, and that some restrictions on speech may be necessary to carry out these functions. But a governmental interest in aesthetics cannot be regarded as sufficiently compelling to justify a restriction of speech based on an assertion that the content of the speech is, in itself, aesthetically displeasing. Because aesthetic judgments are so subjective, however, it is too easy for government to enact restrictions on speech for just such illegitimate reasons and to evade effective judicial review by asserting that the restriction is aimed at some displeasing aspect of the speech that is not solely communicative—for example, its sound, its appearance, or its location. An objective standard for evaluating claimed aesthetic judgments is therefore essential; for without one, courts have no reliable means of assessing the genuineness of such claims.

For example, in evaluating the ordinance before us in this case, the City might be pursuing either of two objectives, motivated by two very different judgments. One objective might be the elimination of "visual clutter," attributable in whole or in part to signs posted on public property. The aesthetic judgment underlying this objective would be that the clutter created by these signs offends the community's desire for an orderly, visually pleasing environment. A second objective might simply be the elimination of the messages typically carried by the signs. In that case, the aesthetic judgment would be that the signs' messages are themselves displeasing. The first objective is lawful, of course, but the second is not. Yet the City might easily mask the second objective by asserting the first and declaring that signs constitute visual clutter. In short, we must avoid unquestioned acceptance of the City's bare declaration of an aesthetic objective lest we fail in our duty to prevent unlawful trespasses upon First Amendment protections.

A total ban on an important medium of communication may be upheld only if the government proves that the ban (1) furthers a substantial government objective, and (2) constitutes the least speech-restrictive means of achieving that objective. Here too, however, meaningful judicial application of these standards is seriously frustrated.

No one doubts the importance of a general governmental interest in aesthetics, but in order to justify a restriction of speech, the particular objective behind the restriction must be substantial. Therefore, in order to uphold a restriction of speech imposed to further an aesthetic objective, a court must ascertain the substantiality of the specific objective pursued. Although courts ordinarily defer to the government's assertion that its objective is substantial, that assertion is not immune from critical examination. This is particularly true when aesthetic objectives underlie the restrictions. But in such cases independent judicial assessment of the substantiality of the government's interest is difficult. Because aesthetic judgments are entirely subjective, the government may too easily overstate the substantiality of its goals. Accordingly, unless courts carefully scrutinize aesthetics-based restrictions of speech, they risk standing idly by while important media of communication are foreclosed for the sake of insubstantial governmental objectives.

Similarly, when a total ban is justified solely in terms of aesthetics, the means inquiry necessary to evaluate the constitutionality of the ban may be impeded by deliberate or unintended government manipulation. Governmental objectives that are purely aesthetic can usually be expressed in a virtually limitless variety of ways. Consequently, objectives can be tailored to fit whatever program the government devises to promote its general aesthetic interests. Once the government has identified a substantial aesthetic objective and has selected a preferred means of achieving its objective, it will be possible for the government to correct any mismatch between means and ends by redefining the ends to conform with the means.

In this case, for example, any of several objectives might be the City's actual substantial goal in banning temporary signs: (1) the elimination of all signs throughout the City, (2) the elimination of all signs in certain parts of the City, or (3) a reduction of the density of signs. Although a total ban on the posting of signs on public property would be the least restrictive means of achieving only the first objective, it would be a very effective means of achieving the other two as well. It is quite possible, therefore, that the City might select such a ban as the means by which to further its general interest in solving its sign problem, without explicitly considering which of the three specific objectives is really substantial. Then, having selected the total ban as its preferred means, the City would be strongly inclined to characterize the first objective as the substantial one. This might be done purposefully in order to conform the ban to the least-restrictive-means requirement, or it might be done inadvertently as a natural concomitant of considering means and ends together. But regardless of why it is done, a reviewing court will be confronted with a statement of substantiality the subjectivity of which makes it impossible to question on its face.

This possibility of interdependence between means and ends in the development of policies to promote aesthetics poses a major obstacle to judicial review of the availability of alternative means that are less restrictive of speech. Indeed, when a court reviews a restriction of speech imposed in order to promote an aesthetic objective, there is a significant possibility that the court will be able to do little more than pay lipservice to the First Amendment inquiry into the availability of less restrictive alternatives. The means may fit the ends only because the ends were defined with the means in mind. In this case, for example, the City has expressed an aesthetic judgment that signs on public property constitute visual clutter throughout the City and that its objective is to eliminate visual clutter. We are then asked to determine whether that objective could have been achieved with less restriction of speech. But to ask the question is to highlight the circularity of the inquiry. Since the goal at least as currently expressed, is essentially to eliminate all signs, the only available means of achieving that goal is to eliminate all signs.

The ease with which means can be equated with aesthetic ends only confirms the importance of close judicial scrutiny of the substantiality of such ends. In this case, for example, it is essential that the Court assess the City's ban on signs by evaluating whether the City has a substantial interest in eliminating the visual clutter caused by all posted signs throughout the City—as distinguished from an interest in banning signs in some areas or in preventing densely packed signs. If, in fact, either of the latter two objectives constitute the substantial interest underlying this ordinance, they could be achieved by means far less restrictive of speech than a total ban on signs, and the ban, therefore, would be invalid.

Regrettably, the Court's analysis is seriously inadequate. Because the Court has failed to develop a reliable means of gauging the nature or depth of the City's commitment to pursuing the goal of eradicating "visual clutter," it simply approves the ordinance with only the most cursory degree of judicial oversight. Without stopping to consider carefully whether this supposed commitment is genuine or substantial, the Court essentially defers to the City's aesthetic judgment and in so doing precludes serious assessment of the availability of alternative means.

The Court begins by simply affirming that "[t]he problem addressed by this ordinance—the visual assault on the citizens of Los Angeles presented by an accumulation of signs posted on public property—constitutes a significant substantive end within the City's power to prohibit." Then, addressing the availability of less restrictive alternatives, the Court can do little more than state the unsurprising conclusion that "[b]y banning these signs, the City did no more than eliminate the exact source of the evil it sought to remedy." Finally, as if to explain the ease with which it reaches its conclusion, the Court notes that "[w]ith respect to signs posted by appellees . . . it is the tangible medium of expressing the message that has adverse impact on the appearance of the landscape." But, as I have demonstrated, it is precisely the ability of the State to make this judgment that should lead us to approach these cases with more caution.

The fact that there are difficulties inherent in judicial review of aesthetics-based restrictions of speech does not imply that government may not engage in such activities. As I have said, improvement and preservation of the aesthetic environment are often legitimate and important governmental functions. But because the implementation of these functions creates special dangers to our First Amendment freedoms, there is a need for more stringent judicial scrutiny than the Court seems willing to exercise.

In cases like this, where a total ban is imposed on a particularly valuable method of communication, a court should require the government to provide tangible proof of the legitimacy and substantiality of its aesthetic objective. Justifications for such restrictions articulated by the government should be critically examined to determine whether the government has committed itself to addressing the identified aesthetic problem.

In my view, such statements of aesthetic objectives should be accepted as substantial and unrelated to the suppression of speech only if the government demonstrates that it is pursuing an identified objective seriously and comprehensively and in ways that are unrelated to the restriction of speech. Without such a demonstration, I would invalidate the restriction as violative of the First Amendment. By requiring this type of showing, courts can ensure that governmental regulation of the aesthetic environment remains within the constraints established by the First Amendment. First, we would have a reasonably reliable indication that it is not the content or communicative aspect of speech that the government finds unaesthetic. Second, when a restriction of speech is part of a comprehensive and seriously pursued program to promote an aesthetic objective, we have a more reliable indication of the government's own assessment of the substantiality of its objective. And finally, when an aesthetic objective is pursued on more than one front, we have a better basis upon which to ascertain its precise nature and thereby determine whether the means selected are the least restrictive ones for achieving the objective.[6]

This does not mean that a government must address all aesthetic problems at one time or that a government should hesitate to pursue aesthetic objectives. What it does mean, however, is that when such an objective is pursued, it may not be pursued solely at the expense of First Amendment freedoms, nor may it be pursued by arbitrarily discriminating against a form of speech that has the same aesthetic characteristics as other forms of speech that are also present in the community.

Accordingly, in order for Los Angeles to succeed in defending its total ban on the posting of signs, the City would have to demonstrate that it is pursuing its goal of eliminating visual clutter in a serious and comprehensive manner. Most importantly, the City would have to show that it is pursuing its goal through programs other than its ban on signs, that at least some of those programs address the visual clutter problem through means that do not entail the restriction of speech, and that the programs parallel the ban in their stringency, geographical scope, and aesthetic focus. In this case, however, as the Court of Appeals found, there is no indication that the City has addressed its visual clutter problem in any way other than by prohibiting the posting of signs—throughout the City and without regard to the density of their presence. Therefore, I would hold that the prohibition violates appellees' First Amendment rights.

In light of the extreme stringency of Los Angeles' ban—barring all signs from being posted—and its wide geographical scope—covering the entire City—it might be difficult for Los Angeles to make the type of showing I have suggested. A more limited approach to the visual clutter problem, however, might well pass constitutional muster. I have no doubt that signs posted on public property in certain areas—including, perhaps, parts of Los Angeles—could contribute to the type of eyesore that a city would genuinely have a substantial interest in eliminating. These areas might include parts of the City that are particularly pristine, reserved for certain uses, designated to reflect certain themes, or so blighted that broad gauged renovation is necessary. Presumably, in these types of areas, the City would also regulate the aesthetic environment in ways other than the banning of temporary signs. The City might zone such areas for a particular type of development or lack of development; it might actively create a particular type of environment; it might be especially vigilant in keeping the area clean; it might regulate the size and location of permanent signs; or it might reserve particular locations, such as kiosks, for the posting of temporary signs. Similarly, Los Angeles might be able to attack its visual clutter problem in more areas of the City by reducing the stringency of the ban, perhaps by regulating the density of temporary signs, and coupling that approach with additional measures designed to reduce other forms of visual clutter. There are a variety of ways that the aesthetic environment can be regulated, some restrictive of speech and others not, but it is only when aesthetic regulation is addressed in a comprehensive and focused manner that we can ensure that the goals pursued are substantial and that the manner in which they are pursued is no more restrictive of speech than is necessary.

In the absence of such a showing in this case, I believe that Los Angeles' total ban sweeps so broadly and trenches so completely on appellees' use of an important medium of political expression that it must be struck down as violative of the First Amendment. ▬

The Erogenous Zoning Case: City of Renton v. Playtime Theatres, Inc.

Few land uses evoke as much community resistance as "adult entertainment." Nude dancing, adults-only movies and the selling of pornographic books, magazines, videotapes and paraphernalia inexorably trigger local efforts to ban or limit these activities. For many people, the problem is the content of the message: they are morally offended by pornography. Others are not disturbed by the message per se, but are concerned about impacts on property values and crime rates.

The Constitution's first amendment proscribing government action "abridging the freedom of speech" not only protects political and ideological speech, but also extends to nonobscene pornographic expression such as nude dancing and many adult films. The qualification "nonobscene" is needed since obscenity is one of the few categories of speech unprotected by the first amendment and thus is subject to total government regulation (including criminalization). Obscenity is pornography, only more so.

Because the first amendment is understood to prevent communities from enacting total bans on pornography (as opposed to obscenity) used within their borders, local governments have been forced to develop alternative approaches. Two diverse zoning strategies have been used. Under one, the municipality concentrates adult entertainment within one geographical district. Under the other, the municipality disperses adult businesses by prohibiting their location within certain distances of one another.

The *Renton* case, involving an adult entertainment zoning ordinance that forced neither concentration nor dispersal, provided Justice Brennan with his second opportunity, again in dissent, to embellish his

Metromedia theory that land use regulations infringing on first amendment rights must be justified by evidence of a serious and comprehensive effort addressing land use problems.

In May 1980 the mayor of Renton, Wash., a community of 32,000 located just south of Seattle, proposed that the city explore zoning laws to regulate adult businesses, even though no such uses existed at the time. The city's planning and development committee investigated the approaches of other cities such as Seattle and held public hearings. Following the recommendation of the committee, the city council in 1981 adopted a zoning regulation prohibiting buildings used for adult movies, videos or related visual media from locating within 1,000 feet of residential zoning districts, single- or multifamily dwellings, churches or parks, or within one mile of any school. The one-mile school rule was subsequently reduced to 1,000 feet.

In 1982 a film exhibitor acquired two existing downtown Renton movie theaters in which to show adult features. Because the zoning ordinance operated to prohibit such use, the film exhibitor sued the city in federal district court on first and fourteenth amendment grounds. Although the federal district court ruled for Renton, the federal court of appeals reversed the decision and found that the ordinance violated the first amendment.

In its seven-to-two decision, the U.S. Supreme Court in 1986 sided with the city. Justice Rehnquist, joined by Chief Justice Burger and Justices White, Powell, Stevens and O'Connor, wrote the majority opinion. Justice Blackmun concurred in the result but not in the opinion. Justice Brennan, joined by Justice Marshall, dissented. The majority concluded that Renton's ordinance was "content-neutral," concerned not with the content of adult films but with their secondary effects on the surrounding community. Thus, the appropriate standard of first amendment review was significantly more deferential to the local government than if the ordinance had been directed at the content of the speech. As long as the law served a substantial governmental interest and did not unreasonably limit alternative avenues of communication, stated the majority, it was to be upheld. For the lower court of appeals, the city's failure to conduct its own studies about the impact of adult theaters in Renton, and its necessary reliance on studies and experiences of Seattle and other cities, made Renton's justifications "conclusory and speculative." Justice Rehnquist's majority disagreed, holding that nothing in the first amendment required Renton to produce its own independent study. That conclusion set the stage for Justice Brennan's application of his *Metromedia-Vincent* reasoning. For him, the first amendment interests implicated by billboard and poster bans were equally evident here. Reliance on studies documenting the so-called secondary effects of adult theaters in Seattle and elsewhere was insufficient to prove the same secondary effects in Renton.

JUSTICE BRENNAN

Renton's zoning ordinance selectively imposes limitations on the location of a movie theater based exclusively on the content of the films shown there.

The constitutionality of the ordinance is therefore not correctly analyzed under standards applied to content-neutral time, place and manner restrictions. But even assuming that the ordinance may fairly be characterized as content-neutral, it is plainly unconstitutional under the standards established by the decisions of this Court. Although the Court's analysis is limited to cases involving "businesses that purvey sexually explicit materials," and thus does not affect our holdings in cases involving state regulation of other kinds of speech, I dissent.

"[A] constitutionally permissible time, place or manner restriction may not be based on either the content or subject matter of speech." The Court asserts that the ordinance is "aimed not at the content of the films shown at 'adult motion picture theatres,' but rather at the secondary effects of such theatres on the surrounding community," and thus is simply a time, place, and manner regulation. This analysis is misguided.

The fact that adult movie theaters may cause harmful "secondary" land use effects may arguably give Renton a compelling reason to regulate such establishments; it does not mean, however, that such regulations are content-neutral. Because the ordinance imposes special restrictions on certain kinds of speech on the basis of content, I cannot simply accept, as the Court does, Renton's claim that the ordinance was not designed to suppress the content of adult movies. "[W]hen regulation is based on the content of speech, governmental action must be scrutinized more carefully to ensure that communication has not been prohibited 'merely because public officials disapprove the speaker's views.'" "[B]efore deferring to [Renton's] judgment, [we] must be convinced that the city is seriously and comprehensively addressing" secondary land use effects associated with adult movie theaters. In this case, both the language of the ordinance and its dubious legislative history belie the Court's conclusion "the city's pursuit of its zoning interests here was unrelated to the suppression of free expression."

The ordinance discriminates on its face against certain forms of speech based on content. Movie theaters specializing in "adult motion pictures" may not be located within 1,000 feet of any residential zone, single- or multiple-family dwelling, church, park, or school. Other motion picture theaters, and other forms of "adult entertainment," such as bars, massage parlors, and adult bookstores, are not subject to the same restrictions. This selective treatment strongly suggests that Renton was interested not in controlling the "secondary effects" associated with adult businesses, but in discriminating against adult theaters based on the content of the films they exhibit. The Court ignores this discriminatory treatment, declaring that Renton is free "to address the potential problems created by one particular kind of adult business," and to amend the ordinance in the future to include other adult enterprises. However, because of the First Amendment interests at stake here, this one-step-at-a-time analysis is wholly inappropriate.

This Court frequently has upheld underinclusive classifications on the sound theory that a legislature may deal with one part of a problem without addressing all of it. This presumption of statutory validity, however, has less force when a classification turns on the subject matter of expression. "[A]bove all else, the

First Amendment means that government has no power to restrict expression because of its message, its ideas, its subject matter, or its content."

In this case, the city has not justified treating adult movie theaters differently from other adult entertainment businesses. The ordinance's underinclusiveness is cogent evidence that it was aimed at the content of the films shown in adult movie theaters.

Shortly after this lawsuit commenced, the Renton City Council amended the ordinance, adding a provision explaining that its intention in adopting the ordinance had been "to promote the City of Renton's great interest in protecting and preserving the quality of its neighborhoods, commercial districts, and the quality of urban life through effective land use planning." The amended ordinance also lists certain conclusory "findings" concerning adult entertainment land uses that the Council purportedly relied upon in adopting the ordinance. The city points to these provisions as evidence that the ordinance was designed to control the secondary effects associated with adult movie theaters, rather than to suppress the content of the films they exhibit. However, the "legislative history" of the ordinance strongly suggests otherwise.

Prior to the amendment, there was no indication that the ordinance was designed to address any "secondary effects" a single adult theater might create. In addition to the suspiciously coincidental timing of the amendment, many of the City Council's "findings" do not relate to legitimate land use concerns. As the Court of Appeals observed, "[B]oth the magistrate and the district court recognized that many of the stated reasons for the ordinance were no more than expressions of dislike for the subject matter." That some residents may be offended by the content of the films shown at adult movie theaters cannot form the basis for state regulation of speech.

Some of the "findings" added by the City Council do relate to supposed "secondary effects" associated with adult movie theaters. However, the Court cannot, as it does, merely accept these *post-hoc* statements at face value. "[T]he presumption of validity that traditionally attends a local government's exercise of its zoning powers carries little, if any, weight where the zoning regulation trenches on rights of expression protected under the First Amendment." As the Court of Appeals concluded, "[T]he record presented by Renton to support its asserted interest in enacting the zoning ordinance is very thin."

The amended ordinance states that its "findings" summarize testimony received by the City Council at certain public hearings. While none of this testimony was ever recorded or preserved, a city official reported that residents had objected to having adult movie theaters located in their community. However, the official was unable to recount any testimony as to how adult movie theaters would specifically affect the schools, churches, parks, or residences "protected" by the ordinance. The City Council conducted no studies, and heard no expert testimony, on how the protected uses would be affected by the presence of an adult movie theater, and never considered whether residents' concerns could be met by "restrictions that are less intrusive on protected forms of expression." As a result, any "findings" regarding "secondary effects" caused by adult movie theaters, or the need to adopt specific locational requirements to combat such effects, were not "findings" at all, but purely speculative conclusions. Such "findings" were not such as are required to justify the burdens the ordinance imposed upon constitutionally protected expression.

The Court holds that Renton was entitled to rely on the experiences of cities like Detroit and Seattle, which had enacted special zoning regulations for adult entertainment businesses after studying the adverse effects caused by such establishments. However, even assuming that Renton was concerned with the same problems as Seattle and Detroit, it never actually reviewed any of the studies conducted by those cities. Renton had no basis for determining if any of the "findings" made by these cities were relevant to Renton's problems or needs. Moreover, since Renton ultimately adopted zoning regulations different from either Detroit or Seattle, these "studies" provide no basis for assessing the effectiveness of the particular restrictions adopted under the ordinance. Renton cannot merely rely on the general experiences of Seattle or Detroit, for it must "justify its ordinance in the context of Renton's problems—not Seattle's or Detroit's problems."

In sum, the circumstances here strongly suggest that the ordinance was designed to suppress expression, even that constitutionally protected, and thus was not to be analyzed as a content-neutral time, place, and manner restriction. The Court allows Renton to conceal its illicit motives, however, by reliance on the fact that other communities adopted similar restrictions. The Court's approach largely immunizes such measures from judicial scrutiny, since a municipality can readily find other municipal ordinances to rely upon, thus always retrospectively justifying special zoning regulations for adult theaters. Rather than speculate about Renton's motives for adopting such measures, our cases require that the ordinance, like any other content-based restriction on speech, is constitutional "only if the [city] can show that [it] is a precisely drawn means of serving a compelling [governmental] interest." Only this strict approach can insure that cities will not use their zoning powers as a pretext for suppressing constitutionally protected expression.

Applying this standard to the facts of this case, the ordinance is patently unconstitutional. Renton has not shown that locating adult movie theaters in proximity to its churches, schools, parks, and residences will necessarily result in undesirable "secondary effects," or that these problems could not be effectively addressed by less intrusive restrictions.

Even assuming that the ordinance should be treated like a content-neutral time, place, and manner restriction, I would still find it unconstitutional. "[R]estrictions of this kind are valid provided . . . that they are narrowly tailored to serve a significant governmental interest, and that they leave open ample alternative channels for communication of the information." In applying this standard, the Court "fails to subject the alleged interests of the [city] to the degree of scrutiny required to ensure that expressive activity protected by the First Amendment remains free of unnecessary limitations." The Court "evidently [and wrongly] assumes that the balance struck by [Renton] officials is deserving of deference so long as it does not appear to be tainted by content discrimination." Under a proper application of the relevant standards, the ordinance is clearly unconstitutional.

The Court finds that the ordinance was designed to further Renton's substantial interest in "preserv[ing] the quality of urban life." As explained above, the record here is simply insufficient to support this assertion. The city made no showing as to how uses "protected" by the ordinance would be affected by the presence of an adult movie theater. Thus, the Renton ordinance is clearly distinguishable from the Detroit zoning ordinance upheld in *Young v. American Mini Theatres, Inc.* The Detroit ordinance, which was designed to disperse adult theaters throughout the city, was supported by the testimony of urban planners and real estate experts regarding the adverse effects of locating several such businesses in the same neighborhood. Here, the Renton Council was aware only that some residents had complained about adult movie theaters, and that other localities had adopted special zoning restrictions for such establishments. These are not "facts" sufficient to justify the burdens the ordinance imposed upon constitutionally protected expression.

Finally, the ordinance is invalid because it does not provide for reasonable alternative avenues of communication. The District Court found that the ordinance left 520 acres in Renton available for adult theater sites, an area comprising about five percent of the city. However, the Court of Appeals found that because much of this land was already occupied, "[l]imiting adult theater uses to these areas is a substantial restriction on speech." Many "available" sites are also largely unsuited for use by movie theaters. Again, these facts serve to distinguish this case from *American Mini Theatres*, where there was no indication that the Detroit zoning ordinance seriously limited the locations available for adult businesses.

Despite the evidence in the record, the Court reasons that the fact "that respondents must fend for themselves in the real estate market, on an equal footing with other prospective purchasers and lessees, does not give rise to a First Amendment violation." However, respondents are not on equal footing with other prospective purchasers and lessees, but must conduct business under severe restrictions not imposed upon other establishments. The Court also argues that the First Amendment does not compel "the government to ensure that adult theatres, or any other kinds of speech-related businesses for that matter, will be able to obtain sites at bargain prices." However, respondents do not ask Renton to guarantee low-price sites for their businesses, but seek only a reasonable opportunity to operate adult theaters in the city. By denying them this opportunity, Renton can effectively ban a form of protected speech from its borders. The ordinance "greatly restrict[s] access to, lawful speech," and is plainly unconstitutional. ▬

9 PRIVATE PROPERTY, PRESERVATION AND PUBLIC POLICY

Site for a proposed nuclear power plant in San Diego.
From **San Diego Gas & Electric Co. v. City of San Diego.**
(Jerold S. Kayden)

"Nor shall private property be taken for public use, without just compensation." More than any other provision of the U.S. Constitution, the just compensation, or takings, clause of the fifth amendment has set the ground rules for the battle between private and public rights in the use of land. During the past decade, the U.S. Supreme Court, and especially Justice Brennan, has given renewed attention to interpreting the clause's four key concepts: private property, taking, public use and just compensation.

The most elusive of the four, private property, has puzzled philosophers and kings no less than lawyers and judges. Bentham, Locke, Marx and Henry VIII struggled to suggest answers no less than Maitland, Blackstone, Hohfeld and Brennan. American private property derives its meaning from an uncertain alliance of custom, common law, constitutions, state law and judicial decisions. The English statute of 1290, *Quia Emptores*, or the venerable Magna Carta of 1215 find modern analogues in both constitutions and legislative enactments. Overworked, the metaphor of a bundle of sticks or rights nonetheless provides a useful baseline. The most important sticks are the right of possession, the right to use land in noninjurious ways, the right to exclude others and the right to sell or transfer property.

The Constitution's just compensation clause protects these rights from government takings without compensation. Traditional land takings appropriate the entire bundle for such purposes as the construction of highways and civic centers and thus clearly call for payment of compensation. During this century, however, government has increasingly relied on regulation to achieve many of its public goals; in these cases, only part of the bundle has been taken from the owner, and the complex question is whether too much has been taken, thereby also requiring payment of compensation.

Justice Brennan has played a central role in interpreting the just compensation clause. His three opinions in this chapter are among the most influential and thoughtful judicial statements on its meaning and scope. His opinion for the Court in the 1978 *Penn Central* "Grand Central Terminal" case was a comprehensive review of Supreme Court takings law—and a clear-cut, if sheepish, reminder that no one really knows what the clause means. Pragmatically, his decision not only saved Grand Central Terminal, it also signaled the basic constitutionality of landmark regulation across the country.

His opinion in the 1981 *San Diego Gas & Electric Co.* "Nuclear Power Plant" case was the most pivotal land use dissent ever written. It set the stage for a Supreme Court decision, rendered seven years later in *First English Evangelical Lutheran Church v. County of Los Angeles*, which, for the first time, held explicitly that just compensation must be paid when a land use regulation goes too far and effects a taking. And his dissent in the 1987 *Nollan* "Beach House" case—in which the majority struck down a government requirement that coastal homeowners allow the public to walk on their beaches—stressed philosophical dimensions in the discourse on property rights by emphasizing how such rights are inextricably tied to public and private expectations. He was back to the basic question that has haunted major thinkers for centuries: who and what defines private property?

The Grand Central Terminal Case:
Penn Central Transportation Co. v.
New York City

The dominant planning orthodoxy of the 1950s and 1960s labeled old and poor city neighborhoods as urban blight, cancers to be eradicated and replaced by new highrise office and housing blocks, monumental public buildings, convention centers and interstate highways. Generously financed by federal dollars, local urban renewal programs sponsored the taking of private property on a massive scale, the clearance of so-called slums and the selling of land at greatly reduced cost to the private sector for projects of tomorrow. "New" equaled progress, "old" denoted stagnation.

In a supporting role, the International Style architectural movement, with its sleek steel and glass towers, furnished the visual cues. Cities such as New York modified their zoning ordinances to encourage skyscraper construction, allowing ever greater densities and heights. New commercial buildings sprouted in old downtowns, dwarfing their remaining neighbors.

As quickly as neighborhoods were razed, and new projects constructed, doubts surfaced about the entire evolutionary process. The contribution of old neighborhoods to city vitality and diversity was understood in their absence. Lower-scale older buildings suddenly seemed humane in comparison to their hulking and anonymous replacements. The uprooting of poor families by the federal bulldozer—critics bitterly referred to urban renewal as black removal—created enormous resentment, psychological scars and greater poverty. City residents felt the sterility of new development, the increased congestion, the loss of sunlight at street level and wondered what their city was about.

One of the lasting legacies of this period was the emergence of a strong historic preservation movement. With a growing consensus that landmark buildings and historic districts needed heightened legal protection against real estate market pressures, cities enacted, strengthened or applied with renewed vigor their landmark preservation laws. The major political and legal battles between private rights to property and public rights to landmarks were about to begin.

In 1965 the city of New York enacted its celebrated landmarks preservation law designed to protect the city's vast inventory of historic buildings and neighborhoods. The law established an 11-member Landmarks Preservation Commission to designate landmarks and historic districts having "a special character or special historical or aesthetic interest or value as part of the development, heritage or cultural characteristics of the city, state or nation." Individual landmarks had to be at least 30 years old to qualify. Once designated, the owner of a landmark would be required to apply to the commission for permission to alter the structure. The landmarks law in all cases guaranteed that owners would be entitled to a reasonable return on their buildings and that they would be able to sell or transfer from the land-mark site to nearby sites the unused buildable air rights authorized by appli-cable zoning.

Two years later, in 1967, the commission designated the city's Beaux Arts masterpiece, the 54-year-old Grand Central Terminal (1903–13, Reed and Stem; Warren and Wetmore) a landmark. Soon thereafter, the owner of the terminal building, the Penn Central Transportation Company, presented to the commission plans for, first a 55-story, then a 53-story office tower designed by noted architect Marcel Breuer to rise above the terminal proper. Following a review and public hearing, the commission rejected the proposals because of their inappropriate impact on the landmark qualities of Grand Central Terminal. The Penn Central Transportation Company sued the city, claiming that the landmarks law had effected a taking of its property and thus violated the just compensation clause. Although a state trial court decided in favor of Penn Central, the two state appellate courts ruled for the city. Penn Central turned to the U.S. Supreme Court for a remedy. At the time of the case, more than 400 individual landmarks and 31 historic dis-tricts had been designated by the commission.

The U.S. Supreme Court, in its six-to-three decision, upheld the general validity of New York's landmarks preservation law and its applica-tion to Penn Central's property. As Justice Brennan described the issue at the beginning of his opinion in the *Penn Central* case,

> The question presented is whether a city may, as part of a comprehensive pro-gram to preserve historic landmarks and historic districts, place restrictions on the development of individual historic landmarks—in addition to those imposed by applicable zoning ordinances—without effecting a "taking" requiring the pay-ment of "just compensation." Specifically, we must decide whether the applica-tion of New York City's Landmarks Preservation Law to the parcel of land occupied by Grand Central Terminal has "taken" its owners' property in viola-tion of the Fifth and Fourteenth Amendments.

Writing for the majority, Justice Brennan, joined by Justices Stewart, White, Marshall, Blackmun and Powell, presented the most detailed Supreme Court discussion yet on the applicability of the just com-pensation clause to land use regulations. He proffered no simplified formula for answering the question, When does a regulation cross the constitutional line and effect a taking? Instead, he directed judicial inquiries to the charac-ter of the government's action and the nature and extent of the interference with private property rights. He further focused the "interference with pri-vate property rights" inquiry to the owner's distinct investment-backed expectations. Finally, he provided a degree of judicial endorsement for the transfer of development rights, a land use technique in which owners trans-fer or sell unused air rights above their properties to other properties else-where in the city.

In dissent, Justice Rehnquist, joined by Chief Justice Burger and Justice Stevens, immediately indicated (somewhat tongue in cheek) his grounds for disagreement with Justice Brennan:

Of the over one million buildings and structures in the city of New York, [the relevant public agencies] have singled out 400 for designation as official landmarks. . . . The owner of a building might initially be pleased that his property has been chosen by a distinguished committee of architects, historians, and city planners for such a singular distinction. But he may well discover, as appellant Penn Central Transportation Co. did here, that the landmark designation imposes upon him a substantial cost, with little or no offsetting benefit except for the honor of the designation. The question in this case is whether the cost associated with the city of New York's desire to preserve a limited number of "landmarks" within its borders must be borne by all of its taxpayers or whether it can instead be imposed entirely on the owners of the individual properties.

For Justice Rehnquist, the ordinance unfairly asked landmark owners alone to bear a burden more properly borne by the public as a whole:

If the cost of preserving Grand Central Terminal were spread evenly across the entire population of the city of New York, the burden per person would be in cents per year—a minor cost [the city] would surely concede for the benefit accrued. Instead, however, [the city] would impose the entire cost of several million dollars per year on Penn Central. But it is precisely this sort of discrimination that the Fifth Amendment prohibits.

Justice Brennan saw the regulation differently and indeed partially relied on his constant comprehensiveness predicate in upholding its constitutionality.

JUSTICE BRENNAN   (selected notes included)

The question presented is whether a city may, as part of a comprehensive program to preserve historic landmarks and historic districts, place restrictions on the development of individual historic landmarks—in addition to those imposed by applicable zoning ordinances—without effecting a "taking" requiring the payment of "just compensation." Specifically, we must decide whether the application of New York City's Landmarks Preservation Law to the parcel of land occupied by Grand Central Terminal has "taken" its owners' property in violation of the Fifth and Fourteenth Amendments.

Over the past 50 years, all 50 States and over 500 municipalities have enacted laws to encourage or require the preservation of buildings and areas with historic or aesthetic importance.[1] These nationwide legislative efforts have been precipitated by two concerns. The first is recognition that, in recent years, large numbers of historic structures, landmarks, and areas have been destroyed without adequate consideration of either the values represented therein or the possibility of preserving the destroyed properties for use in economically productive ways. The second is a widely shared belief that structures with special historic, cultural, or architectural significance enhance the quality of life for all. Not only do these buildings and their workmanship represent the lessons of the past and embody precious features of our heritage, they serve as examples of quality for today. "[H]istoric conservation is but one aspect of the much larger problem, basically an environmental one, of enhancing—or perhaps developing for the first time—the quality of life for people."

New York City, responding to similar concerns and acting pursuant to a New York State enabling Act, adopted its Landmarks Preservation Law in 1965. The city acted from the conviction that "the standing of [New York City] as a world-wide tourist center and world capital of business, culture and government" would be threatened if legislation were not enacted to protect historic landmarks and neighborhoods from precipitate decisions to destroy or fundamentally alter their character. The city believed that comprehensive measures to safeguard desirable features of the existing urban fabric would benefit its citizens in a variety of ways: e.g., fostering "civic pride in the beauty and noble accomplishments of the past"; protecting and enhancing "the city's attractions to tourists and visitors"; "support[ing] and stimul[ating] business and industry"; "strengthen[ing] the economy of the city"; and promoting "the use of historic districts, landmarks, interior landmarks and scenic landmarks for the education, pleasure and welfare of the people of the city."

The New York City law is typical of many urban landmark laws in that its primary method of achieving its goals is not by acquisitions of historic properties, but rather by involving public entities in land-use decisions affecting these properties and providing services, standards, controls, and incentives that will encourage preservation by private owners and users. While the law does place special restrictions on landmark properties as a necessary feature to the attainment of its larger objectives, the major theme of the law is to ensure the owners of any such properties both a "reasonable return" on their investments and maximum latitude to use their parcels for purposes not inconsistent with the preservation goals.

The operation of the law can be briefly summarized. The primary responsibility for administering the law is vested in the Landmarks Preservation Commission (Commission), a broad based, 11-member agency assisted by a technical staff. The Commission first performs the function, critical to any landmark preservation effort, of identifying properties and areas that have "a special character or special historical or aesthetic interest or value as part of the development, heritage or cultural characteristics of the city, state or nation." If the Commission determines, after giving all interested parties an opportunity to be heard, that a building or area satisfies the ordinance's criteria, it will designate a building to be a "landmark," situated on a particular "landmark site," or will designate an area to be a "historic district." After the Commission makes a designation, New York City's Board of Estimate, after considering the relationship of the designated property "to the master plan, the zoning resolution, projected public improvements and any plans for the renewal of the area involved," may modify or disapprove the designation, and the owner may seek judicial review of the final designation decision. Thus far, 31 historic districts and over 400 individual landmarks have been finally designated, and the process is a continuing one.

Final designation as a landmark results in restrictions upon the property owner's options concerning use of the landmark site. First, the law imposes a duty upon the owner to keep the exterior features of the building "in good repair" to assure that the law's objectives not be defeated by the landmark's falling into a state of irremediable disrepair. Second, the Commission must approve in advance any proposal to alter the exterior architectural features of the landmark or to construct any exterior improvement on the landmark site, thus ensuring that decisions concerning construction on the landmark site are made with due consideration of both the public interest in the maintenance of the structure and the landowner's interest in use of the property.

In the event an owner wishes to alter a landmark site, three separate procedures are available through which administrative approval may be obtained. First, the owner may apply to the Commission for a "certificate of no effect on protected architectural features": that is, for an order approving the improvement or alteration on the ground that it will not change or affect any architectural feature of the landmark and will be in harmony therewith. Denial of the certificate is subject to judicial review.

Second, the owner may apply to the Commission for a certificate of "appropriateness." Such certificates will be granted if the Commission concludes—focusing upon aesthetic, historical, and architectural values—that the proposed construction on the landmark site would not unduly hinder the protection, enhancement, perpetuation, and use of the landmark. Again, denial of the certificate is subject to judicial review. Moreover, the owner who is denied either a certificate of no exterior effect or a certificate of appropriateness may submit an alternative or modified plan for approval. The final procedure—seeking a certificate of appropriateness on the ground of "insufficient return"—provides special mechanisms, which vary depending on whether or not the landmark enjoys a tax exemption, to ensure that designation does not cause economic hardship.

Although the designation of a landmark and landmark site restricts the owner's control over the parcel, designation also enhances the economic position of the landmark owner in one significant respect. Under New York City's zoning laws, owners of real property who have not developed their property to the full extent permitted by the applicable zoning laws are allowed to transfer development rights to contiguous parcels on the same city block. A 1968 ordinance gave the owners of landmark sites additional opportunities to transfer development rights to other parcels. Subject to a restriction that the floor area of the transferee lot may not be increased by more than 20% above its authorized level, the ordinance permitted transfers from a landmark parcel to property across the street or across a street intersection. In 1969, the law governing the conditions under which transfers from landmark parcels could occur was liberalized, apparently to ensure that the Landmarks Law would not unduly restrict the development options of the owners of Grand Central Terminal. The class of recipient lots was expanded to include lots "across a street and opposite to another lot or lots which except for the intervention of streets or street intersections f[or]m a series extending to the lot occupied by the landmark building[, provided that] all lots [are] in the same ownership." In addition, the 1969 amendment permits, in highly commercialized areas like midtown Manhattan, the transfer of all unused development rights to a single parcel.

This case involves the application of New York City's Landmarks Preservation Law to Grand Central Terminal (Terminal). The Terminal, which is owned by the Penn Central Transportation Co. and its affiliates (Penn Central), is one of New York City's most famous buildings. Opened in 1913, it is regarded not only as providing an ingenious engineering solution to the problems presented by urban railroad stations, but also as a magnificent example of the French beaux-arts style.

The Terminal is located in midtown Manhattan. Its south facade faces 42d Street and that street's intersection with Park Avenue. At street level, the Terminal is bounded on the west by Vanderbilt Avenue, on the east by the Commodore Hotel, and on the north by the Pan-American Building. Although a 20-story office tower, to have been located above the Terminal, was part of the original design, the planned tower was never constructed. The Terminal itself is an eight-story structure which Penn Central uses as a railroad station and in which it rents space not needed for railroad purposes to a variety of commercial interests. The Terminal is one of a number of properties owned by appellant Penn Central in this area of midtown Manhattan. The others include the Barclay, Biltmore, Commodore, Roosevelt, and Waldorf-Astoria Hotels, the Pan-American Building and other office buildings along Park Avenue, and the Yale Club. At least eight of these are eligible to be recipients of development rights afforded the Terminal by virtue of landmark designation.

On August 2, 1967, following a public hearing, the Commission designated the Terminal a "landmark" and designated the "city tax block" it occupies a "landmark site." The Board of Estimate confirmed this action on September 21, 1967. Although appellant Penn Central had opposed the designation before the commission, it did not seek judicial review of the final designation decision.

On January 22, 1968, appellant Penn Central, to increase its income, entered into a renewable 50-year lease and sublease agreement with appellant UGP Properties, Inc. (UGP), a wholly owned subsidiary of Union General Properties, Ltd., a United Kingdom corporation. Under the terms of the agreement, UGP was to construct a multistory office building above the Terminal. UGP promised to pay Penn Central $1 million annually during construction and at least $3 million annually thereafter. The rentals would be offset in part by a loss of some $700,000 to $1 million in net rentals presently received from concessionaires displaced by the new building.

Appellants UGP and Penn Central then applied to the Commission for permission to construct an office building atop the Terminal. Two separate plans, both designed by architect Marcel Breuer and both apparently satisfying the terms of the applicable zoning ordinance, were submitted to the Commission for approval. The first, Breuer I, provided for the construction of a 55-story office building, to be cantilevered above the existing facade and to rest on the roof of the Terminal. The second, Breuer II Revised, called for tearing down a portion of the Terminal that included the 42d Street facade, stripping off some of the remaining features of the Terminal's facade, and constructing a 53-story office building. The Commission denied a certificate of no exterior effect on September 20, 1968. Appellants then applied for a certificate of "appropriateness" as to both proposals. After four days of hearings at which over 80 witnesses testified, the Commission denied this application as to both proposals.

The Commission's reasons for rejecting certificates respecting Breuer II Revised are summarized in the following statement: "To protect a Landmark, one does not tear it down. To perpetuate its architectural features, one does not strip them off." Breuer I, which would have preserved the existing vertical facades of the present structure, received more sympathetic consideration. The Commission first focused on the effect that the proposed tower would have on one desirable feature created by the present structure and its surroundings: the dramatic view of the Terminal from Park Avenue South. Although appellants had contended that the Pan-American Building had already destroyed the silhouette of the south facade and that one additional tower could do no further damage and might even provide a better background for the facade, the Commission disagreed, stating that it found the majestic approach from the south to be still unique in the city and that a 55-story tower atop the Terminal would be far more detrimental to its south facade than the Pan-American Building 375 feet away. Moreover, the Commission found that from closer vantage points the Pan-American Building and the other towers were largely cut off from view, which would not be the case of the mass on top of the Terminal planned under Breuer I. In conclusion, the Commission stated:

> [We have] no fixed rule against making additions to designated buildings—it all depends on how they are done. . . . But to balance a 55-story office tower above a flamboyant Beaux-Arts facade seems nothing more than an aesthetic joke. Quite simply, the tower would overwhelm the Terminal by its sheer mass. The "addition" would be four times as high as the existing structure and would reduce the Landmark itself to the status of a curiosity.
>
> Landmarks cannot be divorced from their settings—particularly when the setting is a dramatic and integral part of the original concept. The Terminal, in its setting, is a great example of urban design. Such examples are not so plentiful in New York City that we can afford to lose any of the few we have. And we must preserve them in a meaningful way—with alterations and additions of such character, scale, materials and mass as will protect, enhance and perpetuate the original design rather than overwhelm it.

Appellants did not seek judicial review of the denial of either certificate. Because the Terminal site enjoyed a tax exemption, remained suitable for its present and future uses, and was not the subject of a contract of sale, there were no further administrative remedies available to appellants as to the Breuer I and Breuer II Revised plans. Further, appellants did not avail themselves of the opportunity to develop and submit other plans for the Commission's consideration and approval. Instead, appellants filed suit in New York Supreme Court, Trial Term, claiming, *inter alia*, that the application of the Landmarks Preservation Law had "taken" their property without just compensation in violation of the Fifth and Fourteenth Amendments and arbitrarily deprived them of their property without due process of law in violation of the Fourteenth Amendment. Appellants sought a declaratory judgment, injunctive relief barring the city from using the Landmarks Law to impede the construction of any structure that might otherwise lawfully be constructed on the Terminal site, and damages for the "temporary taking" that occurred between August 2, 1967, the designation date, and the date when the restrictions arising from the Landmarks Law would be lifted. The trial court granted the injunctive and declaratory relief, but severed the question of damages for a "temporary taking."

Appellees appealed, and the New York Supreme Court, Appellate Division, reversed. The Appellate Division held that the restrictions on the development of the Terminal site were necessary to promote the legitimate public purpose of protecting landmarks and therefore that appellants could sustain their constitutional claims only by proof that the regulation deprived them of all reasonable beneficial use of the property. The Appellate Division held that the evidence appellants introduced at trial—"Statements of Revenues and Costs," purporting to show a net operating loss for the years 1969 and 1971, which were prepared for the instant litigation—had not satisfied their burden. First, the court rejected the claim that these statements showed that the Terminal was operating at a loss, for in the court's view, appellants had improperly attributed some railroad operating expenses and taxes to their real estate operations, and compounded that error by failing to impute any rental value to the vast space in the Terminal devoted to railroad purposes. Further, the Appellate Division concluded that appellants had failed to establish either that they were unable to increase the Terminal's commercial income by transforming vacant or underutilized space to revenue-producing use, or that the unused development rights over the Terminal could not have been profitably transferred to one or more nearby sites. The Appellate Division concluded that all appellants had succeeded in showing was that they had been deprived of the property's most profitable use, and that this showing did not establish that appellants had been unconstitutionally deprived of their property.

The New York Court of Appeals affirmed. That court summarily rejected any claim that the Landmarks Law had "taken" property without "just compensation," indicating that there could be no "taking" since the law had not transferred control of the property to the city, but only restricted appellants' exploitation of it. In that circumstance, the Court of Appeals held that appellants' attack on the law could prevail only if the law deprived appellants of their property in violation of the Due Process Clause of the Fourteenth Amendment. Whether or not there was a denial of substantive due process turned on whether the restrictions deprived Penn Central of a "reasonable return" on the "privately created and privately managed ingredient" of the Terminal.[23] The Court of Appeals concluded that the Landmarks Law had not effected a denial of due process because: (1) the landmark regulation permitted the same use as had been made of the Terminal for more than half a century; (2) the appellants had failed to show that they could not earn a reasonable return on their investment in the Terminal itself; (3) even if the Terminal proper could never operate at a reasonable profit, some of the income from Penn Central's extensive real estate holdings in the area, which include hotels and office buildings, must realistically be imputed to the Terminal; and (4) the development rights above the Terminal, which had been made transferable to numerous sites in the vicinity of the Terminal, one or two of which were suitable for the construction of office buildings, were valuable to appellants and provided "significant, perhaps 'fair,' compensation for the loss of rights above the terminal itself."

Observing that its affirmance was "[o]n the present record," and that its analysis had not been fully developed by counsel at any level of the New York judicial system, the Court of Appeals directed that counsel "should be entitled to present . . . any additional submissions which, in the light of [the court's] opinion, may usefully develop further the factors discussed." Appellants chose not to avail themselves of this opportunity and filed a notice of appeal in this Court. We noted probable jurisdiction. We affirm.

The issues presented by appellants are (1) whether the restrictions imposed by New York City's law upon appellants' exploitation of the Terminal site effect a "taking" of appellants' property for a public use within the meaning of the Fifth Amendment, which of course is made applicable to the States through the Fourteenth Amendment, and, (2), if so, whether the transferable development rights afforded appellants constitute "just compensation" within the meaning of the Fifth Amendment. We need only address the question whether a "taking" has occurred.[25]

Before considering appellants' specific contentions, it will be useful to review the factors that have shaped the jurisprudence of the Fifth Amendment injunction "nor shall private property be taken for public use, without just compensation." The question of what constitutes a "taking" for purposes of the Fifth Amendment has proved to be a problem of considerable difficulty. While this Court has recognized that the "Fifth Amendment's guarantee . . . [is] designed to bar Government from forcing some people alone to bear public burdens which, in all fairness and justice, should be borne by the public as a whole," this Court, quite simply, has been unable to develop any "set formula" for determining when "justice and fairness" require that economic injuries caused by public action be compensated by the government, rather than remain disproportionately concentrated on a few persons. Indeed, we have frequently observed that whether a particular restriction will be rendered invalid by the government's failure to pay for any losses proximately caused by it depends largely "upon the particular circumstances [in that] case."

In engaging in these essentially ad hoc, factual inquiries, the Court's decisions have identified several factors that have particular significance. The economic impact of the regulation on the claimant and, particularly, the extent to which the regulation has interfered with distinct investment-backed expectations are, of course, relevant considerations. So, too, is the character of the governmental action. A "taking" may more readily be found when the interference with property can be characterized as a physical invasion by government, than when interference arises from some public program adjusting the benefits and burdens of economic life to promote the common good.

"Government hardly could go on if to some extent values incident to property could not be diminished without paying for every such change in the general law," and this Court has accordingly recognized, in a wide variety of contexts, that government may execute laws or programs that adversely affect recognized economic values. Exercises of the taxing power are one obvious example. A second are the decisions in which this Court has dismissed "taking" challenges on the ground that, while the challenged government action caused economic harm, it did not interfere with interests that were sufficiently bound up with the reasonable expectations of the claimant to constitute "property" for Fifth Amendment purposes.

More importantly for the present case, in instances in which a state tribunal reasonably concluded that "the health, safety, morals, or general welfare" would be promoted by prohibiting particular contemplated uses of land, this Court has upheld land-use regulations that destroyed or adversely affected recognized real property interests. Zoning laws are, of course, the classic example, which have been viewed as permissible governmental action even when prohibiting the most beneficial use of the property.

Zoning laws generally do not affect existing uses of real property, but "taking" challenges have also been held to be without merit in a wide variety of situations when the challenged governmental actions prohibited a beneficial use to which individual parcels had previously been devoted and thus caused substantial individualized harm. *Miller v. Schoene* is illustrative. In that case, a state entomologist, acting pursuant to a state statute, ordered the claimants to cut down a large number of ornamental red cedar trees because they produced cedar rust fatal to apple trees cultivated nearby. Although the statute provided for recovery of any expense incurred in removing the cedars, and permitted claimants to use the felled trees, it did not provide compensation for the value of the standing trees or for the resulting decrease in market value of the properties as a whole. A unanimous Court held that this latter omission did not render the statute invalid. The Court held that the State might properly make "a choice between the preservation of one class of property and that of the other" and since the apple industry was important in the State involved, concluded that the State had not exceeded "its constitutional powers by deciding upon the destruction of one class of property [without compensation] in order to save another which, in the judgment of the legislature, is of greater value to the public."

Again, *Hadacheck v. Sebastian* upheld a law prohibiting the claimant from continuing his otherwise lawful business of operating a brickyard in a particular physical community on the ground that the legislature had reasonably concluded that the presence of the brickyard was inconsistent with neighboring uses.

Goldblatt v. Hempstead is a recent example. There, a 1958 city safety ordinance banned any excavations below the water table and effectively prohibited the claimant from continuing a sand and gravel mining business that had been operated on the particular parcel since 1927. The Court upheld the ordinance against a "taking" challenge, although the ordinance prohibited the present and presumably most beneficial use of the property and had, like the regulations in *Miller* and *Hadacheck*, severely affected a particular owner. The Court assumed that the ordinance did not prevent the owner's reasonable use of the property since the owner made no showing of an adverse effect on the value of the land. Because the restriction served a substantial public purpose, the Court thus held no taking had occurred. It is, of course, implicit in *Goldblatt* that a use restriction on real property may constitute a "taking" if not reasonably necessary to the effectuation of a substantial public purpose, or perhaps if it has an unduly harsh impact upon the owner's use of the property.

Pennsylvania Coal Co. v. Mahon is the leading case for the proposition that a state statute that substantially furthers important public policies may so frustrate distinct investment-backed expectations as to amount to a "taking." There the claimant had sold the surface rights to particular parcels of property, but expressly reserved the right to remove the coal thereunder. A Pennsylvania statute, enacted after the transactions, forbade any mining of coal that caused the subsidence of any house, unless the house was the property of the owner of the underlying coal and was more than 150 feet from the improved property of another. Because the statute made it commercially impracticable to mine the coal, and thus had nearly the same effect as the complete destruction of rights claimant had reserved from the owners of the surface land, the Court held that the statute was invalid as effecting a "taking" without just compensation.

Finally, government actions that may be characterized as acquisitions of resources to permit or facilitate uniquely public functions have often been held to constitute "takings." *United States v. Causby* is illustrative. In holding that direct overflights above the claimant's land, that destroyed the present use of the land as a chicken farm, constituted a "taking," *Causby* emphasized that Government had not "merely destroyed property [but was] using a part of it for the flight of its planes."

In contending that the New York City law has "taken" their property in violation of the Fifth and Fourteenth Amendments, appellants make a series of arguments, which, while tailored to the facts of this case, essentially urge that any substantial restriction imposed pursuant to a landmark law must be accompanied by just compensation if it is to be constitutional. Before considering these, we emphasize what is not in dispute. Because this Court has recognized, in a number of settings, that States and cities may enact land-use restrictions or controls to enhance the quality of life by preserving the character and desirable aesthetic features of a city, appellants do not contest that New York City's objective of preserving structures and areas with special historic, architectural, or cultural significance is an entirely permissible governmental goal. They also do not dispute that the restrictions imposed on its parcel are appropriate means of securing the purposes of the New York City law. Finally, appellants do not challenge any of the specific factual premises of the decision below. They accept for present purposes both that the parcel of land occupied by Grand Central Terminal must, in its present state, be regarded as capable of earning a reasonable return,[26] and that the transferable development rights afforded appellants by virtue of the Terminal's designation as a landmark are valuable, even if not as valuable as the rights to construct above the Terminal. In appellants' view none of these factors derogate from their claim that New York City's law has effected a "taking."

They first observe that the airspace above the Terminal is a valuable property interest, citing *United States v. Causby*. They urge that the Landmarks Law has deprived them of any gainful use of their "air rights" above the Terminal and that, irrespective of the value of the remainder of their parcel, the city has "taken" their right to this superjacent airspace, thus entitling them to "just compensation" measured by the fair market value of these air rights.

Apart from our own disagreement with appellants' characterization of the effect of the New York City law, the submission that appellants may establish a "taking" simply by showing that they have been denied the ability to exploit a property interest that they heretofore had believed was available for development is quite simply untenable. Were this the rule, this Court would have erred not only in upholding laws restricting the development of air rights, but also in approving those prohibiting both the subjacent, and the lateral, development of particular parcels. "Taking" jurisprudence does not divide a single parcel into discrete segments and attempt to determine whether rights in a particular segment have been entirely abrogated. In deciding whether a particular governmental action has effected a taking, this Court focuses rather both on the character of the action and on the nature and extent of the interference with rights in the parcel as a whole—here, the city tax block designated as the "landmark site."

Secondly, appellants, focusing on the character and impact of the New York City law, argue that it effects a "taking" because its operation has significantly diminished the value of the Terminal site. Appellants concede that the decisions sustaining other land-use regulations, which, like the New York City law, are reasonably related to the promotion of the general welfare, uniformly reject the proposition that diminution in property value, standing alone, can establish a "taking," see *Euclid v. Ambler Realty Co.* (75% diminution in value caused by zoning law); *Hadacheck v. Sebastian* (87½% diminution in value); and that the "taking" issue in these contexts is resolved by focusing on the uses the regulations permit. Appellants, moreover, also do not dispute that a showing of diminution in property value would not establish a "taking" if the restriction had been imposed as a result of historic-district legislation, but appellants argue that New York City's regulation of individual landmarks is fundamentally different from zoning or from historic-district legislation because the controls imposed by New York City's law apply only to individuals who own selected properties.

Stated baldly, appellants' position appears to be that the only means of ensuring that selected owners are not singled out to endure financial hardship for no reason is to hold that any restriction imposed on individual landmarks pursuant to the New York City scheme is a "taking" requiring the payment of "just compensation." Agreement with this argument would, of course, invalidate not just New York City's law, but all comparable landmark legislation in the Nation. We find no merit in it.

It is true, as appellants emphasize, that both historic-district legislation and zoning laws regulate all properties within given physical communities whereas landmark laws apply only to selected parcels. But,
contrary to appellants' suggestions, landmark laws are not like discriminatory, or "reverse spot," zoning: that is, a land-use decision which arbitrarily
singles out a particular parcel for different, less favorable treatment than the
neighboring ones. In contrast to discriminatory zoning, which is the antithesis of land-use control as part of some comprehensive plan, the New York
City law embodies a comprehensive plan to preserve structures of historic or
aesthetic interest wherever they might be found in the city, and as noted,
over 400 landmarks and 31 historic districts have been designated pursuant
to this plan.

Equally without merit is the related argument that the decision
to designate a structure as a landmark "is inevitably arbitrary or at least subjective, because it is basically a matter of taste," thus unavoidably singling
out individual landowners for disparate and unfair treatment. The argument
has a particularly hollow ring in this case. For appellants not only did not
seek judicial review of either the designation or of the denials of the certificates of appropriateness and of no exterior effect, but do not even now suggest that the Commission's decisions concerning the Terminal were in any
sense arbitrary or unprincipled. But, in any event, a landmark owner has a
right to judicial review of any Commission decision, and quite simply, there
is no basis whatsoever for a conclusion that courts will have any greater difficulty identifying arbitrary or discriminatory action in the context of landmark regulation than in the context of classic zoning or indeed in any other
context.

Next, appellants observe that New York City's law differs from
zoning laws and historic-district ordinances in that the Landmarks Law does
not impose identical or similar restrictions on all structures located in particular physical communities. It follows, they argue, that New York City's law
is inherently incapable of producing the fair and equitable distribution of
benefits and burdens of governmental action which is characteristic of zoning laws and historic-district legislation and which they maintain is a constitutional requirement if "just compensation" is not to be afforded. It is, of
course, true that the Landmarks Law has a more severe impact on some landowners than on others, but that in itself does not mean that the law effects a
"taking." Legislation designed to promote the general welfare commonly
burdens some more than others. The owners of the brickyard in *Hadacheck*,
of the cedar trees in *Miller v. Schoene*, and of the gravel and sand mine in
Goldblatt v. Hempstead, were uniquely burdened by the legislation sustained in those cases.[30] Similarly, zoning laws often affect some property
owners more severely than others but have not been held to be invalid on
that account. For example, the property owner in Euclid who wished to use
its property for industrial purposes was affected far more severely by the ordinance than its neighbors who wished to use their land for residences.

In any event, appellants' repeated suggestions that they are solely
burdened and unbenefited is factually inaccurate. This contention overlooks

the fact that the New York City law applies to vast numbers of structures in the city in addition to the Terminal—all the structures contained in the 31 historic districts and over 400 individual landmarks, many of which are close to the Terminal. Unless we are to reject the judgment of the New York City Council that the preservation of landmarks benefits all New York citizens and all structures, both economically and by improving the quality of life in the city as a whole—which we are unwilling to do—we cannot conclude that the owners of the Terminal have in no sense been benefited by the Landmarks Law. Doubtless appellants believe they are more burdened than benefited by the law, but that must have been true, too, of the property owners in *Miller, Hadacheck, Euclid,* and *Goldblatt.*

Appellants' final broad-based attack would have us treat the law as an instance, like that in *United States v. Causby,* in which government, acting in an enterprise capacity, has appropriated part of their property for some strictly governmental purpose. Apart from the fact that *Causby* was a case of invasion of airspace that destroyed the use of the farm beneath and this New York City law has in nowise impaired the present use of the Terminal, the Landmarks Law neither exploits appellants' parcel for city purposes nor facilitates nor arises from any entrepreneurial operations of the city. The situation is not remotely like that in *Causby* where the airspace above the property was in the flight pattern for military aircraft. The Landmarks Law's effect is simply to prohibit appellants or anyone else from occupying portions of the airspace above the Terminal, while permitting appellants to use the remainder of the parcel in a gainful fashion. This is no more an appropriation of property by government for its own uses than is a zoning law prohibiting, for "aesthetic" reasons, two or more adult theaters within a specified area, or a safety regulation prohibiting excavations below a certain level.

Rejection of appellants' broad arguments is not, however, the end of our inquiry, for all we thus far have established is that the New York City law is not rendered invalid by its failure to provide "just compensation" whenever a landmark owner is restricted in the exploitation of property interests, such as air rights, to a greater extent than provided for under applicable zoning laws. We now must consider whether the interference with appellants' property is of such a magnitude that "there must be an exercise of eminent domain and compensation to sustain [it]." That inquiry may be narrowed to the question of the severity of the impact of the law on appellants' parcel, and its resolution in turn requires a careful assessment of the impact of the regulation on the Terminal site.

Unlike the governmental acts in *Goldblatt, Miller, Causby, Griggs,* and *Hadacheck,* the New York City law does not interfere in any way with the present uses of the Terminal. Its designation as a landmark not only permits but contemplates that appellants may continue to use the property precisely as it has been used for the past 65 years: as a railroad terminal containing office space and concessions. So the law does not interfere with what must be regarded as Penn Central's primary expectation concerning the use of the parcel. More importantly, on this record, we must regard the New York City law as permitting Penn Central not only to profit from the Terminal but also to obtain a "reasonable return" on its investment.

Appellants, moreover, exaggerate the effect of the law on their ability to make use of the air rights above the Terminal in two respects. First, it simply cannot be maintained, on this record, that appellants have been prohibited from occupying any portion of the airspace above the Terminal. While the Commission's actions in denying applications to construct an office building in excess of 50 stories above the Terminal may indicate that it will refuse to issue a certificate of appropriateness for any comparably sized structure, nothing the Commission has said or done suggests an intention to prohibit any construction above the Terminal. The Commission's report emphasized that whether any construction would be allowed depended upon whether the proposed addition "would harmonize in scale, material, and character with [the Terminal]." Since appellants have not sought approval for the construction of a smaller structure, we do not know that appellants will be denied any use of any portion of the airspace above the Terminal.

Second, to the extent appellants have been denied the right to build above the Terminal, it is not literally accurate to say that they have been denied all use of even those pre-existing air rights. Their ability to use these rights has not been abrogated; they are made transferable to at least eight parcels in the vicinity of the Terminal, one or two of which have been found suitable for the construction of new office buildings. Although appellants and others have argued that New York City's transferable development-rights program is far from ideal, the New York courts here supportably found that, at least in the case of the Terminal, the rights afforded are valuable. While these rights may well not have constituted "just compensation" if a "taking" had occurred, the rights nevertheless undoubtedly mitigate whatever financial burdens the law has imposed on appellants and, for that reason, are to be taken into account in considering the impact of regulation.

On this record, we conclude that the application of New York City's Landmarks Law has not effected a "taking" of appellants' property. The restrictions imposed are substantially related to the promotion of the general welfare and not only permit reasonable beneficial use of the landmark site but also afford appellants opportunities further to enhance not only the Terminal site proper but also other properties.[36] ▬

The Nuclear Power Plant Case: San Diego Gas & Electric Co. v. City of San Diego

If the *Penn Central* case demonstrated the difficulty of establishing a regulatory taking, the 1981 *San Diego Gas & Electric Co.* case indicated the rewards of a favorable outcome. Indeed, Justice Brennan wrote his most famous land use dissent, asserting that if a regulation effects a taking, then the property owner is entitled to just compensation. Later, in 1987, his theory and approach were adopted by a Court majority and became the constitutional law of the land.

The facts in *San Diego* are an interesting adjunct to the major constitutional debate it engendered. At a time when the few new nuclear power plants, fully constructed and ready to operate, are unable to obtain licenses to open, it is jarring to recall an earlier period when utilities were actively pursuing the development of nuclear power. In 1966 the San Diego Gas & Electric Company assembled a 412-acre parcel of land located several hundred feet from the California coast in northwest San Diego. The utility, which paid about $1.77 million for the land, considered the site a possible location for a nuclear power plant, to be constructed in the 1980s. When purchased, 214 of the 412 acres were completely vacant and unimproved. Of the 214, 116 acres were zoned industrial, the balance agricultural, defined as "undeveloped areas not yet ready for urbanization and awaiting development, those areas where agricultural usage may be reasonably expected to persist or areas designated as open space in the general plan." One year later, the city adopted its master plan designating the entire site for industrial use.

In 1973 the city took three actions giving rise to this case. First, it downzoned some of the industrial land to agricultural. Second, it classified the site as open space in a newly adopted plan. Third, the city council tagged the parcel for public acquisition, although funding from a proposed bond issue was never obtained.

Claiming that the three actions together denied beneficial use of its property and effected an unconstitutional regulatory taking without just compensation, the San Diego Gas & Electric Company sued the city in 1974 for $6.15 million and for other relief. Following a nonjury state court trial on the taking issue, the judge decided in favor of the utility. A jury then heard evidence on the question of money damages and awarded more than $3 million to the company. The intermediate appellate court affirmed the judgment of the trial court.

Shortly after San Diego petitioned the California Supreme Court for a hearing, that court issued an opinion in another case, *Agins v. City of Tiburon*, that severely affected the *San Diego* case. In *Agins*, the California Supreme Court announced the constitutional rule that landowners deprived of property through land use regulations were never entitled to money damages and instead must settle exclusively for invalidation of the offending regulation. The California *Agins* opinion was subsequently affirmed, but on another ground, by the U.S. Supreme Court.

Having precluded the award of monetary damages in the *Agins* case, the California Supreme Court sent the *San Diego* case back to the intermediate appellate court for reconsideration. That court then reversed the decision of the trial court awarding damages and added a few ambiguous comments about whether the trial judge had adequately resolved the basic question, Did the city's actions constitute a taking in the first place? The company next appealed that decision to the California Supreme Court, which declined to hear the case, and finally to the U.S. Supreme Court, which took it.

The question presented to the nine justices was whether just compensation must be awarded when regulations deprive landowners of reasonable use of their properties or whether invalidation is constitutionally sufficient. In a five-to-four decision, that question remained unanswered. The majority, in an opinion by Justice Blackmun, joined by Chief Justice Burger and Justices White, Rehnquist and Stevens, held that because the lower California courts never definitively and unambiguously ruled on the threshold question of whether the city's actions effected a taking, the Supreme Court lacked jurisdiction to address the compensation versus invalidation question. Dissenting, Justice Brennan, joined by Justices Stewart, Marshall and Powell, believed that the lower courts had ruled on the taking issue and that the subsequent question of remedy was properly presented for consideration. Thus, Justice Brennan addressed the major constitutional issues.

What gave his landmark dissent added force was a short opinion, concurring with the majority, by Justice Rehnquist. By stating that, were he satisfied that the issue had been properly presented, he "would have little difficulty in agreeing with much of what is said in the dissenting opinion of Justice Brennan," Justice Rehnquist helped convert the dissent's four votes to a *de facto* five—a majority.

JUSTICE BRENNAN (selected notes included)

The Just Compensation Clause of the Fifth Amendment, made applicable to the States through the Fourteenth Amendment, states in clear and unequivocal terms: "[N]or shall private property be taken for public use, without just compensation." The question presented on the merits in this case is whether a government entity must pay just compensation when a police power regulation has effected a "taking" of "private property" for "public use" within the meaning of that constitutional provision. Implicit in this question is the corollary issue whether a government entity's exercise of its regulatory police power can ever effect a "taking" within the meaning of the Just Compensation Clause.

As explained in Part II, the California courts have held that a city's exercise of its police power, however arbitrary or excessive, cannot as a matter of federal constitutional law constitute a "taking" within the meaning of the Fifth Amendment. This holding flatly contradicts clear precedents of this Court. For example, in last Term's *Agins v. City of Tiburon*, the Court noted that "[t]he application of a general zoning law to particular property effects a taking if the ordinance does not substantially advance legitimate state interests . . . or [if it] denies an owner economically viable use of his land. . . ." Applying that principle, the Court examined whether the Tiburon zoning ordinance effected a "taking" of the Agins' property, concluding that it did not have such an effect.

In *Penn Central Transp. Co. v. New York City*, the Court analyzed "whether the restrictions imposed by New York City's [Landmarks Preservation] law upon appellants' exploitation of the [Grand Central] Terminal site effect a 'taking' of appellants' property . . . within the meaning of the Fifth Amendment." Canvassing the appropriate inquiries necessary to determine whether a particular restriction effected a "taking," the Court identified the "economic impact of the regulation on the claimant" and the "character of the governmental action" as particularly relevant considerations. Although the Court ultimately concluded that application of New York's Landmarks Law did not effect a "taking" of the railroad property, it did so only after deciding that "[t]he restrictions imposed are substantially related to the promotion of the general welfare and not only permit reasonable beneficial use of the landmark site but also afford appellants opportunities further to enhance not only the Terminal site proper but also other properties."

The constitutionality of a local ordinance regulating dredging and pit excavating on a property was addressed in *Goldblatt v. Town of Hempstead*. After observing that an otherwise valid zoning ordinance that deprives the owner of the most beneficial use of his property would not be unconstitutional, the Court cautioned: "That is not to say, however, that governmental action in the form of regulation cannot be so onerous as to constitute a taking which constitutionally requires compensation." On many other occasions, the Court has recognized in passing the vitality of the general principle that a regulation can effect a Fifth Amendment "taking."

The principle applied in all these cases has its source in Justice Holmes' opinion for the Court in *Pennsylvania Coal Co. v. Mahon*, in which he stated: "The general rule at least is, that while property may be regulated to a certain extent, if regulation goes too far it will be recognized as a taking."[14] The determination of a "taking" is "a question of degree—and therefore cannot be disposed of by general propositions." While acknowledging that "[g]overnment hardly could go on if to some extent values incident to property could not be diminished without paying for every such change in the general law," the Court rejected the proposition that police power restrictions could never be recognized as a Fifth Amendment "taking."[16] Indeed, the Court concluded that the Pennsylvania statute forbidding the mining of coal that would cause the subsidence of any house effected a "taking."[17]

Not only does the holding of the California Court of Appeal contradict precedents of this Court, but it also fails to recognize the essential similarity of regulatory "takings" and other "takings." The typical "taking" occurs when a government entity formally condemns a landowner's property and obtains the fee simple pursuant to its sovereign power of eminent domain. However, a "taking" may also occur without a formal condemnation proceeding or transfer of fee simple. This Court long ago recognized that

> [i]t would be a very curious and unsatisfactory result, if in construing [the Just Compensation Clause] . . . it shall be held that if the government refrains from the absolute conversion of real property to the uses of the public it can destroy its value entirely, can inflict irreparable and permanent injury to any extent, can in effect, subject it to total destruction without making any compensation, because, in the narrowest sense of that word, it is not taken for the public use.

In service of this principle, the Court frequently has found "takings" outside the context of formal condemnation proceedings or transfer of fee simple, in cases where government action benefiting the public resulted in destruction of the use and enjoyment of private property.

Police power regulations such as zoning ordinances and other land-use restrictions can destroy the use and enjoyment of property in order to promote the public good just as effectively as formal condemnation or physical invasion of property. From the property owner's point of view, it may matter little whether his land is condemned or flooded, or whether it is restricted by regulation to use in its natural state, if the effect in both cases is to deprive him of all beneficial use of it. From the government's point of view, the benefits flowing to the public from preservation of open space through regulation may be equally great as from creating a wildlife refuge through formal condemnation or increasing electricity production through a dam project that floods private property. Appellees implicitly posit the distinction that the government intends to take property through condemnation or physical invasion whereas it does not through police power regulations. But "the Constitution measures a taking of property not by what a State says, or by what it intends, but by what it does." It is only logical, then, that government action other than acquisition of title, occupancy, or physical invasion can be a "taking," and therefore a *de facto* exercise of the power of eminent domain, where the effects completely deprive the owner of all or most of his interest in the property.

Having determined that property may be "taken for public use" by police power regulation within the meaning of the Just Compensation Clause of the Fifth Amendment, the question remains whether a government entity may constitutionally deny payment of just compensation to the property owner and limit his remedy to mere invalidation of the regulation instead. Appellant argues that it is entitled to the full fair market value of the property. Appellees argue that invalidation of the regulation is sufficient without payment of monetary compensation. In my view, once a court establishes that there was a regulatory "taking," the Constitution demands that the government entity pay just compensation for the period commencing on the date the regulation first effected the "taking," and ending on the date the government entity chooses to rescind or otherwise amend the regulation. This interpretation, I believe, is supported by the express words and purpose of the Just Compensation Clause, as well as by cases of this Court construing it.

The language of the Fifth Amendment prohibits the "tak[ing]" of private property for "public use" without payment of "just compensation." As soon as private property has been taken, whether through formal condemnation proceedings, occupancy, physical invasion, or regulation, the landowner has already suffered a constitutional violation, and " 'the self-executing character of the constitutional provision with respect to compensation,' " is triggered. This Court has consistently recognized that the just compensation requirement in the Fifth Amendment is not precatory: once there is a "taking," compensation must be awarded. In *Jacobs v. United States*, for example, a Government dam project creating intermittent overflows onto petitioners' property resulted in the "taking" of a servitude. Petitioners brought suit against the Government to recover just compensation for the partial "taking." Commenting on the nature of the landowners' action, the Court observed:

The suits were based on the right to recover just compensation for property taken by the United States for public use in the exercise of its power of eminent domain. That right was guaranteed by the Constitution. The fact that condemnation proceedings were not instituted and that the right was asserted in suits by the owners did not change the essential nature of the claim. The form of the remedy did not qualify the right. It rested upon the Fifth Amendment. Statutory recognition was not necessary. A promise to pay was not necessary. Such a promise was implied because of the duty to pay imposed by the Amendment.

Invalidation unaccompanied by payment of damages would hardly compensate the landowner for any economic loss suffered during the time his property was taken.[22]

Moreover, mere invalidation would fall far short of fulfilling the fundamental purpose of the Just Compensation Clause. That guarantee was designed to bar the government from forcing some individuals to bear burdens which, in all fairness, should be borne by the public as a whole. When one person is asked to assume more than a fair share of the public burden, the payment of just compensation operates to redistribute that economic cost from the individual to the public at large. Because police power regulations must be substantially related to the advancement of the public health, safety, morals, or general welfare, it is axiomatic that the public receives a benefit while the offending regulation is in effect. If the regulation denies the private property owner the use and enjoyment of his land and is found to effect a "taking," it is only fair that the public bear the cost of benefits received during the interim period between application of the regulation and the government entity's rescission of it. The payment of just compensation serves to place the landowner in the same position monetarily as he would have occupied if his property had not been taken.

The fact that a regulatory "taking" may be temporary, by virtue of the government's power to rescind or amend the regulation, does not make it any less of a constitutional "taking." Nothing in the Just Compensation Clause suggests that "takings" must be permanent and irrevocable. Nor does the temporary reversible quality of a regulatory "taking" render compensation for the time of the "taking" any less obligatory. This Court more than once has recognized that temporary reversible "takings" should be analyzed according to the same constitutional framework applied to permanent irreversible "takings." For example, in *United States v. Causby*, the United States had executed a lease to use an airport for a one-year term "ending June 30, 1942, with a provision for renewals until June 30, 1967, or six months after the end of the national emergency, whichever [was] the earlier." The Court held that the frequent low-level flights of Army and Navy airplanes over respondents' chicken farm, located near the airport, effected a "taking" of an easement on respondents' property. However, because the flights could be discontinued by the Government at any time, the Court remanded the case to the Court of Claims: "Since on this record it is not clear whether the easement taken is a permanent or a temporary one, it would be premature for us to consider whether the amount of the award made by the Court of Claims was proper." In other cases where the Government has taken only temporary use of a building, land, or equipment, the Court has not hesitated to determine the appropriate measure of just compensation.

But contrary to appellant's claim that San Diego must formally condemn its property and pay full fair market value, nothing in the Just Compensation Clause empowers a court to order a government entity to condemn the property and pay its full fair market value, where the "taking" already effected is temporary and reversible and the government wants to halt the "taking." Just as the government may cancel condemnation proceedings before passage of title, or abandon property it has temporarily occupied or invaded, it must have the same power to rescind a regulatory "taking." As the Court has noted: "[A]n abandonment does not prejudice the property owner. It merely results in an alteration of the property interest taken—from full ownership to one of temporary use and occupation. . . . In such cases compensation would be measured by the principles normally governing the taking of a right to use property temporarily."

The constitutional rule I propose requires that, once a court finds that a police power regulation has effected a "taking," the government entity must pay just compensation for the period commencing on the date the regulation first effected the "taking," and ending on the date the government entity chooses to rescind or otherwise amend the regulation. Ordinary principles determining the proper measure of just compensation, regularly applied in cases of permanent and temporary "takings" involving formal condemnation proceedings, occupations, and physical invasions, should provide guidance to the courts in the award of compensation for a regulatory "taking." As a starting point, the value of the property taken may be ascertained as of the date of the "taking." The government must inform the court of its intentions vis-à-vis the regulation with sufficient clarity to guarantee a correct assessment of the just compensation award. Should the government decide immediately to revoke or otherwise amend the regulation, it would be liable for payment of compensation only for the interim during which the regulation effected a "taking." Rules of valuation already developed for temporary "takings" may be particularly useful to the courts in their quest for assessing the proper measure of monetary relief in cases of revocation or amendment, although additional rules may need to be developed. Alternatively the government may choose formally to condemn the property, or otherwise to continue the offending regulation: in either case the action must be sustained by proper measures of just compensation.

It should be noted that the Constitution does not embody any specific procedure or form of remedy that the States must adopt: "The Fifth Amendment expresses a principle of fairness and not a technical rule of procedure enshrining old or new niceties regarding 'causes of action'—when they are born, whether they proliferate, and when they die." The States should be free to experiment in the implementation of this rule, provided that their chosen procedures and remedies comport with the fundamental constitutional command. The only constitutional requirement is that the landowner must be able meaningfully to challenge a regulation that allegedly effects a "taking," and recover just compensation if it does so. He may not be forced to resort to piecemeal litigation or otherwise unfair procedures in order to receive his due.

In *Agins v. City of Tiburon*, the California Supreme Court was "persuaded by various policy considerations to the view that inverse condemnation is an inappropriate and undesirable remedy in cases in which unconstitutional regulation is alleged." In particular, the court cited "the need for preserving a degree of freedom in land-use planning function, and the inhibiting financial force which inheres in the inverse condemnation remedy," in reaching its conclusion. But the applicability of express constitutional guarantees is not a matter to be determined on the basis of policy judgments made by the legislative, executive, or judicial branches.[26] Nor can the vindication of those rights depend on the expense in doing so. ▬

The Beach House Case:
Nollan v. California Coastal Commission

Initial public awareness of Supreme Court decisions frequently depends on the vagaries of the day's news. When major world or national events occur, news coverage of Court opinions is relegated to the middle of newspapers and network programs. When the *Nollan* case was announced on the final day of the Supreme Court's 1986 term on June 26, 1987, another story dominated the press and airwaves: Justice Powell's resignation. Where, just one week earlier, the Court's *First English* case (approving Justice Brennan's *San Diego Gas & Electric Co.* constitutional rule that governments must pay compensation when their regulations effect takings of private property) was the lead story in the *New York Times*, the *Nollan* case received scant early notice. Yet, to many close followers of land use constitutional jurisprudence, *Nollan* is more significant than *First English*.

The *Nollan* case featured a confrontation between homeowners and the California Coastal Commission, a controversial state agency regulating all development along the California coastline. California has earned a reputation as the preeminent state battleground between development and environmental interests. Builders and real estate lawyers have railed for years about the antiproperty, proregulation climate dominating the state legislature, local city councils and the state judiciary. At the same time, environmentalists have complained about the loss of open space and scenic landscapes to rapacious, unbridled development. It is hardly a coincidence that, of the six major U.S. Supreme Court cases considering just compensation issues in the 1980s (*Agins*, *San Diego Gas & Electric Co.*, *Williamson*, *MacDonald*, *First English* and *Nollan*), five percolated up from the California courts.

For many developers in California, the Coastal Commission is the embodiment of everything wrong with government regulation: it is viewed as arbitrary, arrogant and at heart ideologically disrespectful of private property rights. Indeed, some developers only half-facetiously refer to the easternmost boundary of the commission's jurisdiction as coterminous with that of the Soviet Union. Thus, when the *Nollan* case first arose, the Pacific Legal Foundation, one of the most active, conservative private property rights advocacy organizations in the country, almost immediately leaped into the fray to represent the Nollans.

      Typical homeowners, Pat and Marilyn Nollan leased a small oceanside lot north of Los Angeles in Ventura County that contained a 504-square-foot bungalow. Although the Nollans rented out the bungalow to

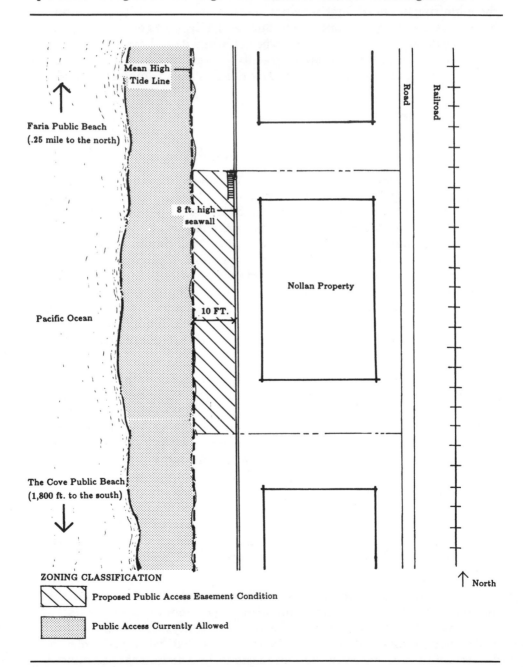

summer tenants, it had deteriorated to a point of uninhabitability. The Nollans had an option to buy the lot, contingent on their agreement to replace the existing bungalow with a new house. Desiring to purchase the property, demolish the bungalow and replace it with a three-bedroom house, they applied to the California Coastal Commission, as required by law, for a special permit to develop the property. The commission granted the permit but only on the condition that the Nollans allow the public the right to walk up and down the beachfront part of their property.

Under California law, the public already owned the beach from the ocean east to the mean high tide line. Thus, when the tide was out, people could walk on dry sand in front of the Nollans' property without trespassing on their land. However, at high tide, only swimmers could proceed north and south in front of their house. The commission's special permit condition would alleviate this problem by making public that portion of the Nollans' beach between the mean high tide line and the seawall some 10 feet to the east. The Nollans' proposed house would be located east of the seawall on land eight feet higher than the beach.

The commission made certain factual findings to support its special permit public access condition. It found, for example, that the Nollans' proposed house would add to "a 'wall' of residential structures" preventing people "psychologically . . . from realizing a stretch of coastline exists nearby that they have every right to visit." The house would also contribute to increased private use of the coast, which, together with other existing and proposed coastal development, would "burden the public's ability to traverse to and along the shorefront." Of 60 other coastline developments, the commission had imposed the same condition on 43, with 14 others approved without conditions at a time when the commission lacked administrative guidelines to impose them.

The Nollans sued the commission in state trial court, alleging that the condition constituted a taking of their property without payment of just compensation in violation of the just compensation clause. The trial court ruled in favor of the Nollans, although not on federal constitutional grounds. While the commission appealed, the Nollans built their three-bedroom house and purchased the property outright. The court of appeal reversed the trial court and found for the commission on the basis that, even if the Nollans' new house alone had not created the need for additional public beach access, there was nevertheless a sufficient relationship between burdens on access generated by the new house and the special permit condition.

Completing the seesaw history, the U.S. Supreme Court reversed the appellate court and ruled for the Nollans in a closely divided five-to-four decision. Justice Antonin Scalia, joined by Chief Justice Rehnquist and Justices White, Powell and O'Connor, wrote the majority, while Justice Brennan, joined by Justice Marshall, wrote the major dissent. Justice Blackmun contributed his own dissenting opinion and also joined Justice Stevens's dissent.

For Justice Scalia, the case was rather simple. Clearly, he reasoned, the commission could not *ex cathedra* require the Nollans to allow people onto their property. That would take from the Nollans, without compensation, one of the most essential sticks in the bundle of rights known as private property—the right to exclude others. Thus, observed Justice Scalia, the question became whether imposing the public access requirement as a condition of their proposed new development fundamentally changed the analysis. Citing Court precedents, the majority adopted the test that the condition must "substantially advance" legitimate state interests to pass constitutional muster.

Applying this test, the Court found the commission's condition wanting. The commission supported its action on the basis of protecting the public's ability to see the beach, overcoming psychological barriers created by coastal development and preventing beach congestion. Assuming the legitimacy of these purposes, Justice Scalia argued, the commission could have totally banned the new house by maintaining it substantially harmed the public interests the commission was protecting, such as seeing the beach. In the alternative, the commission could have permitted construction of the new house, as long as the Nollans mitigated its harmful impact. Justice Scalia suggested that limiting the height or width of the new house, banning fences or even requiring the Nollans to "provide a viewing spot on their property for passersby with whose sighting of the ocean their new house would interfere" would be constitutionally acceptable conditions related to the asserted public interests.

What made the condition here unacceptable was its lack of connection to the commission's articulated purposes. Wrote Justice Scalia,

> It is quite impossible to understand how a requirement that people already on the public beaches be able to walk across the Nollans' property reduces any obstacles to viewing the beach created by the new house. It is also impossible to understand how it lowers any "psychological barrier" to using the public beaches, or how it helps to remedy any additional congestion on them caused by construction of the Nollans' new house.

In short, Justice Scalia generalized, "unless the permit condition serves the same governmental purpose as the development ban, the building restriction is not a valid regulation of land use but 'an out-and-out plan of extortion' . . . ."

None of the dissenters disagreed with the majority's general notion that requirements imposed on the Nollans must bear some relationship to a harm or need created by their proposed new house. However, all four believed the majority to be overly rigid in its application to the facts of this case. Justice Blackmun opined that "[t]he land-use problems this country faces require creative solutions. These are not advanced by an 'eye for an eye' mentality." For him, the condition permitting public passage sufficiently addressed the diminution in visual and physical access to the beach caused by the new house.

Justice Stevens's dissent came as a surprise: it attacked Justice

Brennan's dissenting position in a wholly different case (*San Diego Gas & Electric Co.*) while implicitly agreeing with his dissent in this case. For several years Justice Stevens had opposed the idea, first advanced by Justice Brennan in his *San Diego* dissent and subsequently adopted by a Court majority in the *First English* case, that regulatory takings give rise to claims for just compensation. For Justice Stevens, invalidation of the offending regulation is all that is constitutionally required. He did not always think this way: he was one of the three dissenters (with Justice Rehnquist and Chief Justice Burger) from Justice Brennan's *Penn Central* majority upholding New York City's landmarks law against a takings challenge. Justice Stevens and his codissenters there concluded that the law effected a taking. Thus, they asked whether proceeds from the transfer to adjacent properties of development rights above Grand Central Terminal would constitute adequate just compensation.

In *Nollan*, Justice Stevens argued, the consequence of Justice Brennan's *San Diego Gas & Electric Co.* dissent had come home to roost:

> I write today to identify the severe tension between that dramatic development [the adoption one week earlier by six justices in the *First English* case of Justice Brennan's *San Diego* rule] and the view expressed by Justice Brennan's dissent in this case that the public interest is served by encouraging state agencies to exercise considerable flexibility in response to private desires for development in a way that threatens the preservation of public resources. . . . I like the hat that Justice Brennan has donned today better than the one he wore in *San Diego*, and I am persuaded that he has the better of the legal arguments here. Even if his position prevailed in this case, however, it would be of little solace to land-use planners who would still be left guessing about how the Court will react to the next case, and the one after that. As this case demonstrates, the rule of liability created by the Court in *First English* is a short-sighted one.

Justice Brennan's *Nollan* dissent speaks for itself.

JUSTICE BRENNAN (selected notes included)

Appellants in this case sought to construct a new dwelling on their beach lot that would both diminish visual access to the beach and move private development closer to the public tidelands. The Commission reasonably concluded that such "buildout," both individually and cumulatively, threatens public access to the shore. It sought to offset this encroachment by obtaining assurance that the public may walk along the shoreline in order to gain access to the ocean. The Court finds this an illegitimate exercise of the police power, because it maintains that there is no reasonable relationship between the effect of the development and the condition imposed.

The first problem with this conclusion is that the Court imposes a standard of precision for the exercise of a State's police power that has been discredited for the better part of this century. Furthermore, even under the Court's cramped standard, the permit condition imposed in this case directly responds to the specific type of burden on access created by appellants' development. Finally, a review of those factors deemed most significant in takings analysis makes clear that the Commission's action implicates none of the concerns underlying the Takings Clause. The Court has thus struck down the Commission's reasonable effort to respond to intensified development along the California coast, on behalf of landowners who can make no claim that their reasonable expectations have been disrupted. The Court has, in short, given appellants a windfall at the expense of the public.

The Court's conclusion that the permit condition imposed on appellants is unreasonable cannot withstand analysis. First, the Court demands a degree of exactitude that is inconsistent with our standard for reviewing the rationality of a state's exercise of its police power for the welfare of its citizens. Second, even if the nature of the public access condition imposed must be identical to the precise burden on access created by appellants, this requirement is plainly satisfied.

There can be no dispute that the police power of the States encompasses the authority to impose conditions on private development. It is also by now commonplace that this Court's review of the rationality of a State's exercise of its police power demands only that the State "could rationally have decided" that the measure adopted might achieve the State's objective.[1] In this case, California has employed its police power in order to condition development upon preservation of public access to the ocean and tidelands. The Coastal Commission, if it had so chosen, could have denied the Nollans' request for a development permit, since the property would have remained economically viable without the requested new development.[2] Instead, the State sought to accommodate the Nollans' desire for new development, on the condition that the development not diminish the overall amount of public access to the coastline. Appellants' proposed development would reduce public access by restricting visual access to the beach, by contributing to an increased need for community facilities, and by moving private development closer to public beach property. The Commission sought to offset this diminution in access, and thereby preserve the overall balance of access, by requesting a deed restriction that would ensure "lateral" access: the right of the public to pass and repass along the dry sand parallel to the shoreline in order to reach the tidelands and the ocean. In the expert opinion of the Coastal Commission, development conditioned on such a restriction would fairly attend to both public and private interests.

The Court finds fault with this measure because it regards the condition as insufficiently tailored to address the precise type of reduction in access produced by the new development. The Nollans' development blocks visual access, the Court tells us, while the Commission seeks to preserve lateral access along the coastline. Thus, it concludes, the State acted irrationally. Such a narrow conception of rationality, however, has long since been discredited as a judicial arrogation of legislative authority. "To make scientific precision a criterion of constitutional power would be to subject the State to an intolerable supervision hostile to the basic principles of our Government." As this Court long ago declared with regard to various forms of restriction on the use of property:

Each interferes in the same way, if not to the same extent, with the owner's general right of dominion over his property. All rest for their justification upon the same reasons which have arisen in recent times as a result of the great increase and concentration of population in urban communities and the vast changes in the extent and complexity of the problems of modern city life. State legislatures and city councils, who deal with the situation from a practical standpoint, are better qualified than the courts to determine the necessity, character, and degree of regulation which these new and perplexing conditions require; and their conclusions should not be disturbed by the courts unless clearly arbitrary and unreasonable.

The Commission is charged by both the state constitution and legislature to preserve overall public access to the California coastline. Furthermore, by virtue of its participation in the Coastal Zone Management Act program, the State must "exercise effectively [its] responsibilities in the coastal zone through the development and implementation of management programs to achieve wise use of the land and water resources of the coastal zone," so as to provide for, *inter alia*, "public access to the coas[t] for recreation purposes." The Commission has sought to discharge its responsibilities in a flexible manner. It has sought to balance private and public interests and to accept tradeoffs: to permit development that reduces access in some ways as long as other means of access are enhanced. In this case, it has determined that the Nollans' burden on access would be offset by a deed restriction that formalizes the public's right to pass along the shore. In its informed judgment, such a tradeoff would preserve the net amount of public access to the coastline. The Court's insistence on a precise fit between the forms of burden and condition on each individual parcel along the California coast would penalize the Commission for its flexibility, hampering the ability to fulfill its public trust mandate.

The Court's demand for this precise fit is based on the assumption that private landowners in this case possess a reasonable expectation regarding the use of their land that the public has attempted to disrupt. In fact, the situation is precisely the reverse: it is private landowners who are the interlopers. The public's expectation of access considerably antedates any private development on the coast. Article X, Section 4 of the California Constitution, adopted in 1879, declares:

> No individual, partnership, or corporation, claiming or possessing the frontage or tidal lands of a harbor, bay, inlet, estuary, or other navigable water in this State, shall be permitted to exclude the right of way to any such water whenever it is required for any public purpose, nor to destroy or obstruct the free navigation of such water; and the Legislature shall enact such laws as will give the most liberal construction to this provision, so that access to the navigable waters of this State shall always be attainable for the people thereof.

It is therefore private landowners who threaten the disruption of settled *public* expectations. Where a private landowner has had a reasonable expectation that his or her property will be used for exclusively private purposes, the disruption of this expectation dictates that the government pay if it wishes the property to be used for a public purpose. In this case, however, the State has sought to protect public expectations of access from disruption by private land use. The State's exercise of its police power for this purpose deserves no less deference than any other measure designed to further the welfare of state citizens.

Congress expressly stated in passing the CZMA that "[i]n light of competing demands and the urgent need to protect and to give high priority to natural systems in the coastal zone, present state and local institutional arrangements for planning and regulating land and water uses in such areas are inadequate." It is thus puzzling that the Court characterizes as a "non-land-use justification," the exercise of the police power to " 'provide continuous public access along Faria Beach as the lots undergo development or redevelopment.' " The Commission's determination that certain types of development jeopardize public access to the ocean, and that such development should be conditioned on preservation of access, is the essence of responsible land use planning. The Court's use of an unreasonably demanding standard for determining the rationality of state regulation in this area thus could hamper innovative efforts to preserve an increasingly fragile national resource.

Even if we accept the Court's unusual demand for a precise match between the condition imposed and the specific type of burden on access created by the appellants, the State's action easily satisfies this requirement. First, the lateral access condition serves to dissipate the impression that the beach that lies behind the wall of homes along the shore is for private use only. It requires no exceptional imaginative powers to find plausible the Commission's point that the average person passing along the road in front of a phalanx of imposing permanent residences, including the appellants' new home, is likely to conclude that this particular portion of the shore is not open to the public. If, however, that person can see that numerous people are passing and repassing along the dry sand, this conveys the message that the beach is in fact open for use by the public. Furthermore, those persons who go down to the public beach a quarter-mile away will be able to look down the coastline and see that persons have continuous access to the tidelands, and will observe signs that proclaim the public's right to access over the dry sand. The burden produced by the diminution in visual access—the impression that the beach is not open to the public—is thus directly alleviated by the provision for public access over the dry sand. The Court therefore has an unrealistically limited conception of what measures could reasonably be chosen to mitigate the burden produced by a diminution of visual access.

The second flaw in the Court's analysis of the fit between burden and exaction is more fundamental. The Court assumes that the only burden with which the Coastal Commission was concerned was blockage of visual access to the beach. This is incorrect. The Commission specifically stated in its report in support of the permit condition that "[t]he Commission finds that the applicants' proposed development would present an increase in view blockage, *an increase in private use of the shorefront*, and that this impact would burden the public's ability to traverse to and along the shorefront." It declared that the possibility that "the public may get the impression that the beachfront is no longer available for public use" would be "due to *the encroaching nature of private use immediately adjacent to the public use, as well as* the visual 'block' of increased residential build-out impacting the visual quality of the beachfront."

The record prepared by the Commission is replete with references to the threat to public access along the coastline resulting from the seaward encroachment of private development along a beach whose mean high tide line is constantly shifting. As the Commission observed in its report, "The Faria Beach shoreline fluctuates during the year depending on the seasons and accompanying storms, and the public is not always able to traverse the shoreline below the mean high tide line." As a result, the boundary between publicly owned tidelands and privately owned beach is not a stable one, and "[t]he existing seawall is located very near to the mean high water line." When the beach is at its largest, the seawall is about 10 feet from the mean high tide mark; "[d]uring the period of the year when the beach suffers erosion, the mean high water line appears to be located either on or beyond the existing seawall." Expansion of private development on appellants' lot toward the seawall would thus "increase private use immediately adjacent to public tidelands, which has the potential of causing adverse impacts on the public's ability to traverse the shoreline." As the Commission explained:

> The placement of more private use adjacent to public tidelands has the potential of creating conflicts between the applicants and the public. The results of new private use encroachment into boundary/buffer areas between private and public property can create situations in which landowners intimidate the public and seek to prevent them from using public tidelands because of disputes between the two parties over where the exact boundary between private and public ownership is located. If the applicants' project would result in further seaward encroachment of private use into an area of clouded title, new private use in the subject encroachment area could result in use conflict between private and public entities on the subject shorefront.

The deed restriction on which permit approval was conditioned would directly address this threat to the public's access to the tidelands. It would provide a formal declaration of the public's right of access, thereby ensuring that the shifting character of the tidelands, and the presence of private development immediately adjacent to it, would not jeopardize enjoyment of that right. The imposition of the permit condition was therefore directly related to the fact that appellants' development would be "located along a unique stretch of coast where lateral access is inadequate due to the construction of private residential structures and shoreline protective devices along a fluctuating shoreline." The deed restriction was crafted to deal with the particular character of the beach along which appellants sought to build, and with the specific problems created by expansion of development toward the public tidelands. In imposing the restriction, the State sought to ensure that such development would not disrupt the historical expectation of the public regarding access to the sea.

The Court is therefore simply wrong that there is no reasonable relationship between the permit condition and the specific type of burden on public access created by the appellants' proposed development. Even were the Court desirous of assuming the added responsibility of closely monitoring the regulation of development along the California coast, this record reveals rational public action by any conceivable standard.

The fact that the Commission's action is a legitimate exercise of the police power does not, of course, insulate it from a takings challenge, for when "regulation goes too far it will be recognized as a taking." Conventional takings analysis underscores the implausibility of the Court's holding, for it demonstrates that this exercise of California's police power implicates none of the concerns that underlie our takings jurisprudence.

In reviewing a Takings Clause claim, we have regarded as particularly significant the nature of the governmental action and the economic impact of regulation, especially the extent to which regulation interferes with investment-backed expectations. The character of the government action in this case is the imposition of a condition on permit approval, which allows the public to continue to have access to the coast. The physical intrusion permitted by the deed restriction is minimal. The public is permitted the right to pass and re-pass along the coast in an area from the seawall to the mean high tide mark. This area is at its widest 10 feet, which means that *even without the permit condition*, the public's right of access permits it to pass on average within a few feet of the seawall. Passage closer to the 8-foot high rocky seawall will make the appellants even less visible to the public than passage along the high tide area farther out on the beach. The intrusiveness of such passage is even less than the intrusion resulting from the required dedication of a sidewalk in front of private residences, exactions which are commonplace conditions on approval of development. Furthermore, the high tide line shifts throughout the year, moving up to and beyond the seawall, so that public passage for a portion of the year would either be impossible or would not occur on appellant's property. Finally, although the Commission had the authority to provide for either passive or active recreational use of the property, it chose the least intrusive alternative: a mere right to pass and repass. As this Court made clear in *PruneYard Shopping Center v. Robins*, physical access to private property in itself creates no takings problem if it does not "unreasonably impair the value or use of [the] property." Appellants can make no tenable claim that either their enjoyment of their property or its value is diminished by the public's ability merely to pass and re-pass a few feet closer to the seawall beyond which appellants' house is located.

PruneYard is also relevant in that we acknowledged in that case that public access rested upon a "state constitutional . . . provision that had been construed to create rights to the use of private property by strangers." In this case, of course, the State is also acting to protect a state constitutional right. The constitutional provision guaranteeing public access to the ocean states that "the Legislature shall enact such laws as will give *the most liberal construction to this provision* so that access to the navigable waters of this State shall always be attainable for the people thereof." This provision is the explicit basis for the statutory directive to provide for public access along the coast in new development projects, and has been construed by the state judiciary to permit passage over private land where necessary to gain access to the tidelands. The physical access to the perimeter of appellants' property at issue in this case thus results directly from the State's enforcement of the state constitution.

Finally, the character of the regulation in this case is not unilateral government action, but a condition on approval of a development request submitted by appellants. The State has not sought to interfere with any pre-existing property interest, but has responded to appellants' proposal to intensify development on the coast. Appellants themselves chose to submit a new development application, and could claim no property interest in its approval. They were aware that approval of such development would be conditioned on preservation of adequate public access to the ocean. The State has initiated no action against appellants' property; had the Nollans not proposed more intensive development in the coastal zone, they would never have been subject to the provision that they challenge.

Examination of the economic impact of the Commission's action reinforces the conclusion that no taking has occurred. Allowing appellants to intensify development along the coast in exchange for ensuring public access to the ocean is a classic instance of government action that produces a "reciprocity of advantage." Appellants have been allowed to replace a one-story 521-square-foot beach home with a two-story 1,674-square-foot residence and an attached two-car garage, resulting in development covering 2,464 square feet of the lot. Such development obviously significantly increases the value of appellants' property; appellants make no contention that this increase is offset by any diminution in value resulting from the deed restriction, much less that the restriction made the property less valuable than it would have been without the new construction. Furthermore, appellants gain an additional benefit from the Commission's permit condition program. They are able to walk along the beach beyond the confines of their own property only because the Commission has required deed restrictions as a condition of approving other new beach developments. Thus, appellants benefit both as private landowners and as members of the public from the fact that new development permit requests are conditioned on preservation of public access.

Ultimately, appellants' claim of economic injury is flawed because it rests on the assumption of entitlement to the full value of their new development. Appellants submitted a proposal for more intensive development of the coast, which the Commission was under no obligation to approve, and now argue that a regulation designed to ameliorate the impact of that development deprives them of the full value of their improvements. Even if this novel claim were somehow cognizable, it is not significant. "[T]he interest in anticipated gains has traditionally been viewed as less compelling than other property-related interests."

With respect to appellants' investment-backed expectations, appellants can make no reasonable claim to any expectation of being able to exclude members of the public from crossing the edge of their property to gain access to the ocean. It is axiomatic, of course, that state law is the source of those strands that constitute a property owner's bundle of property rights. "[A]s a general proposition[,] the law of real property is, under our Constitution, left to the individual States to develop and administer." In this case, the state constitution explicitly states that no one possessing the "frontage" of any "navigable water in this State, shall be permitted to exclude the right of way to such water whenever it is required for any public purpose." The state Code expressly provides that, save for exceptions not relevant here, "[p]ublic access from the nearest public roadway to the shoreline and along the coast shall be provided in new development projects." The Coastal Commission Interpretative Guidelines make clear that fulfillment of the Commission's constitutional and statutory duty require that approval of new coastline development be conditioned upon provisions ensuring lateral public access to the ocean. At the time of appellants' permit request, the Commission had conditioned all 43 of the proposals for coastal new development in the Faria Family Beach Tract on the provision of deed restrictions ensuring lateral access along the shore. Finally, the Faria family had leased the beach property since the early part of this century, and "the Faria family and their lessees [including the Nollans] had not interfered with public use of the beachfront within the Tract, so long as public use was limited to pass and re-pass lateral access along the shore." California therefore has clearly established that the power of exclusion for which appellants seek compensation simply is not a strand in the bundle of appellants' property rights, and appellants have never acted as if it were. Given this state of affairs, appellants cannot claim that the deed restriction has deprived them of a reasonable expectation to exclude from their property persons desiring to gain access to the sea.

Even were we somehow to concede a pre-existing expectation of a right to exclude, appellants were clearly on notice when requesting a new development permit that a condition of approval would be a provision ensuring public lateral access to the shore. Thus, they surely could have had no expectation that they could obtain approval of their new development and exercise any right of exclusion afterward. In this respect, this case is quite similar to *Ruckelshaus v. Monsanto Co.* In *Monsanto*, the respondent had submitted trade data to the Environmental Protection Agency (EPA) for the purpose of obtaining registration of certain pesticides. The company claimed that the agency's disclosure of certain data in accordance with the relevant regulatory statute constituted a taking. The Court conceded that the data in question constituted property under state law. It also found, however, that certain of the data had been submitted to the agency after Congress had made clear that only limited confidentiality would be given data submitted for registration purposes. The Court observed that the statute served to inform Monsanto of the various conditions under which the data might be released, and stated:

> If, despite the data-consideration and data-disclosure provisions in this statute, Monsanto chose to submit the requisite data in order to receive a registration, it can hardly argue that its reasonable investment-backed expectations are disturbed when EPA acts to use or disclose the data in a manner that was authorized by law at the time of the submission.

The Court rejected respondent's argument that the requirement that it relinquish some confidentiality imposed an unconstitutional condition on receipt of a Government benefit:

> [A]s long as Monsanto is aware of the conditions under which the data are submitted, and the conditions are rationally related to a legitimate Government interest, a voluntary submission of data by an applicant in exchange for the economic advantages of a registration can hardly be called a taking.

The similarity of this case to *Monsanto* is obvious. Appellants were aware that stringent regulation of development along the California coast had been in place at least since 1976. The specific deed restriction to which the Commission sought to subject them had been imposed since 1979 on all 43 shoreline new development projects in the Faria Family Beach Tract. Such regulation to ensure public access to the ocean had been directly authorized by California citizens in 1972, and reflected their judgment that restrictions on coastal development represented "the advantage of living and doing business in a civilized community." The deed restriction was "authorized by law at the time of [appellants' permit] submission," and, as earlier analysis demonstrates, was reasonably related to the objective of ensuring public access. Appellants thus were on notice that new developments would be approved only if provisions were made for lateral beach access. In requesting a new development permit from the Commission, they could have no reasonable expectation of, and had no entitlement to, approval of their permit application without any deed restriction ensuring public access to the ocean. As a result, analysis of appellants' investment-backed expectations reveals that "the force of this factor is so overwhelming . . . that it disposes of the taking question."[10]

Standard Takings Clause analysis thus indicates that the Court employs its unduly restrictive standard of police power rationality to find a taking where neither the character of governmental action nor the nature of the private interest affected raise [sic] any takings concern. The result is that the Court invalidates regulation that represents a reasonable adjustment of the burdens and benefits of development along the California coast.

The foregoing analysis makes clear that the State has taken no property from appellants. Imposition of the permit condition in this case represents the State's reasonable exercise of its police power. The Coastal Commission has drawn on its expertise to preserve the balance between private development and public access, by requiring that any project that intensifies development on the increasingly crowded California coast must be offset by gains in public access. Under the normal standard for review of the police power, this provision is eminently reasonable. Even accepting the Court's novel insistence on a precise *quid pro quo* of burdens and benefits, there is a reasonable relationship between the public benefit and the burden created by appellants' development. The movement of development closer to the ocean creates the prospect of encroachment on public tidelands, because of fluctuation in the mean high tide line. The deed restriction ensures that disputes about the boundary between private and public property will not deter the public from exercising its right to have access to the sea.

Furthermore, consideration of the Commission's action under traditional takings analysis underscores the absence of any viable takings claim. The deed restriction permits the public only to pass and repass along a narrow strip of beach, a few feet closer to a seawall at the periphery of appellants' property. Appellants almost surely have enjoyed an increase in the value of their property even with the restriction, because they have been allowed to build a significantly larger new home with a garage on their lot. Finally, appellants can claim the disruption of no expectation interest, both because they have no right to exclude the public under state law, and because, even if they did, they had full advance notice that new development along the coast is conditioned on provisions for continued public access to the ocean.

Fortunately, the Court's decision regarding this application of the Commission's permit program will probably have little ultimate impact either on this parcel in particular or the Commission program in general. A preliminary study by a Senior Lands Agent in the State Attorney General's Office indicates that the portion of the beach at issue in this case likely belongs to the public. Since a full study had not been completed at the time of appellants' permit application, the deed restriction was requested "without regard to the possibility that the applicant is proposing development on public land." Furthermore, analysis by the same Land Agent also indicated that the public had obtained a prescriptive right to the use of Faria Beach from the seawall to the ocean. The Superior Court explicitly stated in its ruling against the Commission on the permit condition issue that "no part of this opinion is intended to foreclose the public's opportunity to adjudicate the possibility that public rights in [appellants'] beach have been acquired through prescriptive use."

With respect to the permit condition program in general, the Commission should have little difficulty in the future in utilizing its expertise to demonstrate a specific connection between provisions for access and burdens on access produced by new development. Neither the Commission in its report nor the State in its briefs and at argument highlighted the particular threat to lateral access created by appellants' development project. In defending its action, the State emphasized the general point that *overall* access to the beach had been preserved, since the diminution of access created by the project had been offset by the gain in lateral access. This approach is understandable, given that the State relied on the reasonable assumption that its action was justified under the normal standard of review for determining legitimate exercises of a State's police power. In the future, alerted to the Court's apparently more demanding requirement, it need only make clear that a provision for public access directly responds to a particular type of burden on access created by a new development. Even if I did not believe that the record in this case satisfies the requirement, I would have to acknowledge that the record's documentation of the impact of coastal development indicates that the Commission should have little problem presenting its findings in a way that avoids a takings problem.

Nonetheless it is important to point out that the Court's insistence on a precise accounting system in this case is insensitive to the fact that increasing intensity of development in many areas calls for far-sighted, comprehensive planning that takes into account both the interdependence of land uses and the cumulative impact of development. As one scholar [Sax] has noted:

> Property does not exist in isolation. Particular parcels are tied to one another in complex ways, and property is more accurately described as being inextricably part of a network of relationships that is neither limited to, nor usefully defined by, the property boundaries with which the legal system is accustomed to dealing. Frequently, use of any given parcel of property is at the same time effectively a use of, or a demand upon, property beyond the border of the user.

As Congress has declared, "The key to more effective protection and use of the land and water resources of the coast [is for the states to] develo[p] land and water use programs for the coastal zone, including unified policies, criteria, standards, methods, and processes for dealing with land and water use decisions of more than local significance." This is clearly a call for a focus on the overall impact of development on coastal areas. State agencies therefore require considerable flexibility in responding to private desires for development in a way that guarantees the preservation of public access to the coast. They should be encouraged to regulate development in the context of the overall balance of competing uses of the shoreline. The Court today does precisely the opposite, overruling an eminently reasonable exercise of an expert state agency's judgment, substituting its own narrow view of how this balance should be struck. Its reasoning is hardly suited to the complex reality of natural resource protection in the twentieth century. I can only hope that today's decision is an aberration, and that a broader vision ultimately prevails.[14] ▬

CONCLUSION
A RIGHTFUL PLACE FOR LAND USE JURISPRUDENCE

Interior of Grand Central Terminal, c. 1930. From Penn
Central Transportation Co. v. New York City.
(Ed Nowak)

Determining a "rightful place" for Justice Brennan's land use jurisprudence requires an understanding of his other legal contributions. Justice Brennan is uniformly regarded as one of the most significant justices in the history of the U.S. Supreme Court.[1] His intellect, persuasiveness, consistency and passion are often identified as his salient judicial attributes.[2] Supreme Court colleagues, former law clerks and friends praise his human qualities.[3]

Justice Brennan's land use opinions have not played a principal part in carving his overall reputation. To the public and scholar alike, he is best known as a staunch defender of the personal civil liberties enumerated in the Bill of Rights.[4] He has said, "Were there a list of principles fundamental to the functioning of a free republic, it would, in addition to guaranteeing that no citizen be denied an education, a house, or a job on account of the color of his skin, certainly include an assurance that each citizen's vote would count no more or no less than that of any other citizen, that his government would take no voice in or interfere with his religion, that he would enjoy freedom of speech and a free press, and that the administration of criminal laws would adhere to civilized standards of fairness and decency."[5] For him, the Constitution encompasses an "ideal of libertarian dignity protected through law,"[6] in which free choice, individual autonomy and equal treatment are paramount values.

More particularly, Justice Brennan understands the structure of the Constitution as imposing on the judicial branch a special and ultimate obligation to safeguard individual rights, lest the "written guarantees of liberty" become "mere paper protections."[7] James Madison's faith that " '[i]ndependent tribunals of justice will consider themselves in a peculiar manner the guardians of [constitutional] rights' " is similarly a Brennan article of faith.[8] And he thinks that courts must be especially sympathetic to those "litigants most in need of judicial protection of their rights—the poor, the underprivileged, the deprived minorities."[9] He is not timid about exercising judicial power, and votes to invalidate legislative and executive action when he believes the Constitution demands it. When that document itself, and the Supreme Court's final authority to interpret and enforce it, are threatened, he unhesitatingly enters the controversial fray.[10]

The Supreme Court's participation in the life of American society has expanded dramatically during Justice Brennan's tenure. In his own words, "[I]t is fair to say that from 1962 to 1969 the very face of the law changed" through the Court's application to the states of protections encompassed in the Bill of Rights.[11] He is acknowledged by many as one of the architects, if not the central one, of the Warren Court era.[12] Although annoyed by a popularly held perception that justices bargain or lobby for votes, Justice Brennan enjoys a special ability to fashion consensus opinions satisfying the differing viewpoints of a majority of his colleagues.[13]

The list of Brennan majorities and pluralities forming the grist for his libertarian mill is long and distinguished. He has written pathbreaking opinions in the areas of voting rights,[14] press freedom,[15] sex discrimination,[16] federal court access,[17] privacy,[18] procedural due process,[19] freedom of association[20] and remedies for constitutional violations.[21] He has been an unwavering and eloquent spokesman on behalf of affirmative action[22] and equal treatment for poor and disadvantaged individuals[23] and against unreasonable searches and seizures[24] and the death penalty.[25] He is a firm believer in the separation of church and state[26] and in religious freedom.[27]

Everyone has a favorite Brennan landmark opinion, but no recitation is complete without *Baker v. Carr*,[28] *New York Times Co. v. Sullivan*,[29] *Fay v. Noia*,[30] *Frontiero v. Richardson*[31] and *Goldberg v. Kelly*.[32] Indeed, these cases affect the contours of communities, even if not directly addressing themselves to the use of land. *Baker* announced the proposition—controversial at the time—that courts have power to review challenges to the apportionment of state legislative districts brought under the equal protection clause.[33] His opinion set the stage for adoption of the bulwark principle of modern-day democracies: the one-person, one-vote rule.[34] *New York Times Co. v. Sullivan* enumerated the now-famous standard requiring public officials, before recovering damages for defamatory statements, to prove that "the statement was made with 'actual malice'—that is, with knowledge that it was false or with reckless disregard of whether it was false or not."[35] Only with such a rule protecting speech and the press can society be assured that debate on public issues is "uninhibited, robust, and wide-open," as contemplated under the first amendment.[36] Justice Brennan's *Fay v. Noia* opinion held that federal district courts, through the writ of *habeas corpus*, have broad powers to review claims of constitutional deficiency made by state prisoners following their convictions in state criminal proceedings.[37] Although substantially cut back by subsequent Court decisions,[38] the case illustrates his concept of federalism as a "double source of protection" for individuals, with both state and federal processes at work.[39] Justice Brennan's plurality opinion in *Frontiero v. Richardson*, one vote short of a majority, proposed to add sex discrimination to the list of suspect classifications, such as race, nationality and alienage, thereby subject to the highest level of judicial scrutiny.[40] He eventually settled for the less stringent, but still elevated, intermediate scrutiny standard of review in his *Craig v. Boren* majority.[41] And *Goldberg v. Kelly* cast government entitlements, such as welfare benefits and public jobs, in a new light—as a form of property—thereby subjecting their withdrawal to the requirements of procedural due process, such as a hearing.[42] Again, while subsequent Court opinions have limited the reach of this opinion,[43] its underlying theory survives.[44]

Justice Brennan's Land Use Jurisprudence

Although several of his land use opinions (*San Diego Gas & Electric Co.*, *Penn Central* and *Katobimar*) have received public and scholarly attention,[45] Justice Brennan's cumulative contribution in this area has until now been unrecognized.[46] This is not altogether surprising, for several reasons. The majority of his land use opinions—13 of the 21—are products of his state court years. Yet most scholars quite naturally focus on the judicial record of

Supreme Court justices after their appointment. Earlier experience is relevant principally for the purpose of approving or disapproving a nominee during his or her confirmation hearing before the Senate Judiciary Committee. Furthermore, because Justice Brennan's eight Supreme Court land use opinions were written years after his activist Warren Court image was established, and because they neither significantly enlarged nor contradicted that image, they have not created the major waves necessary to garner attention.

Moreover, unlike his views on voting rights, privacy, sex discrimination and the like, Justice Brennan's land use opinions are harder to peg on the ideological liberal-conservative spectrum. To the general public, put off by the law's mysterious language and understandably eager for simplifying images, Justice Brennan is the Court's leading liberal light, voting for criminal defendants, the underprivileged, minorities and the press.[47] In the land use field, however, he confounds ideological labeling. He is neither colloquially liberal nor conservative, neither a rabid proponent of private property rights nor an unswerving supporter of government regulation. His *Metromedia*, *Vincent* and *Renton* opinions frustrate environmental liberals but please American Civil Liberties Union first amendment liberals. His *San Diego Gas & Electric Co.* dissent sparks heated disapproval from conservationists but delights (or should delight) low-income housing proponents. His *Penn Central* and *Nollan* opinions anger private property advocates but hearten preservationists. And his New Jersey opinions, such as *Birkfield* and *Guaclides*, may be deemed conservative in their support of zoning schemes today considered exclusionary.

What, then, is Justice Brennan's land use jurisprudence, and does it cohere into an easily comprehensible theory? Perhaps the greatest risk in taking a subject-matter slice (cases affecting the use of land) out of his volumes of judicial opinions is raising expectations that a single, outcome-determinative, all-encompassing land use philosophy exists. That call of the sirens is only partially answered by this book, where Justice Brennan's land use views gleaned from his 21 opinions are encapsulated by a central theme and four substantive propositions.[48]

Land use cases test Justice Brennan's own broad-based reading of the Constitution as encompassing an "ideal of libertarian dignity protected through law." Some of his balancing, especially in *Moore*, *Metromedia*, *Vincent* and *Renton*, resonates fully with this interpretation. In each of these cases, the claimants could place a fundamental personal civil right on their side of the scale and thus increase the government's burden to justify its infringement. In *Moore*, the notion of imposing white America's stereotype of the nuclear family on ethnic and black families socially and economically dependent on an extended family structure offended Justice Brennan. The justifications asserted by the city—minimizing overcrowding, traffic congestion and burdens on schools—seemed trivial by comparison. In *Metromedia*, *Vincent* and *Renton*, he would invoke the free speech clause of the Bill of Rights to guarantee everyone's right to speak. Government could pursue its interest in protecting and beautifying the environment, but infringement of weighty first amendment rights required that government demonstrate a serious and comprehensive effort on behalf of such non-speech interests.

It is where the right to private property, unallied with a supporting personal civil right, is at stake that Justice Brennan's balancing becomes more difficult. The definition of private property is elastic, stretched and narrowed over time by law and custom. Where the common law of the 19th century prohibited only a small number of "nuisance" land uses, the adoption of zoning in the 20th century dramatically expanded potential limitations on private property. With no fixed compass, Justice Brennan would turn to expectations—privately and publicly created or held—to assess the interests. He had already used this approach to delineate "new property" in his procedural due process series of cases starting with *Goldberg v. Kelly.* In land use as well, the owner's property right must be evidenced by expectations, which especially deserve to be honored as serious when backed by distinct financial investment. Correspondingly, the government's regulation must be backed by an investment of comprehensive-planning commitment and energy to illuminate the seriousness with which it values the underlying public purpose.

Thus, in the *Penn Central* case, the landowner's ability to make a reasonable return on its existing terminal use, coupled with the demonstrated comprehensiveness of the city's landmarks program, informed Justice Brennan's striking of the balance. In his *Nollan* opinion, the public's longstanding expectation of beach use, and the private owner's acquiescence to that expectation over many years, coalesced to help swing the balance. And in his New Jersey opinions of *Leimann, Rexon, Struyk* and *Cobble Close Farm*, the owners knew or should have known that they were not entitled to regulatory exceptions that would permit their desired property uses.

A central theme of balancing may seem meek or contentless to some,[49] particularly to those favoring a single outcome-determinative theory. As a field, however, land use does not lend itself easily to a unified theory. Because such cases may trigger any one of four major constitutional clauses (due process, equal protection, just compensation and free speech), each with its own set of jurisprudential twists and turns, they necessarily implicate a wide range of constitutional theories. For example, the first amendment's free speech clause raises concerns quite different from those posed by the just compensation clause, yet both restrict government infringement on exercise of property rights.

Furthermore, debates rage about the relative values of so-called personal versus property rights. On the one hand, it may be argued that private property rights, especially when defined as the right to exploit land for a profit, are less important than personal civil rights along the constitutional spectrum. On the other hand, it may be argued that private property rights are no less important than personal rights when it comes to effective participation in society. If an individual's right to use and own land encompasses libertarian ideals of free choice and autonomy, as well as principles of equal treatment, it does so in ways more complex than personal rights protected by the Constitution.[50] The complexity arises from a fundamental question:

what is private property as expressly cited in the just compensation clause? Is it an absolute right inherent in the land itself, magically transferred to its owner? Or is it the residuum bestowed at the behest of the sovereign? Compare this to free speech, where what could be the same conundrum is resolved in the direction of an absolute inherent right warranting heightened scrutiny. The choice of starting point determines in large measure whether judgments are viewed as deferential or hostile to private property.

Neither hostile nor deferential, Justice Brennan's opinions mirror the law's ultimate ambivalence about property rights. When "rights" are not susceptible to easy classification, as in the land use field, a seamless explanatory web becomes the more elusive. His four propositions become an intermediate route between the particulars and an overarching statement, giving the land use balancing process a context and some objective criteria.

Justice Brennan and the Future of Land Use Law

What can be expected in the future from Justice Brennan in the land use field? State courts will continue to be the battleground for most conflicts, given the local nature of land use problems.[51] Of course, as Justice Brennan himself frequently observes, the Supreme Court does not create issues, but instead responds to cases brought before it.[52] By the same token, most key issues come to the Court sooner or later, and its essentially limitless discretion to choose its docket defines the law it will make. The prediction of future Court decisions, let alone Justice Brennan's specific position, is always a risky business. The easiest way to hedge one's bet is to pinpoint the emerging problems in the land use field, identify the key questions left unanswered by Supreme Court decisions and measure the inclination of the current Court members for judicial intervention. If the recent past is any indication,[53] their judicial land use appetite remains whetted.

Here, then, is a taste of the future. First, government and private property owners will importune the Court to provide additional guidance about what is a regulatory taking and what is the correct measure of financial damages when one occurs. The growing scarcity of land will place particular pressure on remaining open space and environmentally sensitive areas such as wetlands and floodplains. In many cases, any meaningful development on these lands will prove inconsistent with the public goal of preservation. Governments will face the choice of preventing development through police power regulations or public purchase. If the regulatory route is selected, the Court will need to decide its constitutionality and whether owners of properties with important natural resources enjoy a reasonable expectation of economically viable use. Although articulation of a bright-line rule separating the constitutional from the unconstitutional is unlikely ever to emerge, if only because of the immense difficulty in framing one, the Court will grapple with and decide fact-specific cases, providing comparative signposts to exasperated government officials and landowners.

When the Court finally finds a case in which a regulatory taking has occurred, the contours of the *San Diego Gas & Electric Co.* and *First English* remedy, mandating money damages for the period of time the regulation effected a taking, will come into play. Waiting for that other shoe to drop, cities and landowners will continue to wonder how the amount of damages will be measured, whether financial awards will bankrupt small towns and bankroll land speculators, and even whether the mere existence of a monetary remedy ironically will make judges less likely to find a regulatory taking in the first place. As for Justice Brennan, he may be parsimonious in classifying regulatory actions as takings, but resolute in awarding damages when regulations go too far.

Another area ripe for Court exploration involves the setting of constitutional limitations on communities that impose obligations on real estate developers to meet social needs through the land use regulatory system. For years, many local governments have required developers to shoulder the marginal costs of sewer and water, transportation, school and other infrastructure needs resulting from developers' activities.[54] More recently, some cities are asking office developers to provide or pay for low-income housing, day care and job training[55] and residential developers to set aside a percentage of their units for low-income families.[56] The confluence of shrinking federal dollars, tightening local budgets and burgeoning social problems will make communities increasingly bold and the private sector correspondingly unhappy with the additional burdens. The resulting litigation will wend its way to the Supreme Court. The public access easement condition contested in *Nollan v. California Coastal Commission*[57] is only the first round in this fight, and future knockdowns and knockouts are yet to come. Justice Brennan may tolerate a substantial dose of these developer burdens, as long as they do not deprive owners of reasonable economic use, are comprehensively applied and are justified by sound planning.

At the same time that cities and developers fight it out on this ground, they will conversely become ever-closer partners in multimillion-dollar public-private development projects. The practice of selling publicly owned land to private developers for a profit[58] or entering into joint venture deals[59] blurs the model of traditional government activity and may precipitate Court review. Long-time (*Berman v. Parker*) and recent (*Hawaii Housing Authority v. Midkiff*) precedents aside,[60] the Court will be challenged to put some limits on what government can do, before public officials become indistinguishable from private developers. It is too early to predict Justice Brennan's reaction, or the Court's, to this controversial issue.

Municipal efforts to control the design of private buildings may force the Court to ponder whether architectural expression is protected by the first amendment. Cities across the country are enacting design review ordinances authorizing planning departments and review boards to consider the architectural aspects of proposed buildings before approving their construction.[61] For example, Bethesda, Md., and San Francisco hold what are known locally as beauty contests, in which so-called experts judge the architectural merits of proposed projects and select winners for approved development.[62] The San Francisco zoning ordinance effectively prohibits flat roofs on all new office towers, in strict obedience to the postmodernist penchant for embellishment and for rejection of the International Style.[63] Boston has its design review commission.[64] And some suburban communities dictate the choice of exterior building material, color and architectural style in multifamily residential and commercial developments to ensure either a harmonious or diverse neighborhood appearance.[65] Developers, residents and perhaps architects will challenge these laws on the basis that their rights to free speech are improperly impinged. Justice Brennan may agree that architecture is protected by the first amendment but may also find that community interests in quality environments can outweigh the individual speech value, as long as his *Metromedia* comprehensiveness and seriousness test is satisfied.

Interjurisdictional disputes among federal, state and local governments over the use of land will present significant questions about federalism, local control and individual rights. Federal efforts to control pollution or protect wetlands will sometimes conflict with state and local land use planning and real estate development activity.[66] Promotion of offshore oil drilling by federal authorities may enrage local officials concerned about environmental impacts and public coastline use.[67] States harmed by acid rain may challenge states filled with smokestack industries.[68] At least as to the federal-versus-state contests, Justice Brennan may be expected to take an expansive view of federal power, absent congressional legislation granting states the power to ignore federal mandates.[69]

The most exhausting battles may take place intrastate, between local and state levels of government, as the existing balkanization of land use authority matures into a major threat to the solution of regional problems. Local opposition to LULUs (locally undesirable land uses) and NIMBYs (not in my backyard uses), such as drug rehabilitation and mental health centers, halfway houses, AIDS hostels, airport expansions, low-income housing, hazardous waste dumps and prisons, will mount even more. Small towns will close their doors harder and erect their fences higher to keep out new development and undesirable residents, while central cities become home to the poor and minorities. Traffic problems will become more intolerable as comprehensive planning stops at the local jurisdictional boundary. When political solutions founder, parties will turn to the courts as a last resort, reviving old constitutional theories, or fashioning new ones, to empower or enervate local communities. Local governments will press their status as home rule sovereigns entitled to judicial deference.[70] Opponents will employ due process, equal protection and other clauses, advocating innovative individual rights to invalidate local exclusions. And if it is hard to imagine Supreme Court intervention given the Court's present tilt, it must be remembered that today's lineup is tomorrow's history and that cycles of judicial law making can move in unexpected directions. Thus, the Court may find itself a willing or unwilling player in land use planning and regulation, removing impediments to or even ordering the construction of low-income housing,[71] prisons,[72] mental health centers[73] and the like. Justice Brennan will probably oppose local government efforts conflicting with individual civil liberties, absent a strong showing that such efforts are supported by sound planning and a comprehensive approach.[74]

Landmark Justice

In the land use field—as in others—Justice Brennan is a distinguished jurist. With a judicial career now spanning 40 state and federal court years, he has encountered all the land use issues that arise in courtrooms, issues that fundamentally affect the way American society lives as individuals, families and communities. Whether one ultimately agrees with his decisions, one cannot deny the thorough care he applies to each case. Read together, his opinions prompt admiration for their consistent quality of analysis and writing. Beyond themes and propositions, they embody a blend of thoughtfulness and common-sense judgment. A subtext of human values and everyday experience is never far from the surface.[75] Justice Brennan himself would happily accept this evaluation: "I believe that problems are susceptible to rational solution if we work hard at making and understanding arguments that are based on reason and experience."[76] For him, the ultimate control on courts is that "judges have to proceed and to persuade by reasoned argument in a public context."[77] This is not to say that "underneath the robes, I am not, that we are each not, a human being with personal views and moral sensibilities and religious scruples," but, he concludes, "it is to say that above all, I am a judge."[78] In the land use field, he is truly a landmark justice.

NOTES

Chapter 1

1. *See, e.g., Nollan v. California Coastal Comm'n*, 107 S. Ct. 3141, 3143–44 (1987); *Keystone Bituminous Coal Ass'n v. DeBenedictis*, 480 U.S. 470, —— (1987).

2. *See, e.g., Nollan*, 107 S. Ct. at 3143–44; *Penn Central Transp. Co. v. New York City*, 438 U.S. 104, 128–38 (1978).

3. The three key constitutional clauses regularly invoked in land use cases are good examples. The due process clause of the fifth and fourteenth amendments to the U.S. Constitution states only that persons may not be deprived of property without "due process of law." U.S. Const. amends. V, XIV. The meaning of that clause is left to judges to decipher. As Justice Harlan intoned:

> Due process has not been reduced to any formula; its content cannot be determined by reference to any code. The best that can be said is that through the course of this Court's decisions it has represented the balance which our Nation, built upon postulates of respect for the liberty of the individual, has struck between that liberty and the demands of organized society. If the supplying of content to this Constitutional concept has of necessity been a rational process, it certainly has not been one where judges have felt free to roam where unguided speculation might take them. The balance of which I speak is the balance struck by this country, having regard to what history teaches are the traditions from which it developed as well as the traditions from which it broke. That tradition is a living thing. A decision of this Court which radically departs from it could not long survive, while a decision which builds on what has survived is likely to be sound. No formula could serve as a substitute, in this area, for judgment and restraint.

Poe v. Ullman, 367 U.S. 497, 542 (1961) (Harlan, J., dissenting). See *supra* p. 120.

The just compensation clause of the fifth amendment commands, "nor shall private property be taken for public use, without just compensation." U.S. Const. amend. V. Justice Brennan himself observed the difficulty of giving exact content to that phrase: "[T]his Court, quite simply, has been unable to develop any 'set formula' for determining when 'justice and fairness' require that economic injuries caused by public action be compensated by the government. . . ." *Penn Central*, 438 U.S. at 124. Equally opaque is the equal protection clause of the fourteenth amendment, which guarantees "the equal protection of the laws." U.S. Const. amend. XIV. "Equal protection" does not ensure, for example, exactly equal treatment by government of private property. *See, e.g., Pennell v. City of San Jose*, 108 S. Ct. 849, 857 (1988). Justice Brennan himself has spoken about the "patent ambiguities" of the due process and equal protection clauses. *See* W. Brennan, The Fourteenth Amendment, Address to Section on Individual Rights and Responsibilities, American Bar Ass'n, New York University School of Law (Aug. 8, 1986).

State laws authorizing local communities to enact zoning ordinances also have their share of vague language. For example, state acts require that zoning bylaws be "uniform" between and within zoning districts, but the extent of uniformity is never elaborated. *See, e.g.*, Mass. Gen. Laws ch. 40A, § 4 (1979). Variances can be granted only "without substantial detriment to the public good" and "without nullifying or substantially derogating from the intent or purpose" of the zoning ordinance. *Id.*, § 10.

4. *See, e.g., Hawaii Hous. Auth. v. Midkiff*, 467 U.S. 229, 241–42 (1984) (legitimate goal and rational approach, through eminent domain, to end land oligopoly); *Moore v. City of East Cleveland*, 431 U.S. 494, 499–500 (1977) (legitimate goals, but ordinance serves them "marginally, at best").

5. *See, e.g., Village of Arlington Heights v. Metropolitan Hous. Dev. Corp.*, 429 U.S. 252, 268–71 (1977) (no evidence that zoning was racially motivated). In general, the less fundamental the individual right, the more likely courts will accept at face value the asserted government purpose. *See, e.g., City of New Orleans v. Dukes*, 427 U.S. 297, 303 (1976) (ordinance prohibiting pushcart food sales in Vieux Carré but "grandfathering" some operators upheld). Conversely, the more fundamental the individual right, the more likely that courts will delve beyond the asserted purpose. *See, e.g., Schad v. Borough of Mount Ephraim*, 452 U.S. 61, 72–74 (1981) (zoning barring nude dancing and other live entertainment overturned).

6. *See, e.g., Agins v. City of Tiburon*, 447 U.S. 255, 262–63 (1980).

7. *See, e.g., Nollan*, 107 S. Ct. at 3150. In *Nollan*, the Court found that a government decision requiring the Nollans to allow the public to walk up and down their beach property violated the Constitution. *Id.* Whether or not public access along the California coastline is a "good idea," the Court observed, "that does not establish that the Nollans (and other coastal residents) alone can be compelled to contribute to its realization." *Id.*

8. *See, e.g., Johnson v. M'Intosh*, 21 U.S. (8 Wheat.) 543, 571–74 (1823) (sovereignty); *Brumagim v. Bradshaw*, 39 Cal. 24, 43–51 (1870) (ownership of land through possession); *Tapscott v. Lessee of Cobbs*, 52 Va. (11 Gratt.) 172, 179–81 (1854) (title versus possession). *See generally* C. Haar & L. Liebman, Property and Law 35–45 (1977).

9. Justice Brennan began his judicial career in 1949 as a trial judge in the New Jersey Superior Court. One year later he was appointed to the appellate division of the Superior Court. He moved to the New Jersey Supreme Court in 1952. On Oct. 15, 1956, President Dwight D. Eisenhower appointed him an associate justice of the U.S. Supreme Court, and he took office one day later.

10. *See Penn Central*, 438 U.S. at 104.

11. Justice Brennan is a great believer in the value of dissents. *See* Brennan, *In Defense of Dissents*, The Pennsylvania Gazette, February 1986, at 20.

12. *See infra* chapter 3, note 4.

13. For example, Justice Brennan's dissenting opinion in *San Diego Gas & Elec. Co. v. City of San Diego*, 450 U.S. 621 (1981), was followed by six U.S. Courts of Appeal (the Fifth, Sixth, Seventh, Eighth, Ninth and Eleventh Circuits), the U.S. Court of

Claims, five state supreme courts (Arizona, Minnesota, New Hampshire, North Dakota and Wisconsin), *cf.* Berger, Anarchy Reigns Supreme, 29 J. Urb. & Contemp. L. 39, 50–51 (1985), and finally by a majority of the U.S. Supreme Court in *First English Evangelical Lutheran Church v. County of Los Angeles*, 107 S. Ct. 2378 (1987). *See infra* chapter 3, note 104.

14. Because written opinions are the fullest expression of an individual judge's approach, this book focuses on Justice Brennan's land use opinions and not his land use voting record in cases considered by the various courts on which he has served.

15. Indeed, much of Justice Brennan's overall constitutional jurisprudence involves balancing the interests of state and citizen. *See, e.g.*, Friedman, *Mr. Justice Brennan: The First Decade*, 80 Harv. L. Rev. 7, 14–15 (1966) ("[H]e is a balancer of interests and, more than any other member of the liberal wing of the present Court, he has worked to create a coherent yet flexible analytical framework within which to isolate the values to be protected."); Heck, *Justice Brennan and the Heyday of Warren Court Liberalism*, 20 Santa Clara L. Rev. 841, 867–70 (1980) (balancing in criminal law and first amendment cases).

An important group of scholars has mounted a thoughtful critique of judicial balancing. In essence, they argue, balancing and similar so-called objective approaches to decision making are not only incapable of yielding neutrally correct results but disingenuously mask value-laden political decisions. *See, e.g.*, Unger, *The Critical Legal Studies Movement*, 96 Harv. L. Rev. 561, 564–65, 567–76 (1983) (fallacies of "formalism" and "objectivism"); Kennedy, *Form and Substance in Private Law Adjudication*, 89 Harv. L. Rev. 1685, 1708–09 (1984) (judicial legitimization argument that judges neutrally apply rules is unconvincing). *See generally* Denvir, *Justice Brennan, Justice Rehnquist, and Free Speech*, 80 Nw. U.L. Rev. 285, 286–89 (1985). While detailed discussion of the attack is beyond the purview of this book, the power of the critique should not be overlooked.

16. One of the most famous expressions of public rights comes from Justice Douglas:
The concept of the public welfare is broad and inclusive. The values it represents are spiritual as well as physical, aesthetic as well as monetary. It is within the power of the legislature to determine that the community should be beautiful as well as healthy, spacious as well as clean, well-balanced as well as carefully patrolled.
Berman v. Parker, 348 U.S. 26, 33 (1954) (citation omitted).

17. Justice Brennan explained his emphasis on contemporary constitutional interpretation:
[T]here exists in modern America the necessity for protecting all of us from arbitrary action by governments more powerful and more pervasive than any in our ancestors' time. Only if the amendments are construed to preserve their fundamental policies will they ensure the maintenance of our constitutional structure of government for a free society. For the genius of our Constitution resides not in any static meaning that it had in a world that is dead and gone, but in the adaptability of its great principles to cope with the problems of a developing America. A principle to be vital must be of wider application than the mischief that gave it birth. Constitutions are not ephemeral documents, designed to meet passing occasions. The future is their care, and therefore, in their application, our contemplation cannot be only of what has been but of what may be.
Brennan, *State Constitutions and the Protection of Individual Rights*, 90 Harv. L. Rev. 489, 495 (1977).

In his 1986 Oliver Wendell Holmes, Jr., Lecture, sponsored by the Harvard Law School, he elaborated on his mode of constitutional interpretation in a discussion about the eighth amendment's "cruel and unusual punishments" prohibition and the death penalty. *See* Brennan, *Constitutional Adjudication and the Death Penalty: A View from the Court*, 100 Harv. L. Rev. 313 (1986). He firmly rejected a blinders-on historical view of original intent, arguing that "if it were possible to find answers to all constitutional questions by reference to historical practices, we would not need judges," *id.* at 326, musing tongue in cheek that "[c]ourts could be staffed by professional historians who could be instructed to compile a comprehensive master list of life" at the time a constitutional provision was adopted, *id.* Thus, he repeated his well-publicized characterization of "the view that the Constitution could be definitively interpreted by reference to the 'intention of the Framers'" as "nothing more than 'arrogance cloaked as humility.'" *Id.* at 325 (*quoting* W. Brennan, The Constitution of the United States: Contemporary Ratification, Presentation at Georgetown University Text and Teaching Symposium (Oct. 12, 1985)). Arguing that "the choice by the Framers to employ general and relativistic words was a deliberate one," *id.* at 325, he confronted the "original intent of the Framers" proponents on their own turf: "I want to emphasize just one more time that what I am urging is respect for what I believe the Framers insisted of judges: namely, to accept the responsibility and burden and challenge of working with the majestic generalities of their magnificent Constitution," *id.* at 326.

18. *See* W. Brennan, Justice Thurgood Marshall: Defender of Libertarian Dignity Protected Through Law, Address at Dedication of Thurgood Marshall Law Library, University of Maryland Law School (Oct. 9, 1980), *reprinted in* The Reporter, Passaic County Bar Ass'n, vol. VI, at 9 (Spring 1984) (describing approvingly that Justice Marshall teaches that "the vogue for positivism in jurisprudence—the obsession with what the law is, which leaves no room for choice between equally acceptable alternatives—must be replaced by a jurisprudence that recognizes human beings as the most distinctive and important feature of the universe which confronts our senses, and of the function of law as the historic means of guaranteeing that preeminence. . . .").

19. *See Katobimar Realty Co. v. Webster*, 20 N.J. 114, 129, 118 A.2d 824, 832 (1955) (Brennan, J., dissenting).

20. *See supra* note 3.

21. *See, e.g., Penn Central*, 438 U.S. at 124, 134–35; *San Diego Gas & Elec.*, 450 U.S. at 652 (Brennan, J., dissenting).

22. *See, e.g., Penn Central*, 438 U.S. at 124.

23. *See, e.g., Katobimar*, 20 N.J. at 129 (Brennan, J., dissenting); *Conlon v. Board of Pub. Works*, 11 N.J. 363, 94 A.2d 660 (1953); *Casper v. City of Long Branch*, 18 N.J. Super. 90, 86 A.2d 691 (App. Div. 1952); *Birkfield Realty Co. v. Board of Comm'rs*, 12 N.J. Super. 192, 79 A.2d 326 (App. Div.), *cert. denied*, 8 N.J. 319 (1951); *Guaclides v. Borough of Englewood Cliffs*, 11 N.J. Super. 405, 78 A.2d 435 (App. Div. 1951); *cf. Penn Central*, 438 U.S. at 131–35 (comprehensiveness avoids singling out individuals).

24. *See, e.g., City of Renton v. Playtime Theatres, Inc.*, 475 U.S. 41 (1986) (Brennan, J., dissenting); *Members of City Council v. Taxpayers for Vincent*, 466 U.S. 789 (1984) (Brennan, J., dissenting); *Metromedia, Inc. v. City of San Diego*, 453 U.S. 490 (1981) (Brennan, J., concurring); *Moore v. City of East Cleveland*, 431 U.S. 494 (1977) (Brennan, J., concurring); *cf. Warth v. Seldin*, 422 U.S. 490 (1975) (Brennan, J., dissenting) (suggesting he would carefully review suburban zoning ordinance to determine if it is exclusionary).

25. *See, e.g., Metromedia*, 453 U.S. at 521 (Brennan, J., concurring); *Weiner v. Bor-*

ough of Stratford, 15 N.J. 295, 104 A.2d 659 (1954); *Cobble Close Farm v. Board of Adjustment*, 10 N.J. 442, 92 A.2d 4 (1952); *Rexon v. Board of Adjustment*, 10 N.J. 1, 89 A.2d 233 (1952); *Leimann v. Board of Adjustment*, 9 N.J. 336, 88 A.2d 337 (1952).

26. *See, e.g., Nollan*, 107 S. Ct. at 3150 (Brennan, J., dissenting); *San Diego Gas & Elec.*, 450 U.S. at 621 (Brennan, J., dissenting); *Penn Central*, 438 U.S. at 104; *Cobble Close Farm*, 10 N.J. at 442.

27. *See, e.g., Metromedia*, 453 U.S. at 521 (Brennan, J., concurring); *San Diego Gas & Elec.*, 450 U.S. at 621 (Brennan, J., dissenting); *Penn Central*, 438 U.S. at 104; *Katobimar*, 20 N.J. at 129 (Brennan, J., dissenting). The solutions proposed by Justice Brennan in the *San Diego Gas & Elec.* and *Metromedia* cases were not suggested by any of the parties or *amici* in the cases. Justice Frankfurter, a former professor of Justice Brennan, allegedly once said, "I always encouraged my students to think for themselves but Brennan goes too far." *See* B. Schwartz, Super Chief: Earl Warren and His Supreme Court—A Judicial Biography 205 (1983).

28. *See, e.g., Nollan*, 107 S. Ct. at 3150 (Brennan, J., dissenting); *Penn Central*, 438 U.S. at 104; *Katobimar*, 20 N.J. at 129 (Brennan, J., dissenting).

29. *See, e.g., Vincent*, 466 U.S. at 818 (Brennan, J., dissenting); *San Diego Gas & Elec.*, 450 U.S. at 636 (Brennan, J., dissenting); *Warth*, 422 U.S. at 519 (Brennan, J., dissenting); *Katobimar*, 20 N.J. at 129 (Brennan, J., dissenting).

30. *See, e.g., Nollan*, 107 S. Ct. at 3150 (Brennan, J., dissenting); *Cobble Close Farm*, 10 N.J. at 442; *Leimann*, 9 N.J. at 336; *Guaclides*, 11 N.J. Super. at 405.

31. *See, e.g., Moore*, 431 U.S. at 506 (Brennan, J., concurring); *Warth*, 422 U.S. at 519 (Brennan, J., dissenting).

32. Justice Brennan is one of only four Supreme Court justices to be appointed from state courts. The others are Justices Holmes, Cardozo and O'Connor.

33. Not one of Justice Brennan's 13 New Jersey land use opinions was the subject of an appeal or petition to the U.S. Supreme Court for review.

34. Explaining their "patent ambiguity," Justice Brennan suggested that the due process and equal protection clauses were "by design . . . broadly phrased to keep their noble principles adaptable to changing conditions and changing concepts of social justice." W. Brennan, The Fourteenth Amendment, *supra* note 3.

35. State judges also interpret state constitutions. *See, e.g., Southern Burlington County NAACP v. Township of Mount Laurel*, 67 N.J. 151, 336 A.2d 713, *cert. denied and appeal dismissed*, 423 U.S. 808 (1975). Because the U.S. Constitution is the supreme law of the land, *see* U.S. Const. art. VI, however, state courts interpreting state constitutions are analogous to a ratchet: they can expand, but never contract, federal constitutional protections afforded individual liberties. To counteract increasingly parsimonious interpretations of the Bill of Rights by a majority of the U.S. Supreme Court, Justice Brennan has urged state courts to do just that. *See* Brennan, *State Constitutions, supra* note 17.

36. This is not to be confused with accusations of unwarranted judicial activism. In construing state statutes, judges are theoretically law interpreters, not lawmakers. Nonetheless, legislatures frequently find that drafting ambiguous laws is politically expedient, letting courts take the heat for unpopular interpretations.

One commentator suggested that the New Jersey Supreme Court in particular "was more akin functionally to the U.S. Supreme Court than most other state supreme courts." Heck, *The Socialization of a Freshman Justice: The Early Years of Justice Brennan*, 10 Pac. L.J. 707, 723 (1979). He described that state court as especially "policy-oriented," concluding that "[l]ike United States Supreme Court justices, New Jersey Supreme Court justices in Brennan's time were likely to look beyond the words of a statute to the *overall policy goals* underlying acts of the legislature." *Id.* at 725; *see also, e.g., Katobimar*, 20 N.J. at 129 (Brennan, J., dissenting).

37. In several articles, Justice Brennan discussed these differences. *See* Brennan, *The Role of the State Supreme Court Justice and the United States Supreme Court Justice*, 56 N.Y. St. B.J. 6 (Oct. 1984); *Remarks of Associate Justice William J. Brennan, Jr., Seventy-Fifth Anniversary Dinner*, 36 Rutgers L. Rev. 725 (1984); Brennan, *State Supreme Court Judge Versus United States Supreme Court Justice: A Change in Function and Perspective*, 19 U. Fla. L. Rev. 225 (1966).

38. *Remarks of Associate Justice William J. Brennan, Jr., supra* note 37, at 726.

39. Undoubtedly speaking from experience, Justice Brennan personally attested to the difference: "[T]he winds of criticism and controversy that swirl around the Court in Washington are generally of a higher velocity than those blowing in state capitols— and the temperature is hotter." Brennan, *Some Aspects of Federalism*, 39 N.Y.U. L. Rev. 945, 949 (1964). In a 1986 television documentary, Justice Brennan recounted a discussion with his mother, soon after he joined the U.S. Supreme Court, about his then-controversial first-term majority opinion in *Jencks v. United States*, 353 U.S. 657 (1957) (holding that criminal defendant, an alleged communist, was entitled to see government reports prepared by witnesses for the government prosecution who would be testifing at his criminal trial): "As I recall so well, my dear mother, with all the hoopla over [the *Jencks* opinion] . . . had neighbors who said . . . they just couldn't understand it. . . . And Mother said to me, 'Gee, I always liked what you wrote on the New Jersey Supreme Court. Why can't you write the same kinds of opinions?' " *See Justice William J. Brennan, Jr.: Justice For All*, WNET-TV, Channel 13, New York City (Oct. 1986).

40. *See The Federalist* nos. 45 and 46 (J. Madison); *The Federalist* no. 32 (A. Hamilton); *see also* U.S. Const. amend. X.

41. *See New State Ice Co. v. Liebmann*, 285 U.S. 262, 311 (1932) (Brandeis, J., dissenting) ("It is one of the happy incidents of the federal system that a single courageous State may, if its citizens choose, serve as a laboratory. . . .").

42. The doctrine of *stare decisis* (to abide by decided cases) means that inferior courts must follow rulings issued by higher courts. U.S. Supreme Court opinions have *stare decisis* or precedential effect for all federal and state courts. State supreme court rulings bind only the courts of their own states.

Chapter 2

1. *See, e.g.*, E. Hoover & R. Vernon, Anatomy of a Metropolis 126–28 (1962); Tunnard, America's Super-Cities, in Taming Megalopolis 4–6 (H. W. Eldredge ed. 1967).

2. *See, e.g.*, Hoover & Vernon, *supra* note 1, at 243–44; C. Abrams, *The City Is the Frontier* 48–49 (1965). As much as these two federal programs created the transportation and financial conditions necessary for the growth of bedroom suburbs, they also

contributed significantly to the decline of central cities. *See, e.g.*, J. Jacobs, The Death and Life of Great American Cities 308–09 (1961).

3. New York City is credited with adoption of the first comprehensive zoning ordinance in 1916. Ten years later, the U.S. Supreme Court upheld the basic constitutionality of zoning in *Village of Euclid v. Ambler Realty Co.*, 272 U.S. 365 (1926).

4. Through the federal government's section 701 planning grant program, cities and towns hired consultants to prepare comprehensive land use plans and new zoning ordinances. *See generally* M. Scott, American City Planning 504–07 (1969). The deficiencies of old plans and bylaws had become increasingly apparent. For example, original ordinances frequently authorized significantly higher densities citywide than would actually be acceptable were developers to build to the maximum. New York City's first zoning law allegedly would have allowed 77 million residents and 344 million workers, obviously ridiculous figures. *See* S. Toll, Zoned American 205 (1969).

5. *See, e.g.*, *Birkfield Realty Co. v. Board of Comm'rs*, 12 N.J. Super. 192, 194–95, 79 A.2d 326, 327–28 (App. Div.), *cert. denied*, 8 N.J. 319 (1951).

6. *See, e.g.*, *Katobimar Realty Co. v. Webster*, 20 N.J. 114, 122–29, 118 A.2d 824, 826–32 (1955).

7. *Id.* at 129 (Brennan, J., dissenting). The New Jersey statute, like that of many other states, was loosely based on a model law prepared in 1924 by the U.S. Dep't of Commerce to encourage adoption of zoning across the country. *Compare* N.J. Stat. Ann. § 40:55–30 (West 1967) *with* U.S. Dep't of Commerce, A Standard State Zoning Enabling Act, Washington, D.C. (1924). The secretary of commerce at that time, who appointed the model act's drafting committee and wrote its foreword, was Herbert Hoover.

8. In *Lochner v. New York*, 198 U.S. 45 (1905), from which the term "Lochnerian" derives, the Supreme Court held unconstitutional a state law setting a maximum number of working hours (10 hours daily, 60 hours weekly) for bakery employees. Applying a stringent test, the Court found the connection between the law's "end" (protecting workers) and "means" (hour limitation) insufficient. *Id.* at 58–63. A series of subsequent cases struck down other legislation interfering with private business relationships. *See, e.g.*, *Burns Baking Co. v. Bryan*, 264 U.S. 504 (1924) (standard weights for bread law); *Adkins v. Children's Hospital*, 261 U.S. 525 (1923) (minimum wage law for women). Indeed, much of President Franklin D. Roosevelt's New Deal socioeconomic legislation was at risk from a second-guessing Lochnerian judiciary. However, the Court finally abandoned its searching review of economic laws and began deferring to the legislature. *See, e.g.*, *United States v. Carolene Products Co.*, 304 U.S. 144 (1938) (adulterated milk law); *West Coast Hotel Co. v. Parrish*, 300 U.S. 379 (1937) (minimum wage law for women); *Nebbia v. New York*, 291 U.S. 502 (1934) (milk pricing law).

A popular, if apocryphal, story has it that Roosevelt's scheme to pack the Court with additional justices sympathetic to his New Deal program convinced Justice Roberts to change, between 1936 and 1937, from a Lochnerian interventionist to a deferential jurist, as evidenced by his decision to support minimum wage laws (even as he also wrote the 1934 *Nebbia* opinion deferring to the legislature). The expression "switch in time that saved nine" memorializes this version of history. *See* L. Tribe, American Constitutional Law, § 8-7, at 580–81 (2d ed. 1988). Henceforth, if the means of a statute bore a rational relationship to its end, the law would pass constitutional muster. *See, e.g.*, *Williamson v. Lee Optical, Inc.*, 348 U.S. 483, 488 (1955); *Day-Brite Lighting, Inc. v. Missouri*, 342 U.S. 421, 423 (1952); *United States v. Carolene Products Co.*, 304 U.S. at 152–54.

9. *See, e.g.*, Jacobs, *supra* note 2, at 270–72.

10. One of the most stark, dramatic photographic images from the pages of *Life* magazine was the demolition by dynamite in the early 1970s of the disastrous Pruitt-Igoe highrise public housing project in St. Louis.

11. This reliance on procedure is a dominant theme throughout Justice Brennan's jurisprudence. *See, e.g.*, Freund, *William J. Brennan, Jr.*, 86 Yale L.J. 1015, 1016 (1977) (Justice Brennan "has been exceptionally resourceful in fashioning justice with the armament of procedure" and his approach is one of "apprehending substantive rights in terms of procedural variants"); Friedman, *Mr. Justice Brennan: The First Decade*, 80 Harv. L. Rev. 7, 16–21 (1966) (noting Justice Brennan's emphasis on the "role of the judiciary and judicial procedures in protecting individual rights").

12. *Katobimar*, 20 N.J. at 114.

13. *Id.* at 118–19.

14. *Id.* at 119.

15. *Id.* at 126.

16. *Id.* at 128.

17. *Id.*

18. A typical "cumulative" or "pyramidal" ordinance specifies individual zoning districts of increasing intensity: single-family housing districts; multifamily districts allowing both single- and multifamily housing; commercial districts allowing single-family, multifamily and commercial uses; and industrial districts allowing all uses. In other words, as districts become more intense in use, they accumulate the less intense uses.

19. *Katobimar*, 20 N.J. at 129 (Brennan, J., dissenting).

20. *Id.*

21. *Id.* at 130–31.

22. *Id.* at 131.

23. *Id.* "Non-nuisance" industries are those that do not create the traditional problems associated with heavy manufacturing, such as air pollution, odors and noise.

24. *Id.* at 132.

25. *Id.* at 133–34.

26. *Birkfield v. Board of Comm'rs*, 12 N.J. Super. 192, 79 A.2d 326 (App. Div.), *cert. denied*, 8 N.J. 319 (1951).

27. *Id.* at 196.

28. *Id.*

29. *Id.* at 197.

30. *Id.* at 197–98 (citation omitted).

31. *Id.* at 198.

32. *Id.* at 199.

33. *Id.*

34. *See, e.g.*, Candeub, *New Techniques in Making the General Plan*, in Urban Planning in Transition 216–24 (E. Erber ed. 1970).

35. N.J. Stat. Ann. § 40:55–32 (West 1967) (zoning "shall be in accordance with a comprehensive plan").

36. Professional and academic circles have debated at great length whether the comprehensive plan must be a document separate from the zoning ordinance or whether the zoning ordinance itself may be dubbed the comprehensive plan. *See* Haar, *"In Accordance with a Comprehensive Plan"*, 68 Harv. L. Rev. 1154 (1955). The New Jersey courts adopted the "zoning ordinance as comprehensive plan" approach. *See Kozesnik v. Township of Montgomery*, 24 N.J. 154, 166–67, 131 A.2d 1, 7–8 (1957) ("The Zoning Act nowhere provides that the comprehensive plan shall exist in some physical form outside the ordinance itself.").

37. *Guaclides v. Borough of Englewood Cliffs*, 11 N.J. Super. 405, 78 A.2d 435 (App. Div. 1951).

38. *Id.* at 411.

39. *Id.*

40. *Id.*

41. *Id.* at 412.

42. *Id.* Illegal "spot zoning" occurs when a municipality zones one parcel of land differently from similar surrounding land without a reasonable basis for the difference in treatment. *See, e.g., Schertzer v. City of Somerville*, 345 Mass. 747, 189 N.E.2d 555 (1963).

43. *Guaclides*, 11 N.J. Super. at 412–13.

44. *Id.* at 410.

45. *Id.*

46. *Id.*

47. *Conlon v. Board of Pub. Works*, 11 N.J. 363, 94 A.2d 660 (1953).

48. *Id.* at 365.

49. *Id.* at 368.

50. *Id.* at 366.

51. *Id.*

52. *Id.* at 368–69. A variance allowing a landowner to deviate from the applicable zoning theoretically is granted only when unique physical circumstances of the property mean that adherence to the zoning would cause undue hardship to the owner. *See infra* note 58.

53. *Casper v. City of Long Branch*, 18 N.J. Super. 90, 86 A.2d 691 (App. Div. 1952).

54. *Id.* at 92.

55. *Id.* at 93.

56. *Village of Euclid v. Ambler Realty Co.*, 272 U.S. 365 (1926).

57. *See* R. Babcock, The Zoning Game 6–8 (1966).

58. *See* N.J. Stat. Ann. § 40:55–39(c) (West 1967); *Leimann v. Board of Adjustment*, 9 N.J. 336, 340–41, 88 A.2d 337, 339 (1952).

59. *Leimann*, 9 N.J. at 336.

60. *Id.* at 341–42.

61. *Rexon v. Board of Adjustment*, 10 N.J. 1, 89 A.2d 233 (1952).

62. *Id.* at 7.

63. *Id.* at 8–9.

64. *Cobble Close Farm v. Board of Adjustment*, 10 N.J. 442, 92 A.2d 4 (1952).

65. *Id.* at 454.

66. *Id.* at 448.

67. *Cf. infra* chapter 3, notes 73–86 and accompanying text (discussing the role of expectations in Justice Brennan's approach to just compensation clause claims).

68. *Struyk v. Samuel Braen's Sons*, 17 N.J. Super. 1, 85 A.2d 279 (App. Div. 1951), *aff'd*, 9 N.J. 294 (1952).

69. *Id.* at 6.

70. *Id.*

71. *Id.*

72. *See supra* note 67.

73. *See, e.g.*, Jacobs, *supra* note 2, at 8–12; Gans, *The Failure of Urban Renewal*, in Urban Renewal 537–39, 543–45 (J. Wilson ed. 1966)

74. These claims would be heard and sustained two decades later by none other than the New Jersey Supreme Court. *See Southern Burlington County NAACP v. Township of Mount Laurel*, 67 N.J. 151, 336 A.2d 713, *cert. denied and appeal dismissed*, 423 U.S. 808 (1975). In the *Mount Laurel* case, the New Jersey Supreme Court held unconstitutional under its state constitution local zoning ordinances failing to provide for a fair share of a region's low-income housing needs. *Id.* at 174; *see* Kayden & Zax, *Mt. Laurel II: Landmark Decision on Zoning and Low Income Housing*, 1984 Zoning & Planning Law Handbook 365. Through zoning bylaws, suburban communities have required large minimum-lot sizes for houses or proscribed multifamily developments, effectively driving housing prices beyond the reach of low- and moderate-income persons. Cases in the 1950s made fleeting references to this effect. *See, e.g., Lionshead Lake, Inc. v. Township of Wayne*, 10 N.J. 165, 89 A.2d 693 (1952) (Oliphant, J., dissenting), *appeal dismissed*, 344 U.S. 919 (1953). Such strategies, still being used by some communities, have earned the name "exclusionary zoning."

75. *Cf. Warth v. Seldin*, 422 U.S. 490, 523, 528–29 (1975) (Brennan, J., dissenting) (suggesting substantive views on alleged exclusionary zoning conduct of Rochester suburb); Brennan, *State Constitutions and the Protection of Individual Rights*, 90 Harv. L. Rev. 489, 501 (1977) (approval of New Jersey Supreme Court's use of state constitution in *Mount Laurel*).

76. *Metromedia, Inc. v. City of San Diego*, 453 U.S. 490 (1981) (Brennan, J., concurring).

77. *Weiner v. Borough of Stratford*, 15 N.J. 295, 104 A.2d 659 (1954).

78. *Id.* at 297.

79. *Id.*

80. *Id.*

81. *Id.* at 299.

82. *Id.* at 300. Justice Brennan showed a keen understanding of, and distaste for, zoning or other regulations used to protect local businesses. *Cf. United Advertising Corp. v. Borough of Raritan*, 11 N.J. 144, 151–52, 93 A.2d 362, 366 (1952) (nothing in billboard ordinance suggests that it is designed to " 'protect local business and to put plaintiff [billboard company] out of business' ").

83. *Weiner*, 15 N.J. at 300 (citations omitted).

84. *United Advertising*, 11 N.J. at 144.

85. Justice Brennan wrote a concurring opinion in the U.S. Supreme Court billboard case. *See Metromedia*, 453 U.S. at 521 (Brennan, J., concurring).

86. *United Advertising*, 11 N.J. at 147.

87. *Id.* at 151.

88. *Id.*

89. *Metromedia*, 433 U.S. at 531 (Brennan, J., concurring).

90. *United Advertising*, 11 N.J. at 151.

91. In *Valentine v. Chrestensen*, 316 U.S. 52 (1942), the Court held that the first amendment did not protect purely commercial speech. Thus, the government could regulate commercial speech just as it regulated other commercial activities. Only in the 1970s did the Court extend the protections of the first amendment to commercial speech. *See Virginia State Bd. of Pharmacy v. Virginia Citizens Consumer Council, Inc.*, 425 U.S. 748 (1976); *Bigelow v. Virginia*, 421 U.S. 809 (1975).

92. *See, e.g., Minnesota v. Clover Leaf Creamery Co.*, 449 U.S. 456, 466 (1981); *Allied Stores, Inc. v. Bowers*, 358 U.S. 522, 530 (1959); *Williamson v. Lee Optical, Inc.*, 348 U.S. 483, 489 (1955).

93. The eminent domain power refers to the authority of the state to take private property for public use, even if the property owner objects, as long as just compensation is paid. In contrast, the police power refers to the authority of the state to enact regulatory laws that protect the health, safety, morals and general welfare of its citizens. A state enacts zoning legislation as an exercise of its police power authority.
   Justice Brennan addressed the eminent domain power in *Morris May Realty Corp. v. Board of Chosen Freeholders*, 18 N.J. 269, 113 A.2d 649 (1955). There, Monmouth County constructed a concrete roadway across land owned by the New York and Long Branch Railroad, subject to a written agreement providing that the county would vacate the property on 60 days' notice. *Id.* at 273. Morris May Realty acquired the land from the railroad and gave notice to vacate. The county refused and adopted a resolution taking the property from Morris May for a highway. *Id.* at 273–74. Finding that the power of eminent domain "is an inherent attribute of sovereignty," Justice Brennan had no truck for arguments that the public sector can bargain away this power through private agreement. *Id.* at 276. Thus, he invalidated the agreement to vacate.

94. That clause commands, "nor shall private property be taken for public use, without just compensation." U.S. Const. amend. V.

95. *See, e.g., Rindge Co. v. County of Los Angeles*, 262 U.S. 700 (1923).

96. *See, e.g., Kohl v. United States*, 91 U.S. 367 (1876).

97. *See, e.g., Berman v. Parker*, 348 U.S. 26 (1954).

98. *See, e.g., Johnson v. Baltimore*, 158 Md. 93, 148 A. 209 (1930).

99. *See, e.g., Laird v. Pittsburg*, 205 Pa. 1, 54 A. 324 (1903).

100. *See, e.g., New York City Housing Auth. v. Muller*, 270 N.Y. 333, 1 N.E.2d 153 (1936).

101. *Poletown Neighborhood Council v. City of Detroit*, 410 Mich. 616, 304 N.W.2d 455 (1981).

102. *Hawaii Housing Auth. v. Midkiff*, 467 U.S. 229 (1984).

103. *Berman*, 348 U.S. at 26.

104. *Camden Plaza Parking, Inc. v. City of Camden*, 16 N.J. 150, 107 A.2d 1 (1954).

105. *Id.* at 153.

106. *Id.* at 154.

107. *Id.* at 155 (citation omitted).

108. *Tice v. Borough of Woodcliff Lake*, 12 N.J. Super. 20, 78 A.2d 825 (App. Div. 1951).

109. *Id.* at 22.

110. *Id.* at 22–23.

Chapter 3

1. *See Nectow v. City of Cambridge*, 277 U.S. 183 (1928); *Gorieb v. Fox*, 274 U.S. 603 (1927); *Zahn v. Board of Public Works*, 274 U.S. 325 (1927); *Village of Euclid v. Ambler Realty Co.*, 272 U.S. 365 (1926); *see also State of Washington ex rel. Seattle Title Trust Co. v. Roberge*, 278 U.S. 116 (1928) (unlawful delegation of zoning power to neighbors).

2. *Goldblatt v. Town of Hempstead*, 369 U.S. 590 (1962).

3. *Id.* at 592–95.

4. *See Nollan v. California Coastal Comm'n*, 107 S. Ct. 3141 (1987); *First English Evangelical Lutheran Church v. County of Los Angeles*, 107 S. Ct. 2378 (1987); *Keystone Bituminous Coal Ass'n v. DeBenedictis*, 480 U.S. 470 (1987); *MacDonald, Sommer & Frates v. County of Yolo*, 477 U.S. 340 (1986); *City of Renton v. Playtime Theatres, Inc.*, 475 U.S. 41 (1986); *City of Cleburne v. Cleburne Living Center, Inc.*, 473 U.S. 432 (1985); *Williamson County Regional Planning Comm'n v. Hamilton Bank*, 473 U.S. 172 (1985); *Hawaii Hous. Auth. v. Midkiff*, 467 U.S. 229 (1984); *Members of City Council v. Taxpayers for Vincent*, 466 U.S. 789 (1984); *Loretto v. Teleprompter Manhattan CATV Corp.*, 458 U.S. 419 (1982); *Larkin v. Grendel's Den, Inc.*, 456 U.S. 913 (1982); *Metromedia, Inc. v. City of San Diego*, 453 U.S. 490 (1981); *Schad v. Borough of Mount Ephraim*, 452 U.S. 61 (1981); *San Diego Gas & Elec. Co. v. City of San Diego*, 450 U.S. 621 (1981); *Agins v. City of Tiburon*, 447 U.S. 255 (1980); *Kaiser Aetna v. United States*, 444 U.S. 164 (1979); *Penn Central Transp. Co. v. New York City*, 438 U.S. 104 (1978); *Moore v. City of East Cleveland*, 431 U.S. 494 (1977); *Village of Arlington Heights v. Metropolitan Hous. Dev. Corp.*, 429 U.S. 252 (1977); *Young v. American Mini Theatres, Inc.*, 427 U.S. 50 (1976); *City of Eastlake*

v. *Forest City Enters.*, 426 U.S. 668 (1976); *Warth v. Seldin*, 422 U.S. 490 (1975); *Village of Belle Terre v. Boraas*, 416 U.S. 1 (1974).

5. *Metromedia, Inc. v. City of San Diego*, 453 U.S. 490 (1981) (Brennan, J., concurring). Justice Brennan's opinion was joined by Justice Blackmun.

6. *See City of Renton v. Playtime Theatres, Inc.*, 475 U.S. 41 (1986) (Brennan, J., dissenting); *Members of City Council v. Taxpayers for Vincent*, 466 U.S. 789 (1984) (Brennan, J., dissenting).

7. *Metromedia*, 453 U.S. at 509–10, 528.

8. *See Virginia State Bd. of Pharmacy v. Virginia Citizens Consumer Council, Inc.*, 425 U.S. 748 (1976) (overruling *Valentine v. Chrestensen*, 316 U.S. 52 (1942)); *Bigelow v. Virginia*, 421 U.S. 809 (1975).

9. *Metromedia*, 453 U.S. at 528.

10. *Id.*

11. *Id.* at 528, 530.

12. *Id.*

13. *Id.*

14. *Id.* at 528–29.

15. *Id.* at 531.

16. For many years, courts declined to consider the public purpose of aesthetics, standing alone, as a sufficient government justification for exercise of the police power. Only if aesthetics was accompanied by a reason drawn directly from the police power's famous quartet of health, safety, morals or general welfare would the regulation be sustained. For billboard regulations, municipalities routinely proffered traffic safety along with aesthetics to satisfy this "aesthetics plus" doctrine. *See Metromedia*, 453 U.S. at 529–30 n.7; *State v. Diamond Motors, Inc.*, 50 Haw. 33, 36, 429 P.2d 825, 827 (1967).

17. *Metromedia*, 453 U.S. at 531–32.

18. *Id.* at 532.

19. *Id.* at 530–31 (citation omitted).

20. *Id.* at 531.

21. *Id.*

22. *Id.* at 532–33 (footnotes omitted).

23. *See United Advertising Corp. v. Borough of Raritan*, 11 N.J. 144, 151, 93 A.2d 362, 366 (1952).

24. *See supra* chapter 2, note 91.

25. *See Weiner v. Borough of Stratford*, 15 N.J. 295, 104 A.2d 659 (1954).

26. *Id.* at 299–300.

27. *Metromedia*, 453 U.S. at 513.

28. *Id.* at 522 n.26.

29. *Id.* at 536.

30. *Id.* at 536–37; *see also Freedman v. Maryland*, 380 U.S. 51, 56–60 (1965) (insufficient provision in film licensing statute for prompt judicial review of discretionary government decisions). A Supreme Court decision involving newspaper boxes located on public property, decided while this book was in press, addressed the discretion issue. *See City of Lakewood v. Plain Dealer Publishing Co.*, 108 S. Ct. 2138 (1988). A Lakewood, Ohio, ordinance vested the mayor with unlimited discretion to decide which newspaper publishers could place newspaper boxes on public property and where the boxes could be located. The U.S. Supreme Court, in a four-to-three decision written by Justice Brennan, struck down the ordinance, *inter alia*, because it gave the mayor too much discretion in an area where first amendment interests were at stake. *See id.* at 2143–45, 2152; *see also Plain Dealer Publishing Co. v. City of Lakewood*, 794 F.2d 1139, 1143–45 (6th Cir. 1986) (lower court decision).

31. *Metromedia*, 453 U.S. at 538.

32. *City of Renton v. Playtime Theatres, Inc.*, 475 U.S. at 41 (Brennan, J., dissenting); *Members of City Council v. Taxpayers for Vincent*, 466 U.S. at 789 (Brennan, J., dissenting).

33. *Vincent*, 466 U.S. at 789.

34. *Id.* at 817. Unlike *Metromedia*, however, where San Diego's ban applied principally to billboards erected on private property, the Los Angeles ordinance contested in *Vincent* prohibited posters placed on public property.

35. *Id.* at 792–93.

36. *Id.* at 795.

37. *Id.*

38. *Id.* at 821.

39. *Id.* at 822.

40. *Id.* at 824.

41. *Id.* at 827.

42. *Id.* at 828.

43. *Id.*

44. *Renton*, 475 U.S. at 41.

45. *Id.* at 44.

46. *Id.* at 57–63.

47. *Id.* at 60.

48. *Id.* at 61–62.

49. *Penn Central Transp. Co. v. New York City*, 438 U.S. 104 (1978). The pragmatic factual issue, preservation of Grand Central Terminal, caused enormous stirrings in New York City architecture and planning circles. A group of luminaries, who included Jacqueline Onassis, New York Sen. Daniel Moynihan and Joan Mondale, actively and publicly supported preservation. The Municipal Art Society, a New York City public-interest organization, arranged a whistle-stopping train convoy, named the Landmark Express, from New York to Washington, D.C., to publicize the fight and also, coincidentally, to bring individuals to witness the Supreme Court oral argument. *See generally* R. Babcock & C. Siemon, The Zoning Game Revisited 67–69 (1985).

50. *Penn Central*, 438 U.S. at 108–11.

51. *Id.* at 110–11 nn.9 & 11.

52. *Id.* at 111.

53. *Id.* at 112.

54. *Id.* at 115.

55. *Id.* at 116–17.

56. *Id.* at 119.

57. *Id.* at 124 (citation omitted).

58. *Id.* at 124.

59. *Id.*

60. *Id.* at 132–35.

61. *Id.* at 132.

62. *Id.*

63. *See Armstrong v. United States*, 364 U.S. 40, 49 (1960).

64. Justice Rehnquist was joined by Chief Justice Burger and Justice Stevens. Justice Stevens later backed away from his view that a regulation can effect a taking and that just compensation must be paid. *See Williamson County Regional Planning Comm'n v. Hamilton Bank*, 473 U.S. 172 (1985) (Stevens, J., concurring). His attempt (not entirely convincing) to reconcile his *Penn Central* vote with his new view was set forth in his dissenting opinion in *First English Evangelical Lutheran Church v. County of Los Angeles*, 107 S. Ct. 2378, 2394 (1987) (Stevens, J., dissenting).

65. *Penn Central*, 438 U.S. at 134–35.

66. *See Pennsylvania Coal Co. v. Mahon*, 260 U.S. 393, 415 (1922). Justice Holmes found that a state statute prohibiting mining companies that owned subterranean rights from digging coal in places where surface structures might be harmed through subsidence constituted a taking. Unlike another coal case, in which a state requirement that pillars of coal be left in the ground to prevent flooding benefited all mining companies, *see Plymouth Coal Co. v. Pennsylvania*, 232 U.S. 531 (1914), Justice Holmes in *Pennsylvania Coal* saw no average reciprocity of advantage between the mining company and the surface homeowners.

67. *Penn Central*, 438 U.S. at 147 (Rehnquist, J., dissenting). It is unclear whether Justice Rehnquist's calculation included buildings located within the 31 historic districts. If it did not, then he underestimated the comprehensiveness of the landmark law's application.

68. Constitutional land use law scholars do not fare much better. Indeed, the question of what is a regulatory taking has perplexed them for years, generating numerous law review articles and several books. Attempts at all-encompassing theories are rarely made and have yet to convince. Some of the interesting writings on the issue include Michelman, *Property, Utility, and Fairness: Comments on the Ethical Foundations of 'Just Compensation' Law*, 80 Harv. L. Rev. 1165 (1967); Sax, *Takings, Private Property and Public Rights*, 81 Yale L.J. 149 (1971); Sax, *Takings and the Police Power*, 74 Yale L.J. 36 (1964); B. Ackerman, Private Property and the Constitution (1977); R. Epstein, Takings: Private Property and the Power of Eminent Domain (1985).

69. *See, e.g., Goldblatt v. Town of Hempstead,* 369 U.S. at 592–93; *Cobble Close Farm v. Board of Adjustment,* 10 N.J. 442, 452, 92 A.2d 4, 9 (1952).

70. *See, e.g., Agins v. City of Tiburon,* 447 U.S. at 260.

71. *Pennsylvania Coal Co. v. Mahon,* 260 U.S. 393 (1922).

72. *See id.* at 413 (diminution of value inquiry).

73. *Penn Central,* 438 U.S. at 124; *see* Michelman, *supra* note 68, at 1229–34.

74. *Penn Central,* 438 U.S. at 131.

75. *Cf. supra* chapter 2, notes 64–72 and accompanying text (discussing *Cobble Close Farm v. Board of Adjustment,* 10 N.J. 442, 92 A.2d 4 (1952); *Struyk v. Samuel Braen's Sons,* 17 N.J. Super. 1, 85 A.2d 279 (App. Div. 1951), *aff'd,* 9 N.J. 294 (1952)).

76. One of Justice Brennan's New Jersey opinions partially relied upon a similar notion of expectations, by not rescuing a landowner from "situations of its own making." *See Cobble Close Farm,* 10 N.J. at 453–54 (property acquisition with full knowledge of applicable zoning militates against finding of undue hardship adequate for grant of variance).

77. *See, e.g.,* W. Brueggeman & L. Stone, Real Estate Finance 331 (1981).

78. *See, e.g., Ruckelshaus v. Monsanto Co.,* 467 U.S. 986 (1984).

79. *Penn Central,* 438 U.S. at 129 & n.26.

80. *See* Reich, *Individual Rights and Social Welfare: The Emerging Legal Issues,* 74 Yale L.J. 1245, 1255–56 (1965); Reich, *The New Property,* 73 Yale L.J. 733, 785–86 (1964).

81. It is interesting to speculate whether individuals must receive compensation under the fifth amendment's just compensation clause when "new property" rights are improperly withdrawn. *See generally First English,* 107 S. Ct. at 2378.

82. *Goldberg v. Kelly,* 397 U.S. 254, 262 n.8 (1970). The death knell was sounding for the "rights-privilege" distinction—whereby categorizing entitlements as privileges (rather than rights) allowed them to be terminated without any process at all.

83. *See, e.g., Bishop v. Wood,* 426 U.S. 341 (1976). *See generally* Rubin, *Due Process in the Administrative State,* 72 Calif. L. Rev. 1044, 1074 (1984).

84. *Bishop,* 426 U.S. at 353 (citation omitted) (Brennan, J., dissenting).

85. *Id.* (quoting *Board of Regents v. Roth,* 408 U.S. 564, 577 (1972)). Justice Brennan further emphasized expectations in defining property rights: "At a minimum, [determination of the property right] would require in this case an analysis of the common practices utilized and the expectations generated by [the government], and the manner in which the local ordinance would reasonably be read by [the government's] employees." *Bishop,* 426 U.S. at 353–54 (Brennan, J., dissenting). Some scholars have identified an apparent dissimilarity between Justice Brennan's treatment of new property and traditional private property. Michelman noted the "possible appearance of inconsistent attitudes on the Justice's part towards constitutional protection for property interests—cavalier (as an unsympathetic critic might say) in . . . *Penn Central,* solicitous in *Goldberg* and *Bishop.*" Michelman, *Mr. Justice Brennan: A Property Teacher's Appreciation,* 15 Harv. C.R.-C.L. L. Rev. 296, 302 (1980). Explaining the difference, Michelman suggested a "principled account" that explored the relative importance of the property interest to "the maintenance of the conditions of one's fair and effective participation in the constituted order." *Id.* at 305–06. Under this

"structural" view of property rights, the denial of welfare benefits or a public job comes much closer to threatening an individual's effective participation in society and the political order than does the denial of development rights suffered by, for example, Penn Central: "Loss—even great loss—of the economic value of one's property holdings does not as such violate" that participation, while "exposure to sudden changes in the major elements and crucial determinants of one's established position in the world" does. *Id.* at 306. Michelman added, "[T]hat, if true, would go far towards explaining Brennan's adherence to the Holmesian idea that a legislative regulation becomes a compensable taking when it has the effect of largely destroying the utility of any of a person's significant holdings," *id.* (footnote omitted), but not before the regulation has that destructive effect.

Doubtless, Justice Brennan is especially concerned about the lower-end needs of individuals. He has explained, for example, that "[r]ecognition of so-called 'new property' rights in those receiving government entitlements affirms the essential dignity of the least fortunate among us by demanding that government treat with decency, integrity and consistency those dependent on its benefits for their very survival." W. Brennan, The Constitution of the United States: Contemporary Ratification, Presentation at Georgetown University Text & Teaching Symposium (Oct. 12, 1985), *quoted in* Defeis, *Justice William J. Brennan, Jr.*, 18 Seton Hall L. Rev. 429, 438–39 (1986); *see also, e.g., Shapiro v. Thompson*, 394 U.S. 618, 627 (1969) (per Justice Brennan) (one-year residency requirement for welfare benefits unconstitutionally penalizes fundamental right to travel; welfare benefits may be critical for obtaining "food, shelter, and other necessities of life," the "very means to subsist"). And much of his overall jurisprudence is informed by the general goal of ensuring the effective participation of all individuals in society and self-government. *Cf., e.g.,* Denvir, *Justice Brennan, Justice Rehnquist, and Free Speech*, 80 Nw. U.L. Rev. 285, 304–05 (1985) (Justice Brennan's "structural" view of free press and free speech, derived from A. Meiklejohn); Brennan, *The Supreme Court and the Meiklejohn Interpretation of the First Amendment*, 79 Harv. L. Rev. 1 (1965).

Michelman's interesting theory of reconciliation need not obscure, however, the similarity of Justice Brennan's analytical reliance on reasonable expectations as the core determinant defining the contours of the property right in both new and traditional property lines of cases. Furthermore, the different remedies invoked in each case make it perilous to posit that Justice Brennan favors new property over private property. After all, in *Goldberg* and *Bishop*, the remedial question was what process must accompany deprivation of new property. In *Penn Central*, the remedy sought was not process, but the payment of just compensation and an injunction against the deprivation itself. Justice Brennan never disputed, in any of the due process cases, the government's ultimate right to deprive the welfare recipient or public employee of the entitlement (unless, perhaps, that right were defined as permanent and irrevocable). *But cf.* Michelman, *supra*, 15 Harv. C.R.-C.L. L. Rev. at 304 (citing Justice Brennan's majority opinion in *Shapiro v. Thompson*, 394 U.S. 618 (1969), as a harbinger of his view on the deprivation issue); *supra* note 81. Finally, it should be remembered that Justice Brennan joined the majority opinion in *Lynch v. Household Fin. Corp.*, in which the Court stated that "the dichotomy between personal liberties and property rights is a false one" and the "right to enjoy property without unlawful deprivation, no less than the right to speak or the right to travel, is in truth a 'personal' right, whether the 'property' in question be a welfare check, a home, or a saving's account." 405 U.S. 538, 552 (1972) ("rights in property are basic civil rights").

86. *Penn Central*, 438 U.S. at 130–31.

87. *Id.* at 130.

88. Penn Central was denied permission only to build the two towers above Grand

Central Terminal that it proposed to the commission. Other proposals that meshed better with the landmark terminal might have been approved. *See id.* at 137 & n.34.

89. *Id.* at 113–15.

90. *Id.* at 137.

91. *Id.* at 113–15.

92. *Id.* at 150.

93. *Id.* at 152.

94. *See* N.Y. Times, Sept. 17, 1986, at B1, col. 3. Subsequent negotiations over the number of square feet to be transferred have continued to focus on the 800,000-square-foot figure. One of the requirements under the landmarks law transfer provision is a certain degree of adjacency between the "sending site," in this case the property owned by Penn Central, and the "receiving site," the Madison Avenue parcel. But can Penn Central claim that other sites, adjacent to its underground rail lines miles away from the terminal itself, also qualify as receiving sites?

95. *See* Duerksen & Bonderman, *Preservation Law: Where It's Been, Where It's Going,* and Duerksen, *Local Preservation Law,* in A Handbook on Historic Preservation Law 19, 30–31 (1983).

96. *San Diego Gas & Elec. Co. v. City of San Diego,* 450 U.S. 621 (1981).

97. Given his history as a prolific writer of dissents, it is not surprising that Justice Brennan is the author of an article extolling the role of dissenting opinions. *See* Brennan, *In Defense of Dissents,* The Pennsylvania Gazette, Feb. 1986, at 20.

98. *Pennsylvania Coal,* 260 U.S. at 415. Some have insisted that Justice Holmes's phrase be interpreted metaphorically, not literally, and that a regulation can never effect a taking of private property in violation of the just compensation clause. *Compare* Williams, Smith, Sicmon, Mandelker & Babcock, *The White River Junction Manifesto,* 9 Vt. L. Rev. 193, 210 & n.57 (1984) *with* Berger & Kanner, *Thoughts on The White River Junction Manifesto: A Reply to the "Gang of Five's" Views on Just Compensation for Regulatory Taking of Property,* 19 Loy. L.A.L. Rev. 686, 726–28 (1986). *See also infra* note 120.

99. *San Diego Gas & Elec.,* 450 U.S. at 633.

100. *Id.* at 653. Justice Brennan was joined by Justices Stewart, Marshall and Powell.

101. *Id.* at 633 (Rehnquist, J., concurring).

102. *Id.* at 633–34.

103. *See, e.g.,* Bauman, *The Supreme Court, Inverse Condemnation and the Fifth Amendment: Justice Brennan Confronts the Inevitable in Land Use Controls,* 15 Rutgers L.J. 15, 18 (1983).

104. The dissent was followed by six U.S. Courts of Appeal, the U.S. Court of Claims and five state supreme courts. *See Nemmers v. City of Dubuque,* 764 F.2d 502, 505 n.2 (8th Cir. 1985); *Hamilton Bank v. Williamson County Regional Planning Comm'n,* 729 F.2d 402, 408–09 (6th Cir. 1984), *rev'd on other grounds,* 473 U.S. 172 (1985); *United States v. Riverside Bayview Homes, Inc.,* 729 F.2d 391, 398 (6th Cir. 1984), *rev'd on other grounds,* 474 U.S. 121 (1985); *Martino v. Santa Clara Valley Water Dist.,* 703 F.2d 1141, 1148 (9th Cir.), *cert. denied,* 464 U.S. 847 (1983); *Barbian v. Panagis,* 694 F.2d 476, 482 n.5 (7th Cir. 1982); *In re Aircrash in Bali,* 684 F.2d 1301, 1311 n.7 (9th Cir. 1982); *Fountain v. Metropolitan Atlanta Rapid Transit Auth.,* 678

F.2d 1038, 1043 (11th Cir. 1982); *Devines v. Maier*, 665 F.2d 138, 142 (7th Cir. 1981); *Hernandez v. City of Lafayette*, 643 F.2d 1188, 1199-200 (5th Cir. 1981), *cert. denied*, 455 U.S. 907 (1982); *Jentgen v. United States*, 657 F.2d 1210, 1212 & n.3 (Ct. Cl. 1981), *cert. denied*, 455 U.S. 1017 (1982); *Deltona Corp. v. United States*, 657 F.2d 1184, 1190 & n.13 (Ct. Cl. 1981), *cert. denied*, 455 U.S. 1017 (1982); *Corrigan v. City of Scottsdale*, 149 Ariz. 538, 541, 720 P.2d 513, 516 (1986); *Rippley v. City of Lincoln*, 330 N.W.2d 505, 510-11 (N.D. 1983); *Zinn v. State*, 112 Wis. 2d 417, 428-29 & n.6, 334 N.W.2d 67, 72 & n.6 (1983); *Pratt v. Dep't of Natural Resources*, 309 N.W.2d 767, 774 (Minn. 1981) (indicating general agreement with the idea that a regulation can effect a taking); *Burrows v. City of Keene*, 121 N.H. 590, 599, 432 A.2d 15, 20 (1981); *see also Sheerr v. Township of Evesham*, 184 N.J. Super. 11, 61-63, 445 A.2d 46, 73 (1982) (lengthy trial court opinion). In perhaps the most brazen of the state court opinions, the California Court of Appeal, Second District, openly attacked its parent state supreme court for that court's *Agins v. City of Tiburon*, 24 Cal. 3d 266, 598 P.2d 25, 157 Cal. Rptr. 372 (1979), *aff'd on other grounds*, 447 U.S. 255 (1980), decision, observing that "California's position flatly contradicts clear precedent of United States Supreme Court cases," i.e., the *San Diego Gas & Elec.* dissent of Justice Brennan. *See Gilliland v. City of Palmdale*, 127 Cal. App. 3d 396, 179 Cal. Rptr. 627, 631-32 (1981) (opinion withdrawn and deleted from reporter by order of state supreme court, Feb. 10, 1982).

105. *San Diego Gas & Elec.*, 450 U.S. at 624.

106. *Id.*

107. *Id.*

108. *Id.*

109. *Id.* at 625.

110. *Id.*

111. *Id.* at 625-26.

112. *Id.* at 627.

113. *Id.* at 628. The California Supreme Court decision was *Agins v. City of Tiburon*, 24 Cal. 3d 266, 598 P.2d 25, 157 Cal. Rptr. 372 (1979), *aff'd*, 447 U.S. 255 (1980). In *Agins*, five acres of unimproved land in Tiburon, Calif., were downzoned by the city, allowing for construction of a maximum of five single-family homes. 24 Cal. 3d at 271. The landowners sued the city, alleging that the rezoning reduced the value of their land by $2 million and that it constituted a taking of property without just compensation. *Id.* The California Supreme Court found no taking and also stated that property owners would in any event only be entitled to judicial invalidation of an overbearing land use regulation, not to compensation. *Id.* at 273-77. The U.S. Supreme Court agreed that there was no taking and thus declined to reach the invalidation versus compensation remedy question. *See Agins v. City of Tiburon*, 447 U.S. 255, 263 (1980).

114. *San Diego Gas & Elec.*, 450 U.S. at 629-30.

115. *Id.* at 630 & n.10. Justice Blackmun's majority was joined by Chief Justice Burger and Justices White, Rehnquist and Stevens.

116. *Id.* at 639-46.

117. Twelve "friend of the court" briefs were filed in the case.

118. *See San Diego Gas & Elec.*, 450 U.S. at 647 (footnote omitted).

119. Of course, there may be other ways to gain monetary relief, through, for example, the federal civil rights statute, 42 U.S.C. § 1983 (1981).

120. *See Fred F. French Investing Co. v. City of New York*, 39 N.Y.2d 587, 594, 350 N.E.2d 381, 385, 385 N.Y.S.2d 5, 9, *cert. denied and appeal dismissed*, 429 U.S. 990 (1976). In the *French* case, a developer proposed to build apartment towers on two small park sites that he controlled. *Id.* at 592. In response, the city enacted a special park zoning district that allowed only passive recreational uses on the park sites, disallowed the towers but authorized the transfer of development rights above the park sites to other areas in the city. *Id.* Writing for the New York Court of Appeals (the highest court in New York), Chief Judge Breitel struck down the zoning as unconstitutional, *id.* at 597, but not as a taking, *id.* at 595. He observed that, although "many cases have equated an invalid exercise of the regulating zoning power, perhaps only metaphorically, with a 'taking' or a 'confiscation' of property," the "metaphor should not be confused with the reality" that a taking cannot occur when government only regulates. *Id.* at 594; *cf. Agins v. City of Tiburon*, 24 Cal. 3d at 274.

121. *See Penn Central Transp. Co. v. City of New York*, 42 N.Y.2d 324, 329, 366 N.E.2d 1271, 1274, 397 N.Y.S.2d 914, 917 (1977), *aff'd*, 438 U.S. 104 (1978).

122. *See supra* notes 98, 120.

123. *San Diego Gas & Elec.*, 450 U.S. at 647–49.

124. *Id.* at 652 (footnote omitted).

125. *Id.* at 652–53.

126. In general, Justice Brennan has no patience for "abstractions without substance." *National League of Cities v. Usery*, 426 U.S. 833, 860 (1976) (Brennan, J., dissenting); *see, e.g.*, W. Brennan, Justice Thurgood Marshall: Defender of Libertarian Dignity Protected Through Law, Address at Dedication of Thurgood Marshall Law Library, University of Maryland Law School (Oct. 9, 1980), *reprinted in* The Reporter, Passaic County Bar Ass'n, vol. VI, at 9 (Spring 1984) ("The shift must be away from finespun technicalities and abstract rules.").

127. Thus, Justice Brennan also implicitly espoused one theoretical track along which both the police and eminent domain powers are exercised. Under this view, use of the police power may travel sufficiently far down the track that it crosses the line separating constitutional from unconstitutional action. When that line is crossed, an "inverse condemnation" action may be brought, inverse because it is the property owner, not the government, that initiates the condemnation or taking proceeding. *See United States v. Clarke*, 445 U.S. 253, 257 (1980).

128. *San Diego Gas & Elec.*, 450 U.S. at 653.

129. *Id.* at 653, 658.

130. *Id.* at 653.

131. *Id.* at 655 n.22.

132. *Id.* at 653 (footnotes omitted).

133. *Id.* at 658.

134. *Id.* at 657.

135. *Id.* at 654.

136. *Id.* at 656.

137. It is important to observe that the period of taking does not necessarily commence as of the day the regulation is enacted. Landowners must attempt to exempt themselves from the regulation, or have the regulation changed, before successfully bringing an as-applied takings challenge. *See MacDonald, Sommer & Frates v. County of Yolo*, 477 U.S. 340 (1986) (denial of development plan not sufficient to conclude no development would be permitted; landowner should apply again); *Williamson County Regional Planning Comm'n v. Hamilton Bank*, 473 U.S. 172 (1985) (failure to seek variance makes claim of regulatory taking premature).

138. *San Diego Gas & Elec.*, 450 U.S. at 660.

139. *Id.* at 659–60. He does refer to general principles of eminent domain valuation as a starting point. *Id.*

140. *Id.* at 661 n.27. Some commentators have been confused on this point, stating incorrectly that Justice Brennan found a regulatory taking on the facts of the *San Diego Gas & Elec.* case. *See, e.g.*, R. Babcock & C. Siemon, The Zoning Game Revisited 60–61 (1985).

141. *See Owen v. City of Independence*, 445 U.S. 622 (1980) (no good faith immunity for § 1983 suits); *Davis v. Passman*, 442 U.S. 228 (1979) (implied right of action for damages under fifth amendment); *Monell v. Dep't of Social Servs.*, 436 U.S. 658 (1978) (cities liable under § 1983); *Bivens v. Six Unknown Named Agents of Fed. Bureau of Narcotics*, 403 U.S. 388 (1971) (implied right of action for damages under fourth amendment). Indeed, Justice Brennan's dissent cited analogously to *Owen v. City of Independence, supra. See San Diego Gas & Elec.*, 450 U.S. at 661 n.26.

142. *See, e.g.*, R. Epstein, Takings: Private Property and the Power of Eminent Domain 191–92 (1985).

143. Williams, *The Constitutional Vulnerability of American Local Government: The Politics of City Status in American Law*, 1986 Wis. L. Rev. 83, 125 & n.220, 135–36. *See generally* Haar & Kayden, *Private Property vs. Public Use*, N.Y. Times, July 29, 1987. at A23, cols. 3–4.

144. *San Diego Gas & Elec.*, 450 U.S. at 661 n.26.

145. *Cf. Bivens*, 403 U.S. at 395–97. In an article comparing the "city status" theories of Thomas M. Cooley, John F. Dillon, the Burger Court's conservative majority and Justice Brennan, one commentator concluded that the Brennan opinions "expanding municipal liability in section 1983, antitrust and inverse condemnation suits . . . are premised on the idea that cities lack inherent sovereignty." Williams, *supra* note 143, at 84 (footnotes omitted) (citing *Owen*, 445 U.S. at 622; *Monell*, 436 U.S. at 658; *Community Communications Co. v. City of Boulder*, 455 U.S. 40 (1982) (antitrust actions lie against "home rule" cities unless clear articulation and affirmative expression of state policy extends antitrust exemption to localities); *City of Lafayette v. Louisiana Power & Light Co.*, 435 U.S. 389 (1978) (plurality opinion) (antitrust actions lie against cities); *San Diego Gas & Elec.*, 450 U.S. at 636); *see also* Williams, *supra* note 143, at 121 ("Brennan often relies heavily on the principle established by Dillon that cities have no inherent sovereignty. . . ."). Indeed, Williams referred to "[w]hat urbanists have considered Brennan's nigh-monomaniacal insistence on broad city liability," *id.* at 125 (footnote omitted), and asserted that "knowledgeable observers believe that if Brennan's positions were to predominate, American cities would lose much of the independence they gained at the turn of the century when home rule statutes gave cities broad authority over local affairs," *id.* at 121 (footnote omitted) (failing, however, to identify these "knowledgeable observers").

While interesting, the effort to shoehorn the three different lines of cases (§ 1983, antitrust and takings liability) into an all-encompassing anti-urban theory is ultimately unconvincing. For purposes of statutory and constitutional analysis, cities are different legal entities from state and federal governments, and Justice Brennan took note of that difference, especially in the antitrust cases (exploring the reach of the *Parker v. Brown*, 317 U.S. 341 (1943), state antitrust exemption). But it is his belief in ensuring effective monetary remedies for violations of constitutional rights against all levels of government, not some anti-city bias, that explains his judicial attitude. He believes, for example, in monetary remedies implied directly under the Constitution against the federal government. *See, e.g., Bivens*, 403 U.S. at 395–97. He dissented from Court decisions broadly interpreting state sovereign immunity under the eleventh amendment. *See, e.g., Atascadero State Hosp. v. Scanlon*, 473 U.S. 234 (1985) (Brennan, J., dissenting) (broad discussion of eleventh amendment sovereign immunity; immunity should not attach when citizen sues his or her own state); *Edelman v. Jordan*, 415 U.S. 651 (1974) (Brennan, J., dissenting) (retroactive money payments). His *San Diego Gas & Elec.* compensation remedy presumably applies to all levels of governments (although the eleventh amendment impinges on direct suits against states *qua* states). He read the federal Tucker Act, 28 U.S.C. § 1491 (1973), as providing a monetary remedy against the federal government for, *inter alia*, takings claims. *See The Regional Rail Reorganization Act Cases*, 419 U.S. 102, 125–36 (1974) (per J. Brennan); *see also id.* at 134 ("[T]here are clearly grave doubts whether the Rail Act would be constitutional if a Tucker Act remedy were not available as compensation for any unconstitutional [taking] not compensated under the Act itself."). Forced by the anti-city theory, Williams ended up characterizing Justice Brennan's *Penn Central* opinion as essentially anti-city, pro-property rights, *id.* at 136 n.279, a position most property owners would find nothing short of astonishing. Even Williams finally adopted the effective remedy explanation, *see id.* at 122, 125, 130, 134 n.266, 137, apparently without recognizing how it made nugatory the "city status" explanation.

146. *See supra* note 104.

147. *See MacDonald, Sommer & Frates v. County of Yolo*, 477 U.S. 340 (1986); *Williamson County Regional Planning Comm'n v. Hamilton Bank*, 473 U.S. 172 (1985). Added to the 1980 *Agins* and 1981 *San Diego Gas & Elec.* cases, the Supreme Court marched up and down the hill four times before it dispelled the Myth of Sisyphus analogy and reached the compensation issue on its fifth try.

148. *Cf.* Berger, *Anarchy Reigns Supreme*, 29 Wash. U.J. Urb. & Contemp. L. 39, 39–42 (1985) (agonizing over three of the five efforts).

149. The Supreme Court, in its six-to-three opinion written by Chief Justice Rehnquist, stated, "We merely hold that where the government's activities have already worked a taking of all use of property, no subsequent action by the government can relieve it of the duty to provide compensation for the period during which the taking was effective." *First English*, 107 S. Ct. at 2389. However, the Court did not decide whether a taking actually occurred under the set of facts presented and thus remanded the case to the lower state courts for further deliberation. *Id.* The facts may make it difficult for the church ultimately to prevail.

The church operated a recreational camp for handicapped children on rural canyon land northeast of Los Angeles. In 1978 a flood destroyed all the camp buildings on its property. Soon thereafter, the county of Los Angeles enacted an ordinance temporarily prohibiting all building construction or reconstruction in an area including the church campground, and the church challenged that ordinance. Several years later, the county enacted a permanent ordinance providing that

A person shall not use, erect, construct, move onto, or . . . alter, modify, enlarge or reconstruct any building or structure within the boundaries of a flood protection district except . . . [a]ccessory buildings and structures that will not substantially impede the flow of water, including sewer, gas, electrical, and water systems, approved by the county engineer . . . [a]utomobile parking facilities incidental to a lawfully established use . . . [and] [f]lood-control structures approved by the chief engineer of the Los Angeles County Flood Control District. *Id.* at 2384–85 n.7 (quoting Los Angeles County Code § 22.44.-220). The question for the state courts will be whether the owners have a constitutional right to "use" their property, even though such use will necessarily endanger the occupants because of the potential flood conditions. *Cf.* 107 S. Ct. at 2384–85. Does the state have authority under its police power to protect the health or welfare of its citizens by banning dangerous activities on private property, or must it pay compensation to the owner? One suspects that, given the onerous nature of the regulation, the frequency and predictability of serious flooding may be central issues at trial.

150. *First English*, 107 S. Ct. at 2378.

151. *Nollan v. California Coastal Comm'n*, 107 S. Ct. 3141, 3163–64 (1987) (Stevens, J., dissenting).

152. *Id.* at 3141.

153. *Id.* at 3143.

154. *Id.; see also id.* at 3158 (Brennan, J., dissenting).

155. *Id.* at 3143.

156. *Id.* at 3143–44.

157. *Id.*

158. *Id.* at 3143.

159. *Id.* at 3150.

160. *Id.* at 3145 (quoting *Loretto v. Teleprompter Manhattan CATV Corp.*, 458 U.S. 419, 433 (1982)).

161. *Nollan*, 107 S. Ct. at 3146.

162. *Id.* at 3146–47, 3150. This formulation was first announced in *Agins v. City of Tiburon*: "The application of a general zoning law to particular property effects a taking if the ordinance does not substantially advance legitimate state interests or denies an owner economically viable use of his land." 447 U.S. at 260 (citations omitted).

163. *Nollan*, 107 S. Ct. at 3147–50.

164. *Id.* at 3147.

165. *Id.* (footnote and citation omitted). The caveat "unless the denial would interfere so drastically with the Nollans' use of their property as to constitute a taking," although on the surface tautological, presumably referred to the constitutional requirement that, in all events, landowners must be left with some reasonable use of their property. One can question whether this is true in cases where all uses of a property, no matter what mitigating conditions are imposed, are harmful. Perhaps Justice Scalia believed that property owners are always entitled to some use, even if harmful, and that when all use is taken, compensation must be paid. *But see, e.g., Hadacheck v. Sebastian*, 239 U.S. 394 (1915); *Mugler v. Kansas*, 123 U.S. 623 (1887).

166. *Nollan*, 107 S. Ct. at 3147.

167. *Id.* at 3147–48. If Justice Scalia's suggestion of a viewing spot on the Nollan property is to be taken seriously, then the decisive problem with the commission's beach easement is surely not the fact that it is a physical invasion.

168. *Id.* at 3149.

169. *Id.*

170. *Id.* at 3148 (citations omitted).

171. *Id.* at 3150 (emphasis in original). The full quotation reads:
[O]ur cases describe the condition for abridgement of property rights through the police power as a "substantial advanc[ing]" of a legitimate State interest. We are inclined to be particularly careful about the adjective where the actual convey-ance of property is made a condition to the lifting of a land use restriction, since in that context there is heightened risk that the purpose is avoidance of the com-pensation requirement, rather than the stated police power objective.
Id. at 3150 (emphasis in original). For those who would like to limit *Nollan*'s applica-bility to conditions or regulations authorizing physical invasions by the public, the language "[w]e are inclined to be particularly careful" is problematic.

172. *Village of Euclid v. Ambler Realty Co.*, 272 U.S. 359, 395 (1926).

173. *Nollan*, 107 S. Ct. at 3147 n.3. Will land use regulations abridging private prop-erty rights now receive the same "intermediate scrutiny" applied in sex discrimina-tion cases, a standard pioneered, ironically, by Justice Brennan himself? *See, e.g., Craig v. Boren*, 429 U.S. 190, 197, 204 (1976) (invalidating law establishing lower drinking age for females than for males under intermediate scrutiny standard). Will Justice Scalia's footnote 3 garner the same level of notoriety with land use aficionados as has Justice Stone's footnote 4, in *United States v. Carolene Prods. Co.*, 304 U.S. 144, 152–53 n.4 (1938) (discussing need for careful judicial scrutiny of infringements on fundamental rights and discrimination against discrete and insular minorities), with constitutional law observers? More important, will Justice Scalia's admonition have the same impact in the development of land use law as the *Carolene Prods.* foot-note has had generally? A 1988 Court decision upholding a municipal rent control law and applying minimum scrutiny analysis implicitly suggests that *Nollan*'s bark may be worse than its bite. *See Pennell v. City of San Jose*, 108 S. Ct. 849, 856–57 (1988). Justice Scalia dissented from Chief Justice Rehnquist's majority opinion. *Id.* at 859.

174. *Nollan*, 107 S. Ct. at 3151 (Brennan, J., dissenting).

175. *Id.* at 3152 n.1.

176. *Id.* at 3152–53.

177. *See Katobimar Realty Co. v. Webster*, 20 N.J. 114, 118 A.2d 824 (1955) (Bren-nan, J., dissenting). In *Nollan*, Justice Brennan criticized the majority for "overruling an eminently reasonable exercise of an expert state agency's judgment, substituting its own narrow view of how this balance [between public access and development] should be struck." 107 S. Ct. at 3162.

178. *Nollan*, 107 S. Ct. at 3153.

179. *Id.* at 3154 (footnote omitted). In another implicit reference to his New Jersey days, Justice Brennan commented that "increasing intensity of development in many areas calls for *far-sighted, comprehensive planning* that takes into account both the interdependence of land uses and the cumulative impact of development." *Id.* at 3161–62 (footnote omitted) (emphasis added). His belief in comprehensive planning remains unshaken 40 years later.

180. *Id.* at 3154.

181. The majority addressed the psychological burden and additional congestion justifications of the commission by dispatching them with an *ipse dixit:* "It is also
impossible to understand how [the easement condition] lowers any 'psychological
barrier' to using the public beaches, or how it helps to remedy any additional congestion on them caused by construction of the Nollans' new house." *Id.* at 3149. It is
hardly "impossible to understand" how the easement may meet these concerns: for
example, it may ensure easy access from one beach to another if one becomes too
crowded. The majority could have been more forthright by stating that, under its test,
speculation was simply no substitute for proof.

182. *Id.* at 3155.

183. *Id.* at 3155–56.

184. *Id.* at 3154.

185. *Id.* at 3150.

186. The majority avoided this consideration because it found a taking under its own
newly fashioned test.

187. *Nollan,* 107 S. Ct. at 3156.

188. *See Loretto v. Teleprompter Manhattan CATV Corp.*, 458 U.S. 419 (1982). It is
possible, however, to distinguish *Loretto,* where the physical occupation of property
was "permanent," *id.* at 434–35, 438, from the *Nollan* case. In *Nollan,* the proposed
easement granted the public the right to pass and repass, but not to stop permanently,
on the Nollans' property. That distinction may have been more convincing to the
converted than to the opposition. Justice Brennan was one of the three dissenters in
the *Loretto* case, joining Justice Blackmun's opinion. The third dissenter was Justice
White.

189. *See Kaiser Aetna v. United States*, 444 U.S. 164, 176 (1979).

190. *Nollan,* 107 S. Ct. at 3157.

191. *Id.* at 3158–59.

192. *Id.* at 3159.

193. *Id.* at 3158–59. In a separate dissenting opinion, Justice Blackmun expressly dis-
avowed reliance on any state constitutional argument and interpreted the majority as
holding the same view. *Id.*

194. *Id.* at 3153–54. Although Justice Brennan did not present this argument in the
section of his opinion dealing with distinct investment-backed expectations, its
applicability to that analysis is easy to understand.

195. *Id.* at 3153.

196. *Id.* at 3154.

197. *Id.* at 3158.

198. U.S. Const. amend. V.

199. *Bishop v. Wood,* 426 U.S. at 354 n.4 (citations omitted) (Brennan, J., dissenting); *see also id.* at 353 ("There is certainly a federal dimension to the determination
of 'property' in the Federal Constitution."). Justice Rehnquist's notorious view that
"where the grant of a substantive right is inextricably intertwined with the limitations on the procedures which are to be employed in determining that right, a litigant

. . . must take the bitter with the sweet," *Arnett v. Kennedy*, 416 U.S. 134, 153–54 (1974) (plurality opinion), was obviously not shared by Justice Brennan.

200. *Nollan*, 107 S. Ct. at 3158.

201. *Id.* at 3146 n.2.

202. *Id.* at 3160 n.10. The majority and dissent debated the applicability of a prior Supreme Court case in which a chemical company, seeking to register certain pesticides, submitted secret trade data to the federal Environmental Protection Agency (EPA). *See Ruckelshaus v. Monsanto Co.*, 467 U.S. 986 (1984). The laws under which EPA operated could allow some of this information to become public, and the company claimed such disclosure constituted a government taking of its property. *Id.* at 998–99. The Court held that, because the registration statute granted only limited confidentiality, the company should not have expected that the information would be kept secret. *Id.* at 1006–08. For Justice Brennan, just as the chemical company sought the government benefit of registration and thereby voluntarily subjected itself to the limited confidentiality terms of the registration statute, so too did the Nollans seek the "benefit" of permission to build their new house and thus voluntarily subjected themselves to the easement condition.

203. *Nollan*, 107 S. Ct. at 3161.

204. *Id.*

205. *Id.* at 3150.

206. *Id.*

207. In a related joust, Justice Brennan suggested that the Court's decision may be academic. *Id.* at 3161. He cited a preliminary study prepared by an official in the California state attorney general's office indicating that the contested area may already belong to the public. *Id.* The study noted that the mean high tide line may extend farther east than previously thought and that, in any event, prescriptive public use of the area for passive recreation had created public rights to the Nollans' beach. *Id.* at 3161 nn.11–12.

208. *Id.* at 3163–64 (Stevens, J., dissenting). Like Justice Brennan, Justice Stevens has a clear affinity for land use cases. He has written a number of important opinions, *see, e.g., First English Evangelical Lutheran Church v. County of Los Angeles*, 107 S. Ct. 2378, 2389 (1987) (Stevens, J., dissenting); *Keystone Bituminous Coal Ass'n v. DeBenedictis*, 480 U.S. 470 (1987); *Members of City Council v. Taxpayers for Vincent*, 466 U.S. 789 (1984); *Young v. American Mini Theatres, Inc.*, 427 U.S. 50 (1976) (plurality opinion), and, second only to Justice Brennan, bears watching in the future.

209. *Nollan*, 107 S. Ct. at 3163–64 (Stevens, J., dissenting).

210. *Id.* at 3162 n.14 (Brennan, J., dissenting).

211. *Warth v. Seldin*, 422 U.S. 490 (1975).

212. *See Southern Burlington County NAACP v. Township of Mount Laurel*, 67 N.J. 151, 336 A.2d 713, *cert. denied and appeal dismissed*, 423 U.S. 808 (1975).

213. *Warth*, 422 U.S. at 493.

214. *Id.* at 502–17.

215. *Id.* at 520.

216. *Id.*

217. Indeed, Justice Brennan is an ardent foe of virtually all door-closing rules that prevent individuals from immediately pursuing their constitutional claims in a judicial (and especially federal) forum. *See* Brennan, *State Constitutions and the Protection of Individual Rights*, 90 Harv. L. Rev. 489, 498, 502–03 (1977); *Remarks of Associate Justice William J. Brennan, Jr., Seventy-Fifth Anniversary Dinner*, 36 Rutgers L. Rev. 725, 728 (1984). Some of his most well-known opinions deal with this important aspect of judicial access. *See, e.g., Fay v. Noia*, 372 U.S. 391 (1963) (approving federal court *habeas corpus* review of state convictions unless defendant "deliberately by-passed" state court chances to make claim); *Dombrowski v. Pfister*, 380 U.S. 479, 482–85 (1965) (approving federal enjoining of state prosecutions affecting first amendment rights); *Wainwright v. Sykes*, 433 U.S. 72 (1977) (Brennan, J., dissenting) (objecting to majority's abandonment of *Fay v. Noia* "deliberate by-pass" standard and replacement of tougher standard for federal *habeas* review); *Stone v. Powell*, 428 U.S. 465 (1976) (Brennan, J., dissenting) (objecting to exclusion from federal *habeas* review of all fourth amendment claims made in state court, unless there was evidence that defendant lacked "full and fair opportunity" in state court); *Rose v. Lundy*, 455 U.S. 509 (1982) (Brennan, J., concurring in part and dissenting in part) (objecting to total exhaustion requirement in state court before federal *habeas* review allowed); *Huffman v. Pursue, Ltd.*, 420 U.S. 592 (1975) (Brennan, J., dissenting) (objecting to refusal to allow federal intervention in state civil proceedings); *see also* Brennan, *How Goes the Supreme Court*, 36 Mercer L. Rev. 781 (1985).

218. *Warth*, 422 U.S. at 523.

219. *Id.*

220. *Id.* at 528–29 (citations omitted).

221. *Village of Arlington Heights v. Metropolitan Hous. Dev. Corp.*, 429 U.S. 252 (1977).

222. *Id.* at 264–66. The housing developer alleged that the village's refusal to rezone a parcel of land from single- to multifamily housing was an act of racial discrimination prohibited by the equal protection clause. Siding with the village, the Court held that proof of discriminatory intent, not just discriminatory effect, was required to establish a constitutional violation. *Id.; see Washington v. Davis*, 426 U.S. 229, 242 (1976). Among the interesting facts in the case was the statistic that, according to the 1970 U.S. Census, only 27 of the village's 64,000 residents were black.

223. *See* Brennan, *State Constitutions, supra* note 217, at 491, 495–98. He wrote, "State constitutions, too, are a font of individual liberties, their protections often extending beyond those required by the Supreme Court's interpretation of federal law. The legal revolution which has brought federal law to the fore must not be allowed to inhibit the independent protective force of state law—for without it, the full realization of our liberties cannot be guaranteed." *Id.* at 491.

224. *Mount Laurel*, 67 N.J. at 151, 336 A.2d at 713. Justice Brennan was especially delighted that, because the New Jersey Supreme Court had based its decision expanding individual rights on its state constitution, the U.S. Supreme Court was precluded from reviewing its opinion. *See* Brennan, *State Constitutions, supra* note 217, at 501.

225. *Moore v. City of East Cleveland*, 431 U.S. 494 (1977).

226. *Id.* at 496 & n.2.

227. *Id.* at 496–97.

228. *Id.* at 496 n.2.

229. Justice Powell was joined by Justices Brennan, Marshall and Blackmun.

230. *Moore*, 431 U.S. at 499, 501.

231. *Id.* at 503 (footnote omitted).

232. *Id.* at 499–500.

233. The three dissents were written by Chief Justice Burger, Justice Stewart (joined by Justice Rehnquist) and Justice White.

234. *Id.* at 543–44. Ten years later, Justice White appeared to have the current "last laugh" on the broad constitutional argument. In *Bowers v. Hardwick*, 478 U.S. 186 (1986), he wrote the five-to-four majority decision upholding a Georgia statute criminalizing sodomy. For Justice White, the Constitution did not extend any fundamental right (of privacy or other right) to "homosexuals to engage in sodomy." *Id.* at 190. For Justice Blackmun and fellow dissenters (including Justice Brennan), the case, rather, was about " 'the right to be let alone.' " *Id.* at 199 (quoting *Olmstead v. United States*, 277 U.S. 438, 478 (Brandeis, J., dissenting)).

235. *Moore*, 431 U.S. at 506 (footnotes omitted).

236. *Id.* at 507.

237. In *Muller v. Oregon*, 208 U.S. 412 (1908), then lawyer and eventual Supreme Court Justice Louis Brandeis wrote a brief filled with sociological, economic and statistical information about the working conditions of women in order to support government regulations enforcing maximum hour limits for women laborers. A brief composed of such information became known as a Brandeis brief.

In his *Moore* concurrence, Justice Brennan in Brandeisian style cited sociological studies of the West Enders and Irish that discussed the importance of the extended family in providing social, economic and emotional support. 431 U.S. at 508 n.5. As early as 1957 he opposed a legal isolationism that deprives judges of the learning of other disciplines. *See* McQuade & Kardos, *Mr. Justice Brennan and His Legal Philosophy*, 33 Notre Dame L. Rev. 321, 349 (1958).

238. *See, e.g., Harris v. McRae*, 448 U.S. 297 (1980) (Brennan, J., dissenting). In *Harris*, the Court upheld a federal statute (the Hyde Amendment) denying Medicaid assistance for abortions but allowing it for childbirth expenses. Justice Brennan wrote:

> [T]he Hyde Amendment is a transparent attempt by the Legislative Branch to impose the political majority's judgment of the morally acceptable and socially desirable preference on a sensitive and intimate decision that the Constitution entrusts to the individual. Worse yet, the Hyde Amendment does not foist that majoritarian viewpoint with equal measure on everyone in our Nation, rich and poor alike; rather, it imposes that viewpoint only on that segment of our society which, because of its position of political powerlessness, is least able to defend its privacy rights from the encroachments of state-mandated morality.

Id. at 332.

239. N.Y. Times, Apr. 16, 1986, at B8, col. 3.

240. *Moore*, 431 U.S. at 508.

241. *Id.* Indeed, in a 1986 television documentary, Justice Brennan described how his own grandmother lived in his house when he was growing up in Newark, N.J. *See Justice William J. Brennan, Jr.: Justice For All*, WNET-TV, Channel 13, New York City (October 1986).

242. *Moore*, 431 U.S. at 508.

243. *Id.* Justice Brennan exhibited a consistent concern years later in his dissent from

the Court's opinion in *Bowen v. Gilliard*, 107 S. Ct. 3008 (1987). There, the majority upheld a federal law mandating that the amount of welfare benefits granted to a child's custodial mother and siblings be decreased by any money received by the child from his or her noncustodial father. *Id.* at 3016–17. Although the law may create financial incentives for a custodial mother to send her child to live with the father, the Court concluded, in effect, that the law did not " ' "directly and substantially" interfere with family living arrangements and thereby burden a fundamental right.' " *Id.* at 3018 (citations omitted).

Reflecting a similar understanding, as in *Moore*, for the economic realities faced by poor families, Justice Brennan argued that the law placed undue pressure on the mother either to relinquish custody to the father (to maintain her welfare benefits level) or to prevent the noncustodial father from providing any support at all. *Id.* at 3029. In both cases, Justice Brennan observed, the relationship between parent and child was dangerously and impermissibly affected by government action. *Id.* at 3026, 3029.

Notes to Excerpts from Opinions of Justice Brennan

Following are selected notes from excerpts of Justice Brennan's Supreme Court opinions presented in Part III. The notes here retain their original numbers.

Chapter 7

Moore v. City of East Cleveland

4. See Report of the National Advisory Commission on Civil Disorders 278–281 (1968); Kosa & Nash, Social Ascent of Catholics, 8 Social Order 98–103 (1958); M. Novak, The Rise of the Unmeltable Ethnics 209–210 (1972); B. Yorburg, The Changing Family 106–109 (1973); Kosa, Rachiele, & Schommer, Sharing the Home with Relatives, 22 Marriage and Family Living 129 (1960).

5. See *e.g.*, H. Gans, The Urban Villagers 45–73, 245–249 (1962). "Perhaps the most important—or at least the most visible—difference between the classes is one of family structure. The working class subculture is distinguished by the dominant role of the family circle. . . .

"The specific characteristics of the family circle may differ widely—from the collateral peer group form of the West Enders, to the hierarchical type of the Irish, or to the classical three-generation extended family. . . . What matters most—and distinguishes this subculture from others—is that there be a family circle which is wider than the nuclear family, and that all of the opportunities, temptations, and pressures of the larger society be evaluated in terms of how they affect the ongoing way of life that has been built around this circle."

6. Yorburg. "Within the black lower-class it has been quite common for several generations, or parts of the kin, to live together under one roof. Often a maternal grandmother is the acknowledged head of this type of household which has given rise to the term 'matrifocal' to describe lower-class black family patterns." See J. Scanzoni, The Black Family in Modern Society 134 (1971); see also Anderson, The Pains and Pleasures of Old Black Folks, Ebony 123, 128–130 (Mar. 1973). See generally E. Frazier, The Negro Family in the United States (1939); Lewis, The Changing Negro Family, in E. Ginzberg, ed., The Nation's Children 108 (1960).

The extended family often plays an important role in the rearing of young black children whose parents must work. Many such children frequently "spend all of their growing-up years in the care of extended kin. . . . Often children are 'given' to their grandparents, who rear them to adulthood. . . . Many children normally grow up in a three-generation household and they absorb the influences of grandmother and grandfather as well as mother and father." J. Ladner, Tomorrow's Tomorrow: The Black Woman 60 (1972).

7. The extended family has many strengths not shared by the nuclear family.

"The case histories behind mounting rates of delinquency, addiction, crime, neurotic disabilities, mental illness, and senility in societies in which autonomous nuclear families prevail suggest that frequent failure to develop enduring family ties is a serious inadequacy for both individuals and societies." D. Blitsten, The World of the Family 256 (1963).

Extended families provide services and emotional support not always found in the nuclear family: "The troubles of the nuclear family in industrial societies, generally, and in American society, particularly, stem largely from the inability of this type of family structure to provide certain of the services performed in the past by the extended family. Adequate health, education, and welfare provision, particularly for the two nonproductive generations in modern societies, the young and the old, is increasingly an insurmountable problem for the nuclear family. The unrelieved and sometimes unbearably intense parent-child relationship, where childrearing is not shared at least in part by others, and the loneliness of nuclear family units, increasingly turned in on themselves in contracted and relatively isolated settings, is another major problem." Yorburg.

9. It is estimated that at least 26% of black children live in other than husband-wife families, "including foster parents, the presence of other male or female relatives (grandfather or grandmother, older brother or sister, uncle or aunt), male or female nonrelatives, [or with] only one adult (usually mother) present. . . ." Scanzoni.

10. Novak; Hill; N. Glazer & D. Moynihan, Beyond the Melting Pot 50–53 (2d ed. 1970); L. Rainwater & W. Yancey, The Moynihan Report and the Politics of Controversy 51–60 (1967).

Chapter 8

Metromedia, Inc. v. City of San Diego

4. Perusal of the photographs of billboards included in the appendix to the jurisdictional statement filed in this Court reveals the wide range of noncommercial messages communicated through billboards, including the following: "Welcome to San Diego[:] Home of 1,100 Underpaid Cops"; "Support San Diego's No-Growth Policy[:] Spend Your Money in Los Angeles!"; "Voluntary Integration. Better Education By Choice"; "Support America's First Environment Strike. Don't Buy Shell!"; and "Get US out! of the United Nations."

7. Not 1 of the 11 cases cited by the plurality in its footnote 14 stands for the proposition that reviewing courts have determined that "billboards are real and substantial hazards to traffic safety." These 11 cases merely apply the minimal scrutiny rational relationship test and the presumption of legislative validity to hold that it would not be unreasonable or inconceivable for a legislature or city government to conclude that billboards are traffic hazards. For example, in *New York State Thruway Authority v. Ashley Motor Court, Inc.*, the court held: "There are some, perhaps, who may dispute whether billboards and other advertising devices interfere with safe driving and constitute a traffic hazard . . ., but mere disagreement may not cast doubt on the statute's validity. Matters such as these are reserved for legislative judgment, and the legislative determination, here expressly announced, will not be disturbed unless manifestly unreasonable." Only 5 of the 11 cases even discuss the First Amendment. Therefore, when the plurality states that "[t]here is nothing here to suggest that these judgments are unreasonable," it is really saying that there is nothing unreasonable about other courts finding that there is nothing unreasonable about a legislative judgment. This is hardly a sufficient finding under the heightened scrutiny appropriate for this case. It is not surprising that, of the three cases cited in the plurality's footnote 14 that declined to accept the traffic safety rationale, two were decided under heightened scrutiny.

There is another reason why I would hesitate to accept the purported judgment of lawmakers that billboards are traffic hazards. Until recently, it was thought that aesthetics alone could never be a sufficient justification to support an exercise of the police power, and that aesthetics would have to be accompanied by a more traditional health, safety, morals, or welfare justification. Indeed, the California Supreme Court decision below explicitly repudiated the holding of a prior case that held aesthetics to be an insufficient predicate for police power action. Therefore, in the case of billboard regulations, many cities may have used the justification of traffic safety in order to sustain ordinances where their true motivation was aesthetics. As the Hawaii Supreme Court commented in upholding a comprehensive sign ordinance:

[The City's] answering brief admittedly "does not extend to supporting the proposition that aesthetics alone is a proper objective for the exercise of the City's police power." Perhaps, the "weight of authority" in other jurisdictions persuaded the City to present the more traditional arguments because it felt that it was safer to do so. However, the brief of The Outdoor Circle as amicus curiae presents, as we think, a more modern and forthright position. . . .

. . . We are mindful of the reasoning of most courts that have upheld the validity of ordinances regulating outdoor advertising and of the need felt by them to find some basis in economics, health, safety, or even morality. . . . We do not feel so constrained.

10. Appellants argue that the exceptions to the total ban, such as for on-premises signs, undercut the very goals of traffic safety and aesthetics that the city claims as paramount, and therefore invalidate the whole ordinance. But obviously, a city can have special goals the accomplishment of which would conflict with the overall goals addressed by the total billboard ban. It would make little sense to say that a city has an all-or-nothing proposition—either ban all billboards or none at all. Because I conclude that the San Diego ordinance impermissibly infringes First Amendment rights in that the city has failed to justify the ordinance sufficiently in light of substantial governmental interests, I need not decide, as the plurality does in Part V of its opinion, whether the exceptions to the total ban constitute independent grounds for invalidating the regulation. However, if a city can justify a total ban, I would allow an exception only if it directly furthers an interest that is at least as important as the interest underlying the total ban, if the exception is no broader than necessary to advance the special goal, and if the exception is narrowly drawn so as to impinge as little as possible on the overall goal. To the extent that exceptions rely on content-based distinctions, they must be scrutinized with special care.

The San Diego billboard ordinance is a classic example of conflicting interests. In its section entitled "Purpose and Intent," the ordinance states:

> It is the purpose of these regulations to eliminate excessive and confusing sign displays which do not relate to the premises on which they are located; to eliminate hazards to pedestrians and motorists brought about by distracting sign displays; to ensure that signing is used as identification and not as advertisement; and to preserve and improve the appearance of the City as a place in which to live and work.

> It is the intent of these regulations to protect an important aspect of the economic base of the City by preventing the destruction of the natural beauty and environment of the City, which is instrumental in attracting nonresidents who come to visit, trade, vacation or attend conventions; to safeguard and enhance property values; to protect public and private investment in buildings and open spaces; and to protect the public health, safety and general welfare.

To achieve these purposes, the ordinance effects a general ban on billboards, but with an exception for on-premises identification signs. Of course, each on-premises sign detracts from achieving the city's goals of traffic safety and aesthetics, but contributes to the alternative goal of identification. In this way San Diego seeks to achieve the best compromise between the goals of traffic safety and aesthetics on the one hand, and convenience for the public on the other.

San Diego has shown itself fully capable of drafting narrow exceptions to the general ban. For example, the city has promulgated special regulations for sign control in the La Jolla sign control district. . . . My views in this case make it unnecessary to decide the permissibility of the on-premises exception, but it is not inconceivable that San Diego could incorporate an exception to its overall ban to serve the identification interest without violating the Constitution. I also do not decide the validity of the other exceptions to the San Diego regulation.

13. Of course, as a matter of marketplace economics, such an ordinance may prove the undoing of all billboard advertising, both commercial and noncommercial. It may well be that no company would be able to make a profit maintaining billboards used solely for noncommercial messages. Although the record does not indicate how much of appellants' income is produced by noncommercial communicators, it would not be unreasonable to assume that the bulk of their customers advertise commercial messages. Therefore, noncommercial users may represent such a small percentage of the

billboard business that it would be impossible to stay in business based upon their patronage alone. Therefore, the plurality's prescription may represent a *de facto* ban on both commercial and noncommercial billboards. This is another reason to analyze this case as a "total ban" case.

14. These are not mere hypotheticals that can never occur. The Oil, Chemical and Atomic Workers International Union, AFL-CIO, actually placed a billboard advertisement stating: "Support America's First Environment Strike. Don't Buy Shell!" What if Exxon had placed the advertisement? Could Shell respond in kind?

Members of City Council v. Taxpayers for Vincent

6. It is theoretically, though remotely, possible that a form of speech could be so distinctively unaesthetic that a comprehensive program aimed at eliminating the eyesore it causes would apply only to the unpleasant form of speech. Under the approach I suggest, such a program would be invalid because it would only restrict speech, and the community, therefore, would have to tolerate the displeasing form of speech. This is no doubt a disadvantage of the approach. But at least when the form of speech that is restricted constitutes an important medium of communication and when the restriction would effect a total ban on the use of that medium, that is the price we must pay to protect our First Amendment liberties from those who would use aesthetics alone as a cloak to abridge them.

Chapter 9

Penn Central Transportation Co. v. New York City

1. See National Trust for Historic Preservation, A Guide to State Historic Preservation Programs (1976); National Trust for Historic Preservation, Directory of Landmark and Historic District Commissions (1976). In addition to these state and municipal legislative efforts, Congress has determined that "the historical and cultural foundations of the Nation should be preserved as a living part of our community life and development in order to give a sense of orientation to the American people," National Historic Preservation Act of 1966, and has enacted a series of measures designed to encourage preservation of sites and structures of historic, architectural, or cultural significance.

23. The Court of Appeals suggested that in calculating the value of the property upon which appellants were entitled to earn a reasonable return, the "publicly created" components of the value of the property—i.e., those elements of its value attributable to the "efforts of organized society" or to the "social complex" in which the Terminal is located—had to be excluded. However, since the record upon which the Court of Appeals decided the case did not, as that court recognized, contain a basis for segregating the privately created from the publicly created elements of the value of the Terminal site and since the judgment of the Court of Appeals in any event rests upon

bases that support our affirmance, we have no occasion to address the question whether it is permissible or feasible to separate out the "social increments" of the value of property.

25. As is implicit in our opinion, we do not embrace the proposition that a "taking" can never occur unless government has transferred physical control over a portion of a parcel.

26. Appellants are not seeking review of the New York courts' determination that Penn Central could earn a "reasonable return" on its investment in the Terminal. Although appellants suggest in their reply brief that the factual conclusions of the New York courts cannot be sustained unless we accept the rationale of the New York Court of Appeals, it is apparent that the findings concerning Penn Central's ability to profit from the Terminal depend in no way on the Court of Appeals' rationale.

30. Appellants attempt to distinguish these cases on the ground that, in each, government was prohibiting a "noxious" use of land and that in the present case, in contrast, appellants' proposed construction above the Terminal would be beneficial. We observe that the uses in issue in *Hadacheck, Miller,* and *Goldblatt* were perfectly lawful in themselves. They involved no "blameworthiness, . . . moral wrongdoing or conscious act of dangerous risk-taking which induce[d society] to shift the cost to a pa[rt]icular individual." These cases are better understood as resting not on any supposed "noxious" quality of the prohibited uses but rather on the ground that the restrictions were reasonably related to the implementation of a policy—not unlike historic preservation—expected to produce a widespread public benefit and applicable to all similarly situated property.

Nor, correlatively, can it be asserted that the destruction or fundamental alteration of a historic landmark is not harmful. The suggestion that the beneficial quality of appellants' proposed construction is established by the fact that the construction would have been consistent with applicable zoning laws ignores the development in sensibilities and ideals reflected in landmark legislation like New York City's.

36. We emphasize that our holding today is on the present record, which in turn is based on Penn Central's present ability to use the Terminal for its intended purposes and in a gainful fashion. The city conceded at oral argument that if appellants can demonstrate at some point in the future that circumstances have so changed that the Terminal ceases to be "economically viable," appellants may obtain relief.

San Diego Gas & Electric Co. v. City of San Diego

14. One interpretation of the *Pennsylvania Coal* opinion insists that the word "taking" was used "metaphorically," and that the "gravamen of the constitutional challenge to the regulatory measure was that it was an invalid exercise of the police power under the due process clause, and the [case was] decided under that rubric." *Fred F. French Investing Co. v. City of New York.* In addition to tampering with the express language of the opinion, this view ignores the coal company's repeated claim before the Court that the Pennsylvania statute took its property without just compensation.

16. Justice Brandeis, in dissent, argued the absolute position that a "restriction imposed to protect the public health, safety or morals from dangers threatened is not a taking." In partial reliance on Justice Brandeis' dissent, one report urges that the Court overrule the *Pennsylvania Coal* case and hold that "a regulation of the use of land, if reasonably related to a valid public purpose, can never constitute a taking."

17. The California Supreme Court, in its opinion in *Agins v. City of Tiburon,* interpreted Justice Holmes' use of the word "taking" to "indicate the *limit* by which the

acknowledged social goal of land control could be achieved by regulation rather than by eminent domain." (Emphasis added.) I find such a reading unpersuasive. The Court specifically indicated that a "regulation [that] goes too far . . . *will be recognized as a taking*," and that this determination is "*a question of degree*." *Pennsylvania Coal Co. v. Mahon* (emphasis added). Clearly, then, the Court contemplated that a regulation could cross the boundary surrounding valid police power exercise and become a Fifth Amendment "taking."

The California court further argued that the Court in *Pennsylvania Coal* "did not attempt . . . to transmute the illegal governmental infringement into an exercise of eminent domain and the possibility of compensation was not even considered." This overlooks the factual posture in *Pennsylvania Coal*, where the homeowner, not the coal company, brought an injunction action to prevent the company "from mining under their property in such a way as to remove the supports and cause a subsidence of the surface and of their house." Because no one asked for an award of just compensation, there was no reason for the Court to consider it. The company only sought reversal of the Pennsylvania Supreme Court's decree that enjoined it from mining coal, and this Court granted that request.

22. The instant litigation is a good case in point. The trial court, on April 9, 1976, found that the city's actions effected a "taking" of appellant's property on June 19, 1973. If true, then appellant has been deprived of all beneficial use of its property in violation of the Just Compensation Clause for the past seven years.

Invalidation hardly prevents enactment of subsequent unconstitutional regulations by the government entity. At the 1974 annual conference of the National Institute of Municipal Law Officers in California, a California City Attorney gave fellow City Attorneys the following advice:

> IF ALL ELSE FAILS, MERELY AMEND THE REGULATION AND START OVER AGAIN.
>
> If legal preventive maintenance does not work, and you still receive a claim attacking the land use regulation, or if you try the case and lose, don't worry about it. All is not lost. One of the extra "goodies" contained in the recent [California] Supreme Court case appears to allow the City to change the regulation in question, even after trial and judgment, make it more reasonable, more restrictive, or whatever, and everybody starts over again.
>
> • • • • •
>
> See how easy it is to be a City Attorney. Sometimes you can lose the battle and still win the war. Good luck.

26. Even if I were to concede a role for policy considerations, I am not so sure that they would militate against requiring payment of just compensation. Indeed, land-use planning commentators have suggested that the threat of financial liability for unconstitutional police power regulations would help to produce a more rational basis of decisionmaking that weighs the costs of restrictions against their benefits. Such liability might also encourage municipalities to err on the constitutional side of police power regulations, and to develop internal rules and operating procedures to minimize overzealous regulatory attempts. After all, if a policeman must know the Constitution, then why not a planner? In any event, one may wonder as an empirical matter whether the threat of just compensation will greatly impede the efforts of planners.

Nollan v. California Coastal Commission

1. See also *Williamson v. Lee Optical Co.*, 348 U.S. 483, 487–488, 75 S. Ct. 461, 464–465, 99 L. Ed. 563 (1955) ("[T]he law need not be in every respect logically con-

sistent with its aims to be constitutional. It is enough that there is an evil at hand for correction, and that it might be thought that the particular legislative measure was a rational way to correct it"); *Day-Brite Lighting, Inc. v. Missouri*, 342 U.S. 421, 423, 72 S. Ct. 405, 407, 96 L. Ed. 469 (1952) ("Our recent decisions make it plain that we do not sit as a super-legislature to weigh the wisdom of legislation nor to decide whether the policy which it expresses offends the public welfare. . . . [S]tate legislatures have constitutional authority to experiment with new techniques; they are entitled to their own standard of the public welfare").

Notwithstanding the suggestion otherwise [footnote 3 of Justice Scalia's majority opinion], our standard for reviewing the threshold question whether an exercise of the police power is legitimate is a uniform one. As we stated over 25 years ago in addressing a takings challenge to government regulation:

> The term "police power" connotes the time-tested conceptional limit of public encroachment upon private interests. Except for the substitution of the familiar standard of "reasonableness," this Court has generally refrained from announcing any specific criteria. The classic statement of the rule in *Lawton v. Steele* is still valid today: ". . . [I]t must appear, first, that the interests of the public . . . require [government] interference; and, second, that the means are reasonably necessary for the accomplishment of the purpose, and not unduly oppressive upon individuals." Even this rule is not applied with strict precision, for this Court has often said that "debatable questions as to reasonableness are not for the courts but for the legislature . . ."

In *Connolly v. Pension Benefit Guaranty Corp.*, for instance, we reviewed a takings challenge to statutory provisions that had been held to be a legitimate exercise of the police power under due process analysis in *Pension Benefit Corp. v. R. A. Gray & Co.* *Gray*, in turn, had relied on *Usery v. Turner Elkhorn Mining Co.* In rejecting the takings argument that the provisions were not within Congress' regulatory power, the Court in *Connolly* stated, "Although both *Gray* and *Turner Elkhorn* were due process cases, it would be surprising indeed to discover now that in both cases Congress unconstitutionally had taken the assets of the employers there involved." Our phraseology may differ slightly from case to case—*e.g.*, regulation must "substantially advance," or be "reasonably necessary to" the government's end. These minor differences cannot, however, obscure the fact that the inquiry in each case is the same.

Of course, government action may be a valid exercise of the police power and still violate specific provisions of the Constitution. Justice Scalia is certainly correct in observing that challenges founded upon these provisions are reviewed under different standards. Our consideration of factors such as those identified in *Penn Central*, for instance, provides an analytical framework for protecting the values underlying the Takings Clause, and other distinctive approaches are utilized to give effect to other constitutional provisions. This is far different, however, from the use of different standards of review to address the threshold issue of the rationality of government action.

2. As this Court declared in *United States v. Riverside Bayview Homes, Inc.*:

> A requirement that a person obtain a permit before engaging in a certain use of his or her property does not itself "take" the property in any sense: after all, the very existence of a permit system implies that permission may be granted, leaving the landowner free to use the property as desired. Moreover, even if the permit is denied, there may be other viable uses available to the owner. Only when a permit is denied and the effect of the denial is to prevent "economically viable" use of the land in question can it be said that a taking has occurred.

We also stated in *Kaiser Aetna v. United States*, with respect to dredging to create a private marina:

We have not the slightest doubt that the Government could have refused to allow such dredging on the ground that it would have impaired navigation in the bay, or could have conditioned its approval of the dredging on petitioners' agreement to comply with various measures that it deemed appropriate for the promotion of navigation.

10. The Court suggests that *Ruckelshaus v. Monsanto* is distinguishable, because government regulation of property in that case was a condition on receipt of a "government benefit," while here regulation takes the form of a restriction on "the right to build on one's own property," which "cannot remotely be described as a 'government benefit.'" This proffered distinction is not persuasive. Both Monsanto and the Nollans hold property whose use is subject to regulation; Monsanto may not sell its property without obtaining government approval and the Nollans may not build new development on their property without government approval. Obtaining such approval is as much a "government benefit" for the Nollans as it is for Monsanto. If the Court is somehow suggesting that "the right to build on one's own property" has some privileged natural rights status, the argument is a curious one. By any traditional labor theory of value justification for property rights, for instance, *see, e.g.*, J. Locke, The Second Treatise of Civil Government, Monsanto would have a superior claim, for the chemical formulae which constitute its property only came into being by virtue of Monsanto's efforts.

14. I believe that States should be afforded considerable latitude in regulating private development, without fear that their regulatory efforts will often be found to constitute a taking. "*If* . . . regulation denies the property owner the use and enjoyment of his land and is found to effect a 'taking'", however, I believe that compensation is the appropriate remedy for this constitutional violation. *San Diego Gas & Electric Co. v. San Diego* (Brennan, J., dissenting) (emphasis added). I therefore see my dissent here as completely consistent with my position in *First English Evangelical Church v. Los Angeles County.*

(End of Brennan Notes)

Conclusion

1. *See, e.g.*, Sofaer, *Justice William Brennan After Twenty-Five Years*, 1981 N.Y.U. Ann. Surv. Am. L. xii; Posner, *Tribute to Mr. Justice Brennan*, 1981 N.Y.U. Ann. Surv. Am. L. xi; Michelman, *Mr. Justice Brennan: A Property Teacher's Appreciation*, 15 Harv. C.R.-C.L. L. Rev. 296, 296 (1980); Hall, *Mr. Justice Brennan—The Earlier Years*, 15 Harv. C.R.-C.L. L. Rev. 286, 291 (1980).

2. *See, e.g.*, Freund, *William J. Brennan, Jr.*, 86 Yale L.J. 1015, 1017 (1977); Katz, *Mr. Justice Brennan*, 15 Harv. C.R.-C.L. L. Rev. 292, 294–95 (1980); Michelman, *supra* note 1, at 296, 297–98; Sofaer, *supra* note 1, at xiii, xx. In addition to his copious judicial output, Justice Brennan is a prolific author of law review articles (although never about land use issues).

3. *See, e.g.*, Stewart, *Testimonial to Mr. Justice Brennan*, 15 Harv. C.R.-C.L. L. Rev. 281, 281 (1980); Powell, *The Opinion of the Court*, The Reporter, Passaic County Bar Ass'n, vol. VI, at 14 (Spring 1984); Bazelon, *A Tribute to Justice William J. Brennan*,

Jr., 15 Harv. C.R.-C.L. L. Rev. 282, 282–83, 284 (1980) ("the public man and the private man are one"); Hall, *supra* note 1, at 286; Posner, *supra* note 1, at xi; Sofaer, *supra* note 1, at xix–xx. Justice Goldberg once referred to Justice Brennan as "this kindly, warm, thoughtful man" and "one of the finest human beings there are." Goldberg, *Foreword*, in W. Brennan, An Affair With Freedom viii (S. Friedman ed. 1967).

4. Sacks, *A Tribute to Justice Brennan: Foreword*, 15 Harv. C.R.-C.L. L. Rev. 279, 279 (1980); Freund, *supra* note 2, at 1015; Stewart, *supra* note 3, at 281; Hall, *supra* note 1, at 291; Sofaer, *supra* note 1, at xii. As he himself has observed, "The Bill of Rights is the primary source of expressed information as to what is meant by constitutional liberty." Brennan, *Remarks of Associate Justice William J. Brennan, Jr., Seventy-Fifth Anniversary Dinner*, 36 Rutgers L. Rev. 725, 727 (1984).

5. W. Brennan, The Fourteenth Amendment, Address to Section on Individual Rights and Responsibilities, American Bar Ass'n, New York University School of Law (Aug. 8, 1986).

6. *See, e.g.*, Brennan, *Remarks*, *supra* note 4, at 728; *see also Paul v. Davis*, 424 U.S. 693, 734–35 (1976) (Brennan, J., dissenting) ("I have always thought that one of this Court's most important roles is to provide a formidable bulwark against governmental violation of the constitutional safeguards securing in our free society the legitimate expectations of every person to innate human dignity and sense of worth.").

7. Brennan, The Fourteenth Amendment, *supra* note 5; *see, e.g.*, Brennan, *Remarks*, *supra* note 4, at 727 ("the ultimate protection of individual freedom is found in court enforcement of these constitutional guarantees"). He frequently cites *Boyd v. United States* for the principles that " 'constitutional provisions for the security of person and property should be liberally construed' " and that " '[i]t is the duty of courts to be watchful for the constitutional rights of the citizen, and against any stealthy encroachments thereon.' " *See, e.g.*, Brennan, *State Constitutions and the Protection of Individual Rights*, 90 Harv. L. Rev. 489, 494 (1977) (quoting *Boyd v. United States*, 116 U.S. 616, 635 (1886)); *see also Malloy v. Hogan*, 378 U.S. 1, 8 (1964) (per J. Brennan) (citing "the great case of *Boyd v. United States*").

8. W. Brennan, Justice Thurgood Marshall: Defender of Libertarian Dignity Protected Through Law, Address at Dedication of Thurgood Marshall Law Library, University of Maryland Law School (Oct. 9, 1980) (quoting Annals of Cong. 439 (Gales & Seaton ed. 1834), *reprinted in* The Reporter, Passaic County Bar Ass'n, vol. VI, at 10 (footnote omitted) (Spring 1984)); *see also* Brennan, *Constitutional Adjudication*, 40 Notre Dame L. Rev. 559, 569 (1965).

9. Brennan, *State Constitutions*, *supra* note 7, at 498.

10. *See, e.g.*, *Cooper v. Aaron*, 358 U.S. 1 (1958). There, the Court faced a major challenge to its own authority to interpret the Constitution, specifically to its *Brown v. Board of Education*, 347 U.S. 483 (1954), decision striking down racial segregation in public schools as unconstitutional under the equal protection clause. In early September 1957, Gov. Faubus of Arkansas sent the state's National Guard to Little Rock to prevent nine black students from attending Central High School. *Cooper*, 358 U.S. at 9, 11. After three weeks during which the students could not gain admission, President Eisenhower dispatched federal troops on September 25, and the students were able to enter. *Id.* at 12.

In requiring the Little Rock school system to comply with federal court orders regarding integration, the Court issued one of its most significant statements ever on judicial authority, asserting that *Marbury v. Madison*, 5 U.S. 137 (1803), "declared the basic principle that the federal judiciary is supreme in the exposition of the law of the Constitution, and that principle has ever since been respected by this Court and the Country as a permanent and indispensable feature of our constitutional system. It follows that the interpretation of the fourteenth amendment enunciated by this Court in the *Brown* case is the supreme law of the land." *Cooper*, 358 U.S. at 18. Although announced as a unanimous decision signed by all the justices, an unusual procedure likely employed to emphasize the Court's seriousness, *Cooper* is generally understood to have been written by Justice Brennan. *See* B. Schwartz, Super Chief: Earl Warren and His Supreme Court—A Judicial Biography 295 (1983). One remark in *Cooper* may add some credence to that understanding: "Since the first *Brown* opinion three new Justices have come to the Court. They are at one with the Justices still on the Court who participated in that basic decision as to its correctness, and that decision is now unanimously reaffirmed." *Cooper*, 358 U.S. at 19.

Justice Brennan believes mightily in the institution of the Supreme Court and in maintaining collegiality with other justices through the many disagreements that necessarily ensue in judicial decision making. Sofaer, *supra* note 1, at xvi (respect for institution and colleagues); Katz, *supra* note 2, at 292 (recounting Justice Brennan's complimentary response to arguments made by a Rehnquist dissent to a Brennan opinion).

11. Brennan, *Remarks*, *supra* note 4, at 727; *see, e.g.*, *Malloy v. Hogan*, 378 U.S. 1, 8 (1964) (per J. Brennan) (fifth amendment privilege against self-incrimination secured in states through fourteenth amendment).

12. *See, e.g.*, Gillers, *The Warren Court—It Still Lives*, The Nation, Sept. 17, 1983, at 208; Hutchinson, *Hail to the Chief: Earl Warren and the Supreme Court* (Book Review), 81 Mich. L. Rev. 922, 923, 928–30 (1983) (reviewing B. Schwartz, *supra* note 10) (arguing that Brennan, not Warren, deserves real credit for accomplishments of Warren Court); Katz, *supra* note 2, at 292; Sacks, *supra* note 4, at 280; Sofaer, *supra* note 1, at xii.

13. Redlich, *William J. Brennan, Jr.: New Honor for an Old Friend*, 1981 N.Y.U. Ann. Surv. Am. L. xxv; Sacks, *supra* note 4, at 280; B. Schwartz, *supra* note 10.

14. *Baker v. Carr*, 369 U.S. 186 (1962) (federal courts can review equal protection clause challenges to apportionment of state legislative districts); *see also Katzenbach v. Morgan*, 384 U.S. 641 (1966) (section 5 of fourteenth amendment is positive grant to Congress to enforce equal protection clause through appropriate legislation; constitutionality of provision in federal voting rights act upheld).

15. *New York Times Co. v. Sullivan*, 376 U.S. 254 (1964) (announcing "actual malice" standard for libel suits brought by public figures).

16. *Frontiero v. Richardson*, 411 U.S. 677 (1973) (plurality opinion) (proposing strict scrutiny standard for sex discrimination); *Craig v. Boren*, 429 U.S. 190 (1976) (effectively adopting intermediate scrutiny standard for sex discrimination).

17. *Fay v. Noia*, 372 U.S. 391 (1963) (guaranteeing broad federal *habeas corpus* review of state criminal convictions, although federal court has discretion to deny review if applicant "deliberately by-passed" state procedures for review of claim); *Dombrowski v. Pfister*, 380 U.S. 479 (1965) (federal courts can enjoin state criminal prosecutions based on overly broad statutes chilling first amendment rights).

18. *Eisenstadt v. Baird*, 405 U.S. 438 (1972) (plurality opinion) (upholding right of unmarried persons to contraceptives and citing constitutional right of privacy; nominally based on equal protection clause violation, because married persons were entitled to contraceptives under challenged statute).

19. *Goldberg v. Kelly*, 397 U.S. 254 (1970) (finding property interest in welfare benefits triggering procedural requirement of a pretermination hearing).

20. *NAACP v. Button*, 371 U.S. 415 (1963) (finding right of association under first amendment in efforts of NAACP and others to provide legal and other assistance).

21. *Monell v. Dep't of Social Servs.*, 436 U.S. 658 (1978) (local governments and officials may be sued under § 1983 for unconstitutional actions resulting from policy or custom); *Owen v. City of Independence*, 445 U.S. 622 (1980) (municipalities may not assert good-faith defense against § 1983 suit); *Bivens v. Six Unknown Named Agents of Fed. Bureau of Narcotics*, 403 U.S. 388 (1971) (damages cause of action directly under fourth amendment); *Davis v. Passman*, 442 U.S. 228 (1979) (damages cause of action directly under fifth amendment).

22. *Regents of the Univ. of Cal. v. Bakke*, 438 U.S. 265 (1978) (Brennan, J., concurring in the judgment in part and dissenting in part) (upholding remedial use of race to overcome minority underrepresentation in medical profession through preferential admissions); *Local 28, Sheet Metal Workers' Int'l Ass'n v. E.E.O.C.*, 478 U.S. 471 (1986) (plurality opinion) (federal district court order of affirmative action remedying past discrimination violates neither title VII nor Constitution); *United Steelworkers v. Weber*, 443 U.S. 193 (1979) (private employer's voluntarily adopted affirmative action plan does not violate title VII).

23. *See, e.g., Shapiro v. Thompson*, 394 U.S. 618 (1969) (denial of welfare assistance to those not residing in jurisdiction for at least one year violates equal protection clause and constitutional right to travel interstate); *Plyler v. Doe*, 457 U.S. 202 (1982) (upholding under equal protection clause right of illegally admitted children to free public education provided to children who are U.S. citizens or legally admitted).

24. *See, e.g., United States v. Leon*, 468 U.S. 897 (1984) (Brennan, J., dissenting) (disagreeing with majority view that exclusionary rule preventing admission at trial of illegally seized items does not apply when police reasonably rely on magistrate-issued search warrant violating fourth amendment); *Lopez v. United States*, 373 U.S. 427 (1963) (Brennan, J., dissenting) (disagreeing with majority view that conversation surreptitiously recorded by tax auditor did not violate fourth amendment).

25. *See, e.g., McCleskey v. Kemp*, 481 U.S. 279 (1987) (Brennan, J., dissenting) (disagreeing with majority view that capital death-sentencing procedure did not unconstitutionally discriminate against blacks); *Furman v. Georgia*, 408 U.S. 238 (1972) (Brennan, J., concurring) (evolving standards of decency make death penalty unconstitutional under eighth amendment's cruel and unusual punishments clause).

26. *See, e.g., Lynch v. Donnelly*, 465 U.S. 668 (1984) (Brennan, J., dissenting) (arguing that city's maintenance of nativity scene at public expense violates first amendment's establishment clause); *School Dist. of Abington Township v. Schempp*, 374 U.S. 203 (1963) (Brennan, J., concurring) (state laws requiring prayer and bible reading in public schools unconstitutional).

27. *See, e.g., Sherbert v. Verner*, 374 U.S. 398 (1963) (government refusal to grant unemployment compensation to Seventh Day Adventist refusing to work Saturdays was unconstitutional infringement on free exercise of religion).

28. *Baker v. Carr*, 369 U.S. 186 (1962).

29. *New York Times Co. v. Sullivan*, 376 U.S. 254 (1964).

30. *Fay v. Noia*, 372 U.S. 391 (1963).

31. *Frontiero v. Richardson*, 411 U.S. 677 (1973).

32. *Goldberg v. Kelly*, 397 U.S. 254 (1970).

33. *Baker*, 369 U.S. at 198–200, 209.

34. *See Reynolds v. Sims*, 377 U.S. 533, 556–57, 561–68 (1964) (citing *Baker v. Carr* for authority to review voting rights claims under equal protection clause). Of the cases decided during his tenure on the Court, Chief Justice Warren, who wrote the *Reynolds* majority, selected *Baker v. Carr* as the opinion of greatest consequence to Americans. *See* Brennan, *State Constitutions, supra* note 7, at 492.

35. *New York Times Co. v. Sullivan*, 376 U.S. at 279–80.

36. *Id.* at 270.

37. *Fay*, 372 U.S. at 421–24, 438–39, 440–41. In *Fay*, Justice Brennan cited an article he wrote arguing for broad federal *habeas corpus* review. *Id.* at 399 n.4 (citing Brennan, *Federal Habeas Corpus and State Prisoners: An Exercise in Federalism*, 7 Utah L. Rev. 423 (1961)).

38. *See, e.g., Wainwright v. Sykes*, 433 U.S. 72 (1977) (rejecting *Fay*'s "deliberate bypass" and "knowing waiver" standards and substituting tougher "cause" and "prejudice" standards for state prisoners seeking federal *habeas corpus* review); *Stone v. Powell*, 428 U.S. 465 (1976) (restricting *habeas corpus* review for fourth amendment claims where there was "full and fair consideration" of such claims in state court).

39. Brennan, *State Constitutions, supra* note 7, at 503.

40. *Frontiero*, 411 U.S. at 688.

41. *Craig*, 429 U.S. at 197–98, 204.

42. *Goldberg*, 397 U.S. at 262 & n.8, 264.

43. *See, e.g., Paul v. Davis*, 424 U.S. 693 (1976) (distribution of flyer identifying individual as shoplifter did not deprive him of liberty or property interest under state law); *Bishop v. Wood*, 426 U.S. 341 (1976) (policeman's discharge without hearing did not deprive him of property or liberty interest under state law); *Mathews v. Eldridge*, 424 U.S. 319 (1976) (no evidentiary hearing required before termination of Social Security benefits). Not surprisingly, Justice Brennan wrote dissents in all three cases.

44. Justice Brennan is also well known for substantial contributions in other legal areas, most notably labor law. *See, e.g., Boys Mkts., Inc. v. Retail Clerks Union*, 398 U.S. 235 (1970) (reinstating right of federal district courts to issue injunctions in labor disputes); *Rogers v. Missouri Pac. R.R. Co.*, 352 U.S. 500 (1957) (emphasizing primacy of jury trial for injured workers under Federal Employers Liability Act and obligation of employer to pay damages for injury or death wholly or partially due to its negligence). *See generally* Dorman, *Justice Brennan: The Individual and Labor Law*, 58 Chi.[-]Kent L. Rev. 1003 (1982); Gould, *The Supreme Court's Labor and Employment Docket in the 1980 Term: Justice Brennan's Term*, 53 U. Colo. L. Rev. 1 (1981); Sofaer, *supra* note 1, at xviii–xix.

45. *See, e.g.,* Bauman, *The Supreme Court, Inverse Condemnation and the Fifth Amendment: Justice Brennan Confronts the Inevitable in Land Use Controls*, 15 Rutgers L.J. 15 (1983); Berger & Kanner, *Thoughts on The White River Junction Manifesto: A Reply to the "Gang of Five's" Views on Just Compensation for Regulatory Taking of Property*, 19 Loy. L.A.L. Rev. 685 (1986); Cunningham, *Inverse Condemnation as a Remedy for "Regulatory Takings,"* 8 Hastings Const. L.Q. 517 (1981); Kmiec, *Regulatory Takings: The Supreme Court Runs Out of Gas in San Diego*, 57 Ind. L.J. 45 (1982); Mandelker, *Land Use Takings: The Compensation Issue*, 8 Hastings Const. L.Q. 491 (1981); Williams, Smith, Siemon, Mandelker & Babcock, *The White River Junction Manifesto*, 9 Vt. L. Rev. 193 (1984); Case Comment, *Penn Central Transp. Co. v. New York City: Landmark Designation; Legitimate Preservation*

or *Unconstitutional Taking*, 25 Loy. L. Rev. 205 (1979); Note, *Landmark Preservation—A Solution to the Problem*, 41 U. Pitt. L. Rev. 111 (1979); 24 Vill. L. Rev. 610 (1979) *(Penn Central)*; 54 Wash. L. Rev. 727 (1979) *(Penn Central)*; 16 La. L. Rev. 817 (1956) *(Katobimar)*.

46. One scholar has written an insightful article comparing Justice Brennan's treatment of "traditional" private property and "new" property. *See* Michelman, *supra* note 1; *see also supra* chapter 3, note 85.

47. Whether or not Justice Brennan is a consistent "liberal," he has certainly blurred the liberal image from time to time. *See, e.g., Schmerber v. California*, 384 U.S. 757 (1966) (taking of blood sample from allegedly drunk driver involved in accident does not violate due process, privilege against self-incrimination, right to counsel and right not to be subject to unreasonable search and seizure where there was probable cause for arrest, making the search incident to arrest); *Roth v. United States*, 354 U.S. 476 (1957) (classifying obscenity as speech utterly without redeeming social value and thus unprotected by first amendment). He subsequently rejected his *Roth* test on the ground that it is impossible to distinguish between sexually oriented expression and obscenity without significantly harming first amendment interests. *Paris Adult Theatre v. Slaton*, 413 U.S. 49, 73–74, 113 (1973) (Brennan, J., dissenting).

48. *See supra* chapter 1, notes 14–26 and accompanying text.

49. *See supra* chapter 1, note 15.

50. *See* Berger & Kanner, *supra* note 45, at 719 & nn.138–39; Costonis, *Presumptive and Per Se Takings: A Decisional Model for the Taking Issue*, 58 N.Y.U. L. Rev. 465, 476–77 (1983); Oakes, *"Property Rights" in Constitutional Analysis Today*, 56 Wash. L. Rev. 583, 594, 597, 622–23, 624–25 (1981); Van Alstyne, *The Recrudescence of Property Rights as the Foremost Principle of Civil Liberties: The First Decade of the Burger Court*, 43 Law & Contemp. Probs. 66, 70, 73 (1980); *see also* Kennedy, *Form and Substance in Private Law Adjudication*, 89 Harv. L. Rev. 1685, 1714 n.74 (1976); *cf. Lynch v. Household Fin. Corp.*, 405 U.S. 538, 552 (1972) ("[A] fundamental interdependence exists between the personal right to liberty and the personal right in property. Neither could have meaning without the other.") (property rights and personal rights same for purposes of jurisdiction under 28 U.S.C. § 1343(3)). In tracing this division, Judge Oakes unearthed its modern-day roots in Justice Stone's *United States v. Carolene Products Co.*, 304 U.S. 144 (1938), setting forth a rule and rationale for removing heightened scrutiny of standard socioeconomic legislation, while maintaining it for classifications affecting certain groups and laws impinging on certain fundamental rights: "What we have had since *Carolene Products* . . . is a judicial double standard, with the courts feeling more free to protect the civil rights other than property rights of minorities, political and otherwise, even while there has been great restraint on protection of property rights in the broad sense." Oakes, *supra*, at 594. Van Alstyne sees a coalescence of property with liberty, in a "more conservative view of liberty" represented by John Locke *(Second Treatise of Government*, 1690) or Adam Smith *(The Wealth of Nations*, 1776), rather than John Mill *(On Liberty*, 1859) or John Rawls *(A Theory of Justice*, 1971). Van Alstyne, *supra*, at 70 ("liberty as security of property; liberty as freedom of entrepreneurial skill; liberty from the impositions of government and of third parties from disposing of 'one's own.' ").

51. For example, the Supreme Court has made state courts the likely initial forum, even in major federal constitutional takings cases, by requiring property owners to use state procedures where they exist for obtaining payment of just compensation. *See Williamson County Regional Planning Comm'n v. Hamilton Bank*, 473 U.S. 172, 194–97 (1985).

52. *See, e.g.,* N.Y. Times, June 24, 1986, at A24, col. 3.

53. *See supra* chapter 3, note 4.

54. *See* Bauman & Ethier, *Development Exactions and Impact Fees: A Survey of American Practices*, 50 Law & Contemp. Probs. 51, 57–58 (1987).

55. *See* Alterman & Kayden, *Developer Provisions of Public Benefits: Toward a Consensus Vocabulary*, in Private Supply of Public Services: Evaluation of Real Estate Exactions, Linkage, and Alternative Land Policies 28 (R. Alterman ed. 1988); Boston, Mass., Zoning Code art. 26A (1986) (linkage program asking office developers to create low-income housing or pay $5 per office square foot to housing trust fund); *id.* art. 26B (linkage program asking office developers to pay $1 per office square foot for job training); San Francisco, Calif., Ordinance 358-85 (Aug. 18, 1985) (linkage program asking office developers to create low-income housing); San Francisco, Calif., Municipal Code, pt. II, ch. II, §§ 165, 315 (1985) (requiring office developers to provide on-site or nearby child care services or to pay fee).

56. *See* A. Mallach, Inclusionary Housing Programs (1984).

57. *Nollan v. California Coastal Comm'n*, 107 S. Ct. 3141 (1987).

58. *See* N.Y. Times, Nov. 30, 1986, § 4, at 6, col. 1; Taylor, *The Shadow: The Uproar Over the Big Coliseum Project*, New York, Oct. 5, 1987, at 40.

59. *See* Gruen, *Public/Private Projects*, Urban Land, August 1986, at 2.

60. *Hawaii Housing Auth. v. Midkiff*, 467 U.S. 229 (1984); *Berman v. Parker*, 348 U.S. 26 (1954).

61. *See* C. Duerksen, Aesthetic and Land-Use Controls 5–16 (1986); P. Glassford, Appearance Codes for Small Communities 1–7 (1983).

62. *See* Duerksen, *supra* note 61, at 14–16.

63. *See* San Francisco, Calif., Municipal Code, pt. II, ch. II, §§ 260, 263.9, 309(b) (1985) (also known as Ordinance 414-85). The San Francisco Downtown Plan announced a policy to "[f]oster sculpturing of building form to create less overpowering buildings and more interesting building tops, particularly the tops of towers," emphasizing that "[w]hat is desired is the evolution of a San Francisco imagery that departs from the austere, flat top box—a facade cut off in space." San Francisco, Downtown Plan 82 (Nov. 29, 1984). One can only hope that deconstructivism, the latest architectural fashion in which building geometries and forms are made to clash expressly to create discomfort and unhappiness, does not capture the municipal fancy.

64. *See* Boston, Mass., Zoning Code art. 28 (1986) (establishing Boston Civic Design Commission).

65. *See* Duerksen, *supra* note 61, at 12–14; Glassford, *supra* note 61, at 1–7.

66. *Cf. United States v. Metropolitan Dist. Comm'n*, No. 85-0489 (D. Mass. Sept. 5, 1985) (finding violations of federal statute in local pollution of Boston Harbor). Before the federal district court takeover of the case, a state court trial judge had ordered a temporary ban on new sewer connections for real estate development projects in the Boston metropolitan area because of the continuing pollution of Boston Harbor. *See* Haar, *Introduction*, in Of Judges, Politics and Flounders: Perspectives on the Cleaning Up of Boston Harbor xi (C. Haar ed. 1986).

67. *Cf. Conservation Law Found. v. Watt*, 560 F. Supp. 561 (D. Mass.), *aff'd sub nom. Massachusetts v. Watt*, 716 F.2d 946 (1st Cir. 1983) (issuing preliminary injunction against federal offshore Georges Bank lease sales for oil and natural gas exploration, development and production).

68. *See* N.Y. Times, July 17, 1987, at D15, col. 1.

69. *Cf. Hodel v. Virginia Surface Mining & Reclamation Ass'n*, 452 U.S. 264 (1981) (joined by J. Brennan) (federal land use controls over surface mining lawful exercise under commerce clause and not violation of tenth amendment); *Garcia v. San Antonio Metropolitan Transit Auth.*, 469 U.S. 528 (1985) (joined by J. Brennan) (overruling *National League of Cities* and holding that federal minimum wage and overtime laws may be applied to employees of local public mass-transit authority); *National League of Cities v. Usery*, 426 U.S. 833 (1976) (Brennan, J., dissenting) (disagreeing with majority holding, subsequently overruled, that, because of constitutional concerns of federalism, federal minimum wage and maximum hour laws may not be applied to employees of state and local governments involved in traditional government functions).

70. Some argue for greater empowerment of decentralized jurisdictions in the belief that smaller responsive units can best promote public participation in government decision making. *See, e.g.,* Frug, *The City as a Legal Concept*, 93 Harv. L. Rev. 1057, 1067–73 (1980) (adding the caveat that "the argument for city power rests on what cities have been and what they could become," rather than what they are).

71. *Cf. Southern Burlington County NAACP v. Township of Mount Laurel*, 92 N.J. 158, 456 A.2d 390 (1983) (ordering New Jersey communities to adopt affirmative measures, such as incentive and inclusionary zoning, to ensure a fair share of low-income housing); *United States v. Yonkers Bd. of Educ.*, 624 F. Supp. 1276 (S.D.N.Y. 1985), *aff'd*, 837 F.2d 1181 (2d Cir. 1987) (ordering building of public housing in certain areas of city to remedy past publicly directed racial segregation in housing).

72. *Cf. Pugh v. Locke*, 406 F. Supp. 318 (M.D. Ala. 1976), *aff'd sub nom. Newman v. Alabama*, 559 F.2d 283 (5th Cir. 1977), *rev'd sub nom. on other grounds, Alabama v. Pugh*, 438 U.S. 781 (1978) (finding that prison conditions violate eighth amendment's cruel and unusual punishments clause and ordering remedial action including improvement of physical facilities).

73. *Cf. City of Cleburne v. Cleburne Living Center, Inc.*, 473 U.S. 432 (1985) (striking down as violation of equal protection clause refusal of city council to issue special permit for group home for mentally retarded, as home would no more threaten legitimate community interests than other permitted uses such as boarding houses and hospitals).

74. In predicting "more and more collisions of the individual with his government" and "new and different constitutional stresses and strains," Justice Brennan has observed that "[i]t will remain the business of judges to protect fundamental constitutional rights which will be threatened in ways not possibly envisaged by the framers. Justices yet to sit, like their predecessors, are destined to labor earnestly in that endeavor—we hope with wisdom—to reconcile the complex realities of their times with the principles which mark a free people." Brennan, Justice Thurgood Marshall, *supra* note 8, at 10.

75. In this regard, some of Justice Cardozo's eloquent description of the indescribable in judicial decision making reverberates in Justice Brennan's approach. *See* B. Cardozo, The Nature of the Judicial Process 163–77 (1921).

76. Brennan, *Constitutional Adjudication and the Death Penalty: A View from the Court*, 100 Harv. L. Rev. 313, 331 (1986).

77. *Id.* at 329.

78. *Id.* at 331.

WILLIAM J. BRENNAN, JR.

The second of eight children, William Joseph Brennan, Jr., was born April 25, 1906, in Newark, N.J. Sixteen years earlier, at the age of 20, his father had emigrated from County Roscommon, Ireland, where he worked as a metal polisher and a coal shoveler in a brewery. In Newark, Justice Brennan's father quickly rose through the ranks of the labor movement, becoming business manager of a local union and a delegate to the Essex County Trades and Labor Council. In 1916 the Republican mayor appointed him to the Newark Police Board as labor's representative. One year later, he was elected a city commissioner and director of public safety, in charge of the police, fire and license departments.

While attending public and parochial schools, Justice Brennan worked in a local garage and gas station, delivered milk using horse-drawn wagons and made change for trolley riders. Following high school graduation, he attended the Wharton School of Finance and Commerce at the University of Pennsylvania, majoring in economics and receiving his degree in 1928. He married Marjorie Leonard (with whom he had three children) and entered Harvard Law School, where he was a member of the Legal Aid Society, and earned his law degree in 1931. Returning to his home base of Newark, he began his legal career at Pitney, Hardin and Skinner, a law firm specializing in corporate law and labor-management problems, and became a partner in 1937.

During World War II, he joined the army and worked for the Ordnance Department, separating as a full colonel and receiving the Legion of Merit. Back at his old firm, now renamed Pitney, Hardin, Ward and Brennan, he involved himself in statewide efforts led by New Jersey Supreme Court Chief Justice Arthur Vanderbilt to revise the outdated 1844 New Jersey constitution and especially to improve the administration of the courts. The product of that work was the 1947 New Jersey constitutional convention and a new constitution. In January 1949 Republican Gov. Alfred Driscoll appointed him to the Law Division of the New Jersey Superior Court, the general trial court in New Jersey, and Chief Justice Vanderbilt elevated him to the Appellate Division in September 1950. He was appointed in March 1952 to the New Jersey Supreme Court.

On September 29, 1956, U.S. Attorney General Herbert Brownell, Jr., called and requested Justice Brennan's presence in Washington, D.C. The next day, he was told that President Eisenhower planned to nominate him to the Supreme Court of the United States. He took office on October 16, 1956, as a recess appointment and was formally confirmed by the Senate on March 19, 1957. After 32 years on the Supreme Court bench, Justice Brennan is currently the sixth longest serving justice in Court history.

NOTE: This biographical material is drawn principally from McQuade & Kardos, Mr. Justice Brennan and His Legal Philosophy, 33 Notre Dame Law. 321, 321–26 (1958), and from The Supreme Court: Justice and the Law 157–58 (2d ed. 1977).

Table of Land Use Opinions

Justice Heher delivered the opinion of the court, joined by Chief Justice Vanderbilt and Justices Wachenfeld and Burling. Justice Brennan filed a dissenting opinion, joined by Justice Jacobs. Justice Oliphant dissented.

Leimann v. Board of Adjustment, 9 N.J. 336, 88 A.2d 337 (1952) (The Garden Apartments Case)

Justice Brennan delivered the opinion of the court, joined by Chief Justice Vanderbilt and Justices Heher, Wachenfeld and Jacobs. Justice Oliphant filed a dissenting opinion, joined by Justice Burling.

Members of City Council v. Taxpayers for Vincent, 466 U.S. 789 (1984) (Brennan, J., dissenting) (The Campaign Posters Case)

Justice Stevens delivered the opinion of the Court, joined by Chief Justice Burger and Justices White, Powell, Rehnquist and O'Connor. Justice Brennan filed a dissenting opinion, joined by Justices Marshall and Blackmun.

Metromedia, Inc. v. City of San Diego, 453 U.S. 490 (1981) (Brennan, J., concurring in the judgment) (The Billboards Revisited Case)

Justice White announced the judgment of the Court, joined by Justices Stewart, Marshall and Powell. Justice Brennan filed an opinion concurring in the judgment, joined by Justice Blackmun. Justice Stevens concurred in parts of the plurality opinion and filed an opinion dissenting from other parts and from the judgment. Chief Justice Burger and Justice Rehnquist filed dissenting opinions.

Moore v. City of East Cleveland, 431 U.S. 494 (1977) (Brennan, J., concurring) (The Grandmother Case)

Justice Powell announced the judgment of the Court, joined by Justices Brennan, Marshall and Blackmun. Justice Brennan filed a concurring opinion, joined by Justice Marshall. Justice Stevens filed an opinion concurring in the judgment. Chief Justice Burger filed a dissenting opinion. Justice Stewart filed a dissenting opinion, joined by Justice Rehnquist. Justice White filed a dissenting opinion.

Nollan v. California Coastal Commission, 107 S. Ct. 3141 (1987) (Brennan, J., dissenting) (The Beach House Case)

Justice Scalia delivered the opinion of the Court, joined by Chief Justice Rehnquist and Justices White, Powell and O'Connor. Justice Brennan filed a dissenting opinion, joined by Justice Marshall. Justice Blackmun filed a dissenting opinion. Justice Stevens filed a dissenting opinion, joined by Justice Blackmun.

Penn Central Transportation Co. v. New York City, 438 U.S. 104 (1978) (The Grand Central Terminal Case)

Justice Brennan delivered the opinion of the Court, joined by Justices Stewart, White, Marshall, Blackmun and Powell. Justice Rehnquist filed a dissenting opinion, joined by Chief Justice Burger and Justice Stevens.

Rexon v. Board of Adjustment, 10 N.J. 1, 89 A.2d 233 (1952) (The Machine Shop Case)

Justice Brennan delivered the opinion of the court, joined by Chief Justice Vanderbilt and Justices Oliphant, Wachenfeld, Burling and Jacobs.

San Diego Gas & Electric Co. v. City of San Diego, 450 U.S. 621 (1981) (Brennan, J., dissenting) (The Nuclear Power Plant Case)

Justice Blackmun delivered the opinion of the Court, joined by Chief Justice Burger and Justices White, Rehnquist and Stevens. Justice Rehnquist filed a concurring opinion. Justice Brennan filed a dissenting opinion, joined by Justices Stewart, Marshall and Powell.

Struyk v. Samuel Braen's Sons, 17 N.J. Super. 1, 85 A.2d 279 (App. Div. 1951), *aff'd*, 9 N.J. 294 (1952) (The Quarry Case)

Judge Brennan delivered the opinion of the court, joined by Judges McGeehan and Jayne.

Tice v. Borough of Woodcliff Lake, 12 N.J. Super. 20, 78 A.2d 825 (App. Div. 1951) (The Amusement Park Case)

Judge Brennan delivered the opinion of the court, joined by Judges McGeehan and Jayne.

United Advertising Corp. v. Borough of Raritan, 11 N.J. 144, 93 A.2d 362 (1952) (The New Jersey Billboard Case)

Justice Brennan delivered the opinion of the court, joined by Chief Justice Vanderbilt and Justices Heher, Burling and Jacobs. Justice Oliphant dissented.

Warth v. Seldin, 422 U.S. 490 (1975) (Brennan, J., dissenting) (The Exclusionary Zoning Case)

Justice Powell delivered the opinion of the Court, joined by Chief Justice Burger and Justices Stewart, Blackmun and Rehnquist. Justice Douglas filed a dissenting opinion. Justice Brennan filed a dissenting opinion, joined by Justices White and Marshall.

Weiner v. Borough of Stratford, 15 N.J. 295, 104 A.2d 659 (1954) (The Auction Store Case)

Justice Brennan delivered the opinion of the court, joined by Chief Justice Vanderbilt and Justices Heher, Oliphant, Wachenfeld, Burling and Jacobs.

INDEX

Numbers in *italic* refer to footnote numbers.

AUTHORS

CHARLES M. HAAR is Brandeis Professor of Law at the Harvard Law School in Cambridge, Mass. He served as assistant secretary for metropolitan development in the U.S. Department of Housing and Urban Development during the Johnson administration. Author of numerous books and articles on land use, housing and urban development, including *The Wrong Side of the Tracks* (with Daniel Fessler) and the widely used casebook *Land-Use Planning*, he is coeditor with Jerold Kayden of *Zoning and the American Dream: Promises Still to Keep* (American Planners Press, 1989). Haar is a fellow of the American Academy of Arts and Sciences and past recipient of a Guggenheim Fellowship.

JEROLD S. KAYDEN is currently visiting faculty member at the Lincoln Institute of Land Policy in Cambridge, Mass. He has taught for several years at the Harvard Graduate School of Design, most recently as the Gerald D. Hines Lecturer in Real Estate. A law clerk to Justice Brennan during the Court's 1980 term, Kayden previously served as law clerk to Judge James L. Oakes of the U.S. Court of Appeals for the Second Circuit. Author of many articles on land use, urban development and real estate, he has recently received a major grant from the Twentieth Century Fund for a book on land use regulations. Kayden is the recipient of a Guggenheim Fellowship for 1989–90